ACTION AT BADAMA POST

ACTION AT BADAMA POST

THE THIRD AFGHAN WAR, 1919

Paul Macro

CASEMATE

Oxford & Philadelphia

Published in the United States of America and Great Britain in 2019 by
CASEMATE PUBLISHERS
The Old Music Hall, 106–108 Cowley Road, Oxford OX4 1JE, UK
and
1950 Lawrence Road, Havertown, PA 19083, USA

Hardcover Edition: ISBN 978-1-61200-759-5
Digital Edition: ISBN 978-1-61200-760-1

A CIP record for this book is available from the British Library

Printed and bound in the United Kingdom by TJ International

Typeset in India for Casemate Publishing Services. www.casematepublishingservices.com

For a complete list of Casemate titles, please contact:

CASEMATE PUBLISHERS (UK)
Telephone (01865) 241249
Email: casemate-uk@casematepublishers.co.uk
www.casematepublishers.co.uk

CASEMATE PUBLISHERS (US)
Telephone (610) 853-9131
Fax (610) 853-9146
Email: casemate@casematepublishers.com
www.casematepublishers.com

Ernest William Macro. Almost certainly taken in 1915 on his enlisting into the Motor Machine Gun Service. (Macro family)

Contents

Foreword

I first met Paul Macro, then a Lieutenant, when he arrived freshly commissioned from Sandhurst on the Sennelager training area in Germany in 1990, just before our regiment deployed to Northern Ireland. In the 1990s, we served together in Germany and Canada as squadron leaders, and in the mid-2000s, we were reunited, this time as commanding officer and second-in-command of 2nd Royal Tank Regiment. Most recently, and when not working on the staff in the Ministry of Defence, Lieutenant Colonel Macro has demonstrated his talent as a natural story teller and student of our regiment's history and that of its forebears, which include the Heavy Branch, Machine Gun Corps.

Throughout his service, it has been a characteristic of Lieutenant Colonel Macro's approach to soldiering that he has always put his men before himself. It is, therefore, no surprise that when he decided to write a military history, he chose to build it around a low-level action where the exploits of the subjects – which include his own grandfather, Acting Sergeant Ernest 'Bill' Macro – are the focus.

Most, if not all, readers of this book will know the broad background to the UK's involvement in Afghanistan since the 11 September 2001 attacks on the United States. Some will be familiar with the British army's first and second Afghan campaigns of 1839–42 and 1878–80. But I suspect that few will know about the Third Afghan War (May to August 1919), largely because it has been overshadowed, at the time by the conclusion of the Great War some six months earlier and latterly by our own recent focus on the centenary of that Armistice.

The British military teaches that the nature of conflict is enduring but that its character changes. Conflict has always been an adversarial contest of wills, driven by political objectives but with human dynamics at its heart. In contrast, no two conflicts are the same; each is a product of its time and the prevailing conditions and is heavily influence by the weapons, communications, strategy and tactics of the day.

And so this book is both immediately familiar and also of another time. Lieutenant Colonel Macro's description of the North West Frontier being divided into three theatres will remind today's veterans of the differing operations in Kabul, Helmand and Kandahar or Baghdad, Basra and Anbar. They will recognise the challenges of introducing new equipment and adopting novel tactics; of maintaining logistic support over extended supply lines; of campaigns where complete domination of the air environment is in contrast to a much more evenly balanced fight on the ground; and of operating in neighbourhoods where the rule of the national government is tenuous at best. Readers with experience of places such as Garmsir or Al Amarah will have little difficulty visualising Parachinar or Badama Post.

As with all military endeavours, the most important element of this story is not the locations or the equipment but the people involved: Captain Eastwood and 2nd Lieutenant Lapraik of 20 Squadron Royal Air Force; Major Dodd, Subedar Gul Khan and Lance Daffadar Miru Mian of the Kurram Militia; Captains Jameson and Ferguson of the 3rd Guides and, of course, Acting Sergeant Macro of 22nd Battery Motor Machine Gun Service, and those with whom they served.

The actions described in *Action at Badama Post* could come from any age. That they resonate so well with today's generation is an indication both of our familiarity with small wars in the information age and of the quality of Lieutenant Colonel Macro's telling of a previously untold story. I hope you will enjoy reading this book as much as I have.

Major General John Patterson CB
Colonel Commandant, Royal Tank Regiment
Northwood, December 2018

Introduction and Acknowledgements

My paternal grandfather, Ernest William Macro, died when I was a young boy and well before I was of an age to have a discussion about war and soldiering. Despite his service in both world wars, like many who had been through those experiences, he was a firm believer in the futility of war as a means of solving nations' problems. He also understood the necessity to be prepared to fight for our beliefs as a matter of last resort. But as I grew up, I knew only that 'Grandy' had served in India during World War I, had been in the Home Guard during World War II and that within my father's papers was an album of photos from his time in India. I certainly hadn't heard of the Third Afghan War.

It was not until I was serving in Afghanistan myself, in 2009, that I first heard of Badama Post. While I was in Kandahar my parents sent me a copy of the 'Report by Sgt Macro', a copy of which is now lodged with the National Army Museum and which is reproduced as an appendix in this book. Some considerable searching on the maps finally elicited the confirmation that Badama was in modern-day Pakistan; I was certainly not going to be able to conduct my personal battlefield pilgrimage while on an operational tour on the other side of the border. Whether it will be possible to do so in the future remains to be seen. Reading my grandfather's report, however, was the starting point; the report left so much unanswered. Who were Majors Dodd and 'Malony'? Who were the aircrew that were rescued and what happened to them subsequently? What was the significance of Badama Post and who were the militia? As the search started to progress, answering each of these questions frequently just seemed to throw up further conundrums. But the overarching question remained, who were the men of 22nd Battery Motor Machine Gun Service, who had served with my grandfather on the other side of the world?

The British have a long history of conflict in Afghanistan and along the North West Frontier, from the First Afghan War (1839–42), through to the current campaign against the Taliban. The Third Afghan War (1919), the only occasion on which the Afghans invaded British India, is probably the least well known of these conflicts, partly because of its proximity to World War I. Any war, however, is a very human endeavour; as a contest of wills it brings lives together in a series of encounters, some by chance, and others less so. The outcomes occasioned by these encounters tell the story of that war. In the case of the Third Afghan War, it is a story which deserves to be more widely known, especially as the centenary occurs. This book is an attempt to tell the story of one small action, an aircraft crash and rescue, which in many ways typifies that war.

The action at Badama Post took place after an armistice had been declared but before the formal signing of the peace treaty. It was an all-arms action; the lives of two airmen were saved, but at the cost of the life of an Indian militiaman and of an unknown number of Afghan tribesmen. This book will weave together these elements, the background to the conflict, the Kurram Militia, the history of the squadron and the lives of the key players, in order to bring the story to life. Above all, the story of Badama Post is one which highlights the experience of a virtually unknown group of soldiers, the 22nd Battery Motor Machine Gun Service. They had volunteered to serve as motor machine gunners in France, had been through an intense and very competitive selection process, frequently expending considerable sums of their own money just to attend selection interviews, and had suddenly found themselves despatched half-way around the globe to the heat, dust, snows and monsoons of India and the North West Frontier. This was not the only action 22nd Battery fought during the Third Afghan War, but it is, so far as I am aware, the only one for which a personal account has been left. We are fortunate that this is the case, for personal accounts, particularly by soldiers rather than officers, are very rare. That account was the 'Report by Sgt Macro' which my parents had sent to me in Afghanistan nearly 10 years ago. Acting Sergeant Ernest William 'Bill' Macro was in charge of the section of 22nd Battery despatched to Badama Post in late-July 1919. This is his story and the stories of those other men for whom the climax of their experience of the Third Afghan War came during the action at Badama Post.

I hope the book is a small step towards acknowledging the achievements of all the soldiers of the Machine Gun Corps, of which the Motor Machine Gun Service was a forerunner. The corps was one of the shortest-lived organisations in the British Army; it was in existence from just 1915 to 1922. Yet its legacy was immense. Over 170,00 officers and men served in the corps. More than 62,000 (36 per cent) became casualties, including over 12,000 killed; not for nothing was it known as 'The Suicide Club'. There has never been an official history of the Machine Gun Corps, or the Motor Machine Gun Service, which was incorporated into the corps as the Machine Gun Corps (Motors). Their memory today is honoured by the Machine Gun Corps Old Comrades Association. Yet out of the Machine Gun Corps, particularly the Motors and Heavy Section branches, came the modern Royal Tank Regiment, in addition to the Small Arms School Corps.

I would be delighted to hear from anyone who can add to our under-standing of 22nd Battery in particular, and more generally about those who fought at Badama Post. I would be particularly keen to make contact with any descendants of Corporal Ernest Warburton or descendants of Captain George Eastwood, the pilot of Bristol Fighter F4626, and especially to locate a photograph of him. David Lapraik's photograph is published in this book.

Any mistakes in the text are mine and mine alone. I am attempting to interpret events of 100 years ago on a limited evidence base and without the benefit of getting onto the ground physically. I hope this work will take you to the battlefield in spirit and give you a feel for the action. Throughout, I have tried to indicate what is established fact and what is my interpretation. But I remain open to alternate viewpoints and would be delighted to hear from anyone who can add a further perspective to our collective understanding of the Third Afghan War, the action at Badama Post and the important role that 22nd Battery played in the conflict as a whole. Names, of places in particular but also of persons, have been an issue; not only are there multiple spellings in different Indian dialects, but they are also difficult for the English speaker to record accurately in the contemporary accounts. They have also changed over the years, not least when India gained its independence from Britain in 1947 and the North West Frontier broke off to become a part of Pakistan. I have tried to remain consistent through the text, and to use the most common contemporary spelling. I have no doubt that I have not achieved this perfectly throughout. Machine Gun Corps purists will also notice that I have, throughout, used the rank of 'Sergeant' rather than the Machine Gun Corps version 'Serjeant'. This is in the interest of simplicity and consistency. Bill Macro's official documentation, such as his India General Service Medal and his Mention in Despatches use the 'J' spelling. However, when writing his report, Bill used the 'G' spelling. I decided it would be over complicated and confusing to try to replicate this through the book.

My thanks are due to Major General John Patterson CB, now retired, my former commanding officer, for very kindly writing the foreword. It has been my privilege to serve with General 'JP' over the years, but particularly for me to be able to play a small role in highlighting the achievements of the regiment's founders in 1916 (at Flers with the first use of tanks in action) and 1917 (at Cambrai with the first major tank battle and all-arms action), when the general was Colonel Commandant, Royal Tank Regiment. Those centenaries were memorable and fitting occasions. While the link between the Motors, as the Motor Machine Gun Service and subsequently the Machine Gun Corps (Motors) were inevitably known, and the modern Royal Tank Regiment are more tenuous then those of the Heavy Section, I believe this work adds to the understanding of the forebearers of the Royal Tank Regiment. This is particularly the case in India, where many members of the Motors ended up serving in Armoured Cars, and then subsequently transferred into the Tank Corps.

I owe a considerable debt to the team at Casemate (UK), Clare Litt, Ruth Sheppard and Isobel Nettleton, for guiding me through the processes and steering me clear of the pitfalls which lurk around the corners for first-time authors. Particular thanks go to Declan Ingram for making such a good job of the cover and, more importantly, the maps. The importance of decent maps in a military history is impossible to understate, particularly for a battlefield where it is not possible to get onto the actual ground. With minimal guidance, Declan has delivered in spades, and brought the ground to life.

David Murdoch has been of great assistance with his remarkable knowledge of the men of the Motor Machine Gun Service. Ever on the quest for more information about his own grandfather's service with the Motors in France and then in Mesopotamia, he has nevertheless selflessly applied his considerable research skills to discovering more about the men of 22nd Battery and shared his work without hesitation. The nominal roll of 22nd Battery, in Appendix 2, is largely due to his work. Similarly, the 'Pals' of the Great War Forum (www.greatwarforum.org) have been unstinting in their help and support. It was largely through this forum that I have established contact with other descendants of those who fought with 22nd Battery. I cannot recommend the forum highly enough; if you are stuck with a Great War question, then you will find help there. I would especially thank Stephen Pope, former army officer, author and the world's foremost expert on the first tank crews, for encouraging me to get this story on paper, and for his help and advice.

The Great War Forum has also been largely responsible for enabling me to establish contact with other descendants of 22nd Battery members. Jim Jamieson, now resident in the United States, is the grandson of Corporal James Petrie Jamieson and Alex Bowell the great-grandson of Corporal Walter Patrick. While it appears that neither of these men deployed to Parachinar during the Third Afghan War, they both seem to have been members of the battery throughout their service. They remained in contact long after World War I; it appears right up to World War II. Jim and Alex have both been generous in sharing their ancestors' photos, some of which are published in the book, and unstinting in their efforts to share memories in order to shed more light on the activities of 22nd Battery.

I am also delighted to have established contact with Angie Macpherson and Libby Calvert, the daughters of Percy Dodd. For a long time, I believed Percy must have passed away childless, however, eventually persistence, via Ancestry, paid off and, via a number of third parties, we got in touch. Critically for me, and for telling the story of Badama Post, Angie and Libby hold their late-father's papers, which included his service record and a number of photos they were prepared to share. I am very grateful.

We are fortunate in our great country to have a long and rich history. And while we frequently decry it, we are also fortunate to have citizens dedicated to recording and preserving that history. Amongst that number I certainly include the staff at the National Archives at Kew, the National Army Museum and the Tank Museum at Bovington. All have provided me with help and assistance in different ways, from guiding me to the war diaries, through to searching archives for a particular photo which I was sure they had. The National Archives hold a fascinating range of material and both the National Army and Tank Museums are always interesting to visit.

I am also deeply grateful to my godmother, Dr Elizabeth Saxon. A former army officer and a published historian herself, she has always been the first to provide encouragement, advice and constructive criticism. Liz has also gone well beyond the call of duty in proof reading the text and considerably improving it in a number of places. That said, I have not always heeded her advice and I take full responsibility for any errors.

Words are entirely inadequate to thank my parents, John and Marjorie. As they are both former army officers, and children of servicemen, my career choice had a certain inevitability about it. They have, however, always encouraged me to follow my own paths, with just the right amount of help, advice and support when required. More importantly, so far as this book is concerned, from an early age they instilled in me a joy in reading and an interest in history and family history. Last, but certainly not least, this story would not have been told without the love and support of my wife, Irene. She has 'followed the drum' with me for nearly 25 years, before which she taught in service schools. She has put up with too many house moves and even more absences, whether for operational tours, exercises or simply working late. More recently, she has contended with research trips and my vanishing into the study to write. Throughout, she has been my rock and support. Thank you, Darling; love you always.

Prologue
Aircraft Down – 30 July 1919

On 30 July 1919, an unknown tribesman shot down a Bristol Fighter. It was probably the first aircraft he had ever seen. His dust-coloured robes would have blended into the tortured brown rocks of the Khurmana valley in the North West Frontier, just to the east of the village of Sadda, in what is now Pakistan. If he survived the subsequent action, he might have returned to his remote village boasting of how he alone had been responsible for the destruction of the strange flying machine of the *Feringhees*.

The official history[1] records a large gathering of tribesmen that day. It is, therefore, more likely that a group of tribesmen ambushed the aircraft, rather than firing individually. Exploiting their ability to blend into the landscape, they would have fired a concentrated volley at the aircraft, with their mixture of ancient, but very accurate, traditional jezails. A few tribesmen may also have used more modern firearms. We do not know if shots from such a volley damaged the wire controls of the aircraft or punctured the flying control surfaces to such an extent that the Bristol Fighter was inevitably doomed to crash. However, given the relatively robust nature of the construction of this type of aircraft, this does not seem particularly likely. Despite this, it is not unreasonable to assume that, if a volley was fired, some damage might have been inflicted upon the aircraft. We do know that the pilot, Acting Captain George Eastwood, received a gunshot wound through his chest.[2]

The day, 30 July 1919, had started innocently enough, that is if any day on the North West Frontier of India could be described as starting innocently, particularly in a time of war. The four aircraft of 20 Squadron had probably taken off over the course of the morning from their roughly constructed airstrip at the town of Parachinar, at the northern end of the Kurram valley. Parachinar sits at nearly 2000m and the aircraft had struggled a little to get airborne. This was one of the first flights made by the squadron, as it was still in the process of moving forward to Parachinar. While the aircraft could fly forward, the spares and ground crew had to come up in slow, vulnerable road convoys. The squadron, however, was generally appreciative of the cooler atmosphere, and rather more salubrious surroundings when compared to the heat, dust and fever of its previous station at Risalpur, down on the plains of India. Only four aircraft were available in Parachinar. Gaining altitude above the town, Eastwood circled several times over it, little more than a rough-and-ready collection of mud huts and dusty roads, with a fort and cantonment for the garrison. Once he had orientated himself and his observer, 2nd Lieutenant David Lapraik, who occupied the rear cockpit of Bristol Fighter F4626, the pair headed south, following the track which ran from Parachinar to Thal. They may have been in company with one of the other aircraft. They were flying as protection for a convoy making its way between the two towns. Despite the armistice which had followed the defeat of the recent Afghan invasion of the North West Frontier, there was still no shortage of tribesmen willing to ambush a poorly protected convoy or make trouble in any way they could. However, the tribesmen had proved much more reluctant to attack a convoy that was protected by an aircraft circling overhead. The aircrew were an invaluable reinforcement to the hard-pressed ground escort.

Having found the slow-moving convoy, its several trucks and paltry escort of a section of British infantry and a few natives of the Kurram Militia, inching their way along the rutted, dusty, narrow track, Eastwood and Lapraik would have circled and scouted for as long as they dared. As their fuel supply started to dwindle, they swung back to the north again, heading back towards Parachinar, going upstream along the line of the rushing Kurram river, which, as it flowed south from the hills towards Thal, generally ran parallel to the track. As they reached the tiny village of Sadda, about 20 miles south of Parachinar, Eastwood swung the machine off to the east, to his right, into the Khurmana valley; reports at Parachinar had indicated that tribesmen were gathering in the area and Eastwood had been ordered to conduct a reconnaissance. Low to the rugged, rocky ground, the Bristol Fighter roared up the ridge bounding the valley heading east from Sadda. Flashing past the tiny post of Badama, it crested and dropped into the valley beyond, the sound of the engine reverberating and bouncing around the rocks of the ravine, filling the ears of the tribesmen, to whom the machine was something completely alien. George Eastwood's first hint of trouble was a startling thump in his chest, which knocked him back in his cockpit, and an indescribable pain shooting through him. The machine rocked dangerously as George pulled a hand off the throttle and pressed it to his chest. This did nothing to stop the pain. A fraction of a second later, Eastwood returned his hand to the throttle in order to reduce the engine revs. As he did so, he realised his hand was now covered in blood. He shouted, urgently, towards the voice tube, 'David, David I'm hit. I'm not sure I can control her. I think we're coming down.' He did not hear a reply. Blinking away the tears, he scanned forward and to either side of the big engine nacelle, desperately searching for somewhere flat to put down the aircraft. Nothing. An attempt to push his goggles onto his forehead just resulted in him smearing blood onto the lenses. It was increasingly difficult to feel his hand on the stick, the Bristol Fighter wallowed and fluttered towards the rocky base of the ravine. Trying to climb, to perhaps return towards Badama Post, or even Sadda and the track between Parachinar and Thal, George opened up the throttle. However, he could not find the strength to haul the stick back and, giving up the attempt, he throttled back again. Close to a stall, the Bristol Fighter sank lower in the ravine. The rocks were close now; still nowhere flat, even the river was full of them. Suddenly, the wheels of the fixed undercarriage smashed into the rocks. There was a long ripping sound as the undercarriage partially tore away; almost simultaneously, with a rending crash, the nose tipped forward, smashing the propeller and stalling the engine, and the aircraft's tail rose high in the air. Lapsing into unconsciousness, Eastwood slumped forward against his straps. In the rear, as the tail rose, Lapraik's head slammed forward into the rim of the cockpit. He lifted it groggily, blood streaming from the lacerations on his face. A cloud of dust and rock fragments rose in a plume, and a few bits of tattered fabric drifted off in the breeze. The dust settled slowly; the new silence was now broken only by the ticking sounds of hot metal cooling and then by the popping of rifle fire.

The sun continued to beat down out of the clear, pale-blue sky, broken by just a few fluffy white clouds drifting aimlessly along. At ground level, dust devils whirled around the rocks. A couple of miles to the west of the crashed Bristol Fighter, Sergeant Macro gunned his heavy Triumph motorcycle along the dusty, rock-strewn track, little better than a footpath, which ran along the ridge to link the post at Sadda with that at Badama. Of medium height, rangey, with a thinnish face, blue eyes and sandy brown hair, Sergeant Macro was almost universally known as Bill. On that afternoon in 1919, he was just 23 years old. Risking a disaster on the rough track, he glanced back over his shoulder; a few hundred metres behind him came the rest of his section, Number 3 Section, of 22nd Battery Motor Machine Gun Service (22 MMG). The six Clyno and sidecar combinations, carrying the two heavy Vickers machine guns, the gun crews and ammunition, were followed by a couple of rather battered Ford trucks. All were picking their way carefully along the ridge line. Just a few moments before, they had been sheltering in the shade of the walls of Sadda Post, while Bill had been conferring with the Commanding Officer of the Kurram Militia, Major Percy Dodd. They had been discussing the reports, which had brought them all from Parachinar, that tribesman were gathering in the Khurmana. Dodd had passed on the observation from his militia, who manned the posts at both Sadda and Badama, that it appeared the tribesmen were starting to disperse, possibly due to the arrival of the Motor Machine Gun Section. It had been at that very moment that, its engine roaring, the Bristol Fighter had flashed past Sadda and disappeared over the ridge beyond Badama. Percy Dodd had sensed trouble almost immediately the aircraft had disappeared. Swinging himself onto his horse, he had ordered Bill to prepare his section for action and follow him up to Badama. Percy had then cantered off in that direction with several of his militiamen. Dragging his attention back to the front of his bike, Bill realised he was approaching the post, and that Major Dodd was there waiting for him.

The major dismounted from his horse just as Bill pulled up his Triumph in the shade of Badama Post. Getting off the bike, Bill ran across towards Dodd. 'We were right Sergeant, they've been shot down. They've got themselves out of the machine.' Dodd waved his hand towards the east of the post, 'a few of my chaps are bringing them in now. They're badly bashed up.' Bill looked in the direction indicated. A small party of the Kurram Militia was making its way cautiously towards the post; two militiamen were supporting, half carrying, half dragging one British officer, whose face was masked with blood, while two more militiamen were dragging a bundle on roughly made *dhoolie*. The remaining militiamen crouched for cover behind convenient rocks, taking shots to hold their pursuers at bay whenever they presented a target and then sprinting to catch up with those hauling the casualties. 'They'll need to go to hospital,' Dodd said urgently, 'What about one of your lorries?'

'Right oh, Sir,' Bill responded, and dashed towards his section, which was arriving at the post almost coincidentally with the militiamen bringing in the airmen. 'Corporal Warburton,' Bill spoke with his section corporal, riding the leading Clyno combination, shouting to make himself heard above the bubbling and coughing of the bike's engine, 'Guns into action, arcs, North, through East, to South. Keep your eyes open for the militiamen, there's a number of them out of the post and on the ground. They're bringing the airmen in now. Looks like they'll need some patching up; I'll get one of the lorries cleared and send the medic over.' Without waiting for a response, Bill ran over to the lorries and hopped onto the passenger-side running-board of the leading one. Behind him, he knew, the guns were coming into action in a well-rehearsed drill. The leading combinations, each carrying a heavy Vickers machine gun in the sidecar, slewed to a halt, central to the arcs he had given. The driver had dismounted the motorcycle and moved to assist his passenger, who had promptly loaded the gun. From the other combinations, ammunition numbers had sprinted over, carrying boxes of replenishment .303 cartridge belts, should they be required. Although lacking the full defensive paraphernalia of range cards and distance markers, each gun would have been ready to open fire within 30 seconds of the combination coming to a halt. Bill leaned into the cab of the lorry, 'Warm work, Corporal! Get the lorry cleared as quick as you can. Couple of casualties. We'll need you to take them down to Thal, and probably on to Kohat.'

It quickly became apparent that Eastwood and Lapraik were too badly injured to help themselves. Fortunately, Number 3 Section had one of the battery's supporting medics with it. The two airmen were given first aid, but George Eastwood's injuries, in particular, were beyond that which they were really capable of dealing with. Nevertheless, that initial first aid was probably sufficient to stabilise his situation to enable him to survive transporting on a Ford van, across rough terrain, to Kohat. It was probably only 10 or 15 minutes after the aircrew had been brought into Badama Post that the Ford had been cleared, the airmen had been roughly bandaged and despatched back to Sadda, then down the track to Thal and on to Kohat. The lorry crew would have been carefully briefed by Sergeant Macro and probably given a guide and escort of a couple of militiamen. Watching the van bumping away down the ridge line towards Sadda, Bill turned back to Major Dodd.

'Sir, where is the aircraft? Is the site secure?'

'It crashed into the ravine, just over that crest Sergeant. But it's not secure; I don't have enough militia to picquet the surroundings.'

'I was pilot trained last year Sir. There will be lots of ammunition and probably bombs on the aircraft. If we don't clear it, the tribesmen will. It's all stuff they can use. If I can get down to the aircraft, I should be able to clear it.'

'Right. Bring your guns – let's go and have a look.'

CHAPTER I

Strategic Background

This chapter will provide the strategic background to the Third Anglo-Afghan War of 1919, before we dive into the tactical detail of the battle at Badama Post in subsequent chapters. The chapter includes a description of the ground in the three theatres of operations in the north, south and centre. It will describe the Afghan forces and the British forces facing them; it will also cover the principal fighting in May 1919 in the northern and southern theatres, through the Khyber Pass and at Spin Baldak.

It is probably fair to say that the Third Afghan War is the least well known, certainly by British people, of the various conflicts between English and Afghan forces. In some ways, this is unsurprising because the conflict occurred so soon after the tragedy of the Great War. Indeed, the aftermath of that war was still playing out in Europe as the Bolshevik Revolution and the Paris Peace Conference were both ongoing, and the political and economic reconstruction of Europe had commenced. In India, the shocks of the Amritsar massacre were still reverberating. And all this took place around 5000 miles away from the UK, when short communications could be sent by telegraph, but detailed despatches had to go by ship, with a transit time of around a month in each direction. However, the Third Afghan War was still a vicious little campaign that cost the lives of well over a 1000 British and Indian troops. Further, Afghan tribesmen had an unpleasant reputation for brutality towards prisoners; they basically did not take them, and if they did, they tortured and mutilated them. Not even the dead were spared from mutilation. Even so, those who served on the North West Frontier of India would probably not have claimed that it was in anyway as unpleasant as serving in the trenches of the Western Front.

At its simplest, the Third Afghan War was a classic case of distracting attention from trouble at home by fighting abroad. Habibullah, the amir of

Afghanistan, was assassinated in February 1919, whilst on a shooting trip in Laghman.[1] Habibullah had come to power in 1902 and proven to be shrewd, hard-headed and realistic, although he perhaps was a little less cruel and black-humoured than his father, whom he succeeded. He had resented British control over his external relations. Throughout the war, he had successfully played off both ends against the middle in order to keep Afghanistan out of the war, despite the presence of an effective German delegation under the leadership of Captains Werner Otto von Hentig and Oskar von Niedermayer and various entreaties from Russia, Turkey, Britain and the Indian office. However, in doing so, Habibullah had stirred up trouble for himself, both by angering a powerful anti-British party led by his brother Nasrullah Khan and by alienating the Afghan people through his constant fraud.[2] Habibullah's assassination resulted in a power struggle as his brother, Nasrullah, proclaimed himself as Habibullah's successor, while an Afghan army colonel was made scapegoat for the murder and executed.[3]

Meanwhile, in Kabul, Amanullah, Habibullah's third son, proclaimed himself amir, and seized the throne in April 1919. Amanullah posed as a man of democratic ideals, promising reforms in the system of government. He also had the support of the Afghan Army and a number of the anti-British parties, and he had his uncle Nasrullah arrested. Nasrullah was then sentenced to life imprisonment for Habibullah's murder. Nasrullah had been the leader of a more conservative element in Afghanistan and his treatment rendered Amanullah's position as amir tenuous. However, Amanullah came to power on a surge of Afghan nationalism, which chimed with his own sentiments, fanned by German and Turkish activities, anti-British elements and by the presence of Indian revolutionaries in Kabul. Amanullah probably had little alternative other than to attempt to ride this wave of anti-British nationalism and hope to control it. He was also aware of the rising civil unrest in British India, caused by wartime shortages of food and goods, rising prices and taxation, wartime mobilisation and the enlistment of large numbers of men into the Indian Army. These pressures both led to and were exacerbated by the Amritsar massacre. Amanullah would also have been aware of the disaffected state of British, and to a certain extent Indian, troops in India, frustrated by their retention under arms, when their compatriots in France were being demobilised.[4]

The attitudes of the cross-border tribes of the North West Frontier would also have been an important factor in Amanullah's calculations. The tribes had been stirred by the entry of Turkey into the war against the British and they had provoked a major expedition against them.[5] They were better

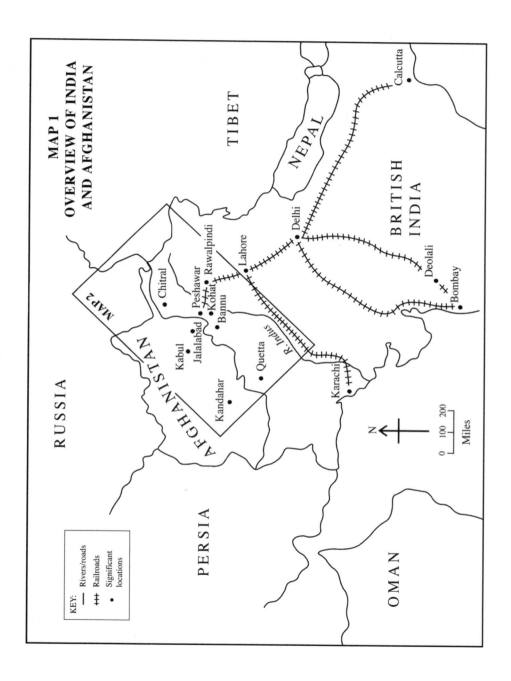

MAP 1
OVERVIEW OF INDIA
AND AFGHANISTAN

RUSSIA

TIBET

NEPAL

AFGHANISTAN

MAP 2

Chitral

Peshawar
Rawalpindi
Kohat
Bannu
Kabul
Jalalabad

Lahore

Delhi

BRITISH
INDIA

Deolali

Bombay

Kandahar

Quetta

R. Indus

Karachi

Calcutta

PERSIA

OMAN

N

0   100   200
Miles

KEY: Rivers/roads
        Railroads
        Significant
        locations

armed than they ever had been, and if they could be properly coordinated, they could have a major impact. However, the tribes were characterised by their independence and unreliability; in practice a simultaneous uprising was almost impossible to coordinate, despite the best efforts of Afghan agents to do so through the early part of 1919. Amanullah, therefore, attempted to relieve the pressure on himself at home by invading British India; his major objective was probably to re-establish his own control over his country's external affairs. With the benefit of hindsight, it is easy to suggest that Amanullah signposted these intentions very clearly. His letter to the Viceroy of India, immediately after taking the throne, his *firmans* to the people of Afghanistan and to the tribes, and his first *durbar*, all clearly indicate his intent to control both the external and internal affairs of Afghanistan. Nevertheless, the Afghans achieved strategic surprise. Whether this was due to Amanullah himself only deciding on invasion at the last minute, as the Viceroy Lord Chelmsford later stated,[6] or whether it was a case of the British Indian establishment and officials consistently refusing to take the Afghan threat seriously, is difficult to determine. In truth, there were probably elements of both factors at play.[7]

The ground of the North West Frontier is dominated by high mountains; a southward-trending offshoot of the eastern Hindu Kush. These mountains separate Afghanistan from the plains of northern India. From Chitral in the north to New Chaman in the south, in a straight line, the frontier between British India and Afghanistan ran for roughly 500 miles. With various twists and turns through mountainous terrain, the actual length was closer to 800 miles. In 1919, it was known as the Durand Line, after Sir Mortimer Durand, the British diplomat who signed the convention at Kabul in November 1893 to define the boundary between Afghanistan and British India. The two parties later camped at Parachinar during the demarcation of the frontier, which took place between 1894 and 1896. In 1919, the boundary was marked by pillars from Chitral going south-west to where the frontiers of India, Persia and Afghanistan meet, with the exception, a stretch of a little over 50 miles between Nawa Sar and the Kabul river and onto Landi Kotal in the Khyber. Even here, where the line was unmarked by boundary pillars, its position on the map was known and agreed by both sides. To the east of boundary, in British territory, lies a swath of land inhabited by the Pathans (who also spread across the line into Afghanistan), loosely under the control of Indian government political officers. However, the Pathans paid no taxes, recognised no border and managed their own tribal affairs. The independent tribal territory is then separated from settled India by the administrative border, which roughly runs from Amb on the Indus to Sherani country south of the Gomal and then along this river to the Durand Line. A narrow belt alongside the Kurram river forms a finger sticking north from Thal into tribal territory.[8] East of the mountains, in India, the Indus river provides a natural barrier to defend against invaders coming down from the mountains onto the Indian Plain. There were, however, a few routes through the mountains and down to the Indus capable of taking large formed bodies of troops or wheeled vehicles and guns.[9]

In 1919, there were no railways in Afghanistan or in the tribal lands. Camels were the main form of transportation because wheeled vehicles were almost non-existent. The routes between Afghanistan and India were valleys of the rivers emptying into the Indus, the Kabul, the Kurram, Kaitu and Tochi, which combined to form the Gambila and the Gomal. South of Ghazni, the rivers ran into the Helmand system, flowing away from India. With the exception of the Kabul, the rivers could be forded in most locations except during times of flood.[10] On the Indian side, the railhead for the broad-gauge railway from the Punjab was Peshawar, and the Indus valley railway formed the main link behind the front between Peshawar and New Chaman. Kohat was also served by broad-gauge railway, and from here, a narrow-gauge extended to Thal. Narrow-gauge lines also served Bannu and Tank in Waziristan, linking to the broad-gauge system at Man, on the Indus. In Baluchistan, the broad-gauge ran up the Bolan Pass to Quetta and then on to the railhead at New Chaman. Railway material was kept here to allow the extension of the line to Kandahar if required and a narrow-gauge extended to Hindubagh in the Zhob. Of the routes between Afghanistan and India, only the route through the Khyber from Peshawar was metalled road, although most had sections which were passable for motor and wheeled vehicles.[11] Internal to Afghanistan, the main route was the historic road between Kabul and Kandahar. At 310 miles, this was a cart route, with limited metalling and bridging. In 1919, it was in such disrepair that Afghan officials moving between the two cities preferred to travel via India. Here, there was a metalled road between Peshawar and Kohat, which ran on to Bannu and Dera Ismail Khan. In the south, another metalled road linked Fort Sandeman to Loralai and Harnai, which was on the loop line to Quetta. The majority of other routes though the frontier region were cart or camel tracks.[12]

So, in 1919, the North West Frontier could be divided neatly into three theatres, each containing one of the major routes between Afghanistan and India. In the north, lies the Chitral and the Khyber Pass. The Chitral forms a narrow amphitheatre, 180 miles long, surrounded on all sides by mountains which rise to between 6000 and 7000m above sea level. The floor of the amphitheatre, which sits in excess of 3000m, is drained by the Chitral river, which flows out of the south-west corner as the Kunar to join the Kabul river near Jalalabad, in Afghanistan, as the later flowed through the Khyber Pass. Logically and geographically, Chitral was part of Afghanistan but was separated by ethnicity and history. The Kunar offered an easy route in from Afghanistan, but there was then no southward route out onto the plains of India. Indeed, for four months in winter all the passes are obstructed by snow and the Chitral is virtually cut off from both Afghanistan and India.[13] Bordering the southern edge of the Chitral is the Khyber Pass. This was the main route from India, via Peshawar to Kabul and, of course, vice versa. It is the traditional route used by almost all invaders of India, apart from Alexander.[14] The name Khyber also refers to the range of arid, broken hills through which the pass runs and which form the last spurs of the Spin Ghar range. On either side of the connecting ridge are the sources of two small streams; the beds of which form the Khyber gorge. This narrow gorge forms the Khyber Pass; it winds between cliffs of shale and limestone, 180–300m high, enters the Khyber Hills a few miles beyond Jamrud, and continues north west for about 33 miles. Just beyond the fort of Haft Chāh, it opens onto the Loe Dakka plain, which stretches to the Kabul river. After a steep ascent at its southern entrance, the pass rises gradually to Fort Ali Masjid at 975m, where the Khyber river leaves the pass to the south. For five miles from Ali Masjid, the pass becomes a gorge not more than 200m wide, flanked by imposing and precipitous walls. From Zīntara village northwards, the gorge opens into a valley a mile or more wide, with forts, villages and scattered cultivation plots. About 10 miles west of Ali Masjid lies Landi Kotal fort and cantonment at 1080m; this is the highest point in the pass and is also an important market centre. Nearby is the village of Bagh and here the summit widens out northward for two miles. The main pass, however, descends from Landi Kotal to Landi Khāna, where it runs through another gorge and winds another 10 miles down the valley to Loe Dakka.[15]

The southern theatre of operations was Baluchistan and the Zhob. This centres on the garrison town of Quetta. From Ruk, on the Indus river, the railway ran across the Sind desert to Sibi and then through the Bolan Pass up to Quetta. Beyond this, the railway ran some 65 miles up through the Shelabagh Tunnel, under the Khojac Pass, to New Chaman just a mile or so short of the Afghan border. In addition to the Shelabagh Tunnel, through which trains could only pass at intervals of two hours, the railway had numerous steep gradients, all of which served to greatly reduce its carrying capacity.[16] Across the border from New Chaman lay the Afghan fort of Spin Baldak, from which a poor cart track extended the 70 miles to the city of Kandahar.[17] This is the second major route between Afghanistan and India and was used as the main supply route to UK and US forces in Helmand during recent operations in Afghanistan. However, despite its strategic importance, in 1919 this represented an unlikely invasion axis for the Afghans. Quetta was strongly held and had the communications to enable it to be easily reinforced, and there were sound defensive positions between Chaman and Quetta. In contrast, communications on the Afghan side of the border were poor. The Baluchi tribes were not as warlike or as prone to insurrection as the Pathans in the north, and even if the Afghans had managed to take Quetta, there were no obvious strategic targets within easy reach.[18] The territory of the Zhob, north east of Quetta, is named after its main river and forms the link between Waziristan in the centre and Baluchistan in the south. The country is essentially rolling desert with occasional hills bounded particularly to the east by the Suleiman mountains. The river is the principal feature, flowing some 200 miles north east across the district, joining the Gormal river at Khajuri Kach, west of Dera Ismail Khan by 65 miles. In May 1919, the Zhob was lightly held by regular troops and not considered to be a likely invasion target for the Afghans.[19]

The third theatre of operations was the central one, consisting of Waziristan and, to its north, the Kurram valley. Waziristan was the most turbulent area of the frontier; the tribes which inhabited it, the Wazirs and Mashuds were the most aggressive and dangerous in the region. From the north, bounded by the Tochi valley, to the south, marked by the Gomal, it is about 60 miles and from east to west about 80 miles between Bannu and Tank and the Afghan border. But it is exceptionally difficult country, a tangle of rocky mountain ridges which rise to some 3300m and are seamed by river valleys that are largely dry, except in the rainy season. The rivers cut through the mountain ranges in narrow defiles, *tangi*, which offer great potential for ambush. The soil is generally poor and difficult to work, apart from occasional patches of alluvial plain along the rivers, while the landscape is bare and stony, with just a few patches of trees at higher altitudes. In 1919, there were no towns or villages, apart from the capital Kaniguram, which lies at just over 2000m above sea level. The topography meant the population, of perhaps 150,000, was scattered in large numbers of tiny hamlets. There were no roads in central Waziristan; the only avenues in and out, certainly for large formations of troops, were the river valleys, with the Tank river, flowing from the north west to Tank, providing the only real access to Kaniguram. The Wazirs and Mashuds had long earned a living by raiding east into more prosperous areas along the Indus, but they remained fiercely independent and were generally at odds with each other, as well as the British and Hindu India. But they were a formidable foe on their own mountainsides; hardy, mobile, tactically astute and excellent shots. They could move cross country at a pace that regular troops had no chance of matching, or had the patience to observe, be immobile for hours, waiting for their opponents to show weakness or a tactical error. Their weaknesses were their extreme individualism and their lack of any form of strategic thinking.[20] The central ground we are particularly interested in is the Kurram valley, which lies to the north north-east of Waziristan and effectively separates it from the Khyber and Peshawar. The Kurram valley will be described in more detail in the next chapter, but Thal was the principle garrison town and the Kurram river rose in the mountains some 50 miles to its north on the mountain passes that eventually provided an alternative route to Kabul, avoiding the Khyber. From the border, at the relatively easy pass at Peiwar Kotal, the small town of Parachinar lies just some 15 miles to the east. Parachinar was the administrative centre for the Upper Kurram. From here, a track follows the Kurram river a little over 50 miles, roughly south, to the town of Thal. This was the major town of the Kurram and the headquarters of British rule in the area.[21]

The climate of Afghanistan and the North West Frontier is characterised by extremes of temperature, strong winds, low rainfall and rapid transitions between seasons. The annual rainfall averages about 275mm across the country; most of this falls between December and April, with the majority as snow at altitudes above 2000m. Spring comes abruptly, and a few weeks after the last of the snow, the heat of the sun is tropical. Temperature extremes are both seasonal and diurnal; cases of both chilblains and heat exhaustion were admitted to hospital in Chaman on the same day in May 1919. The hot weather season on the Frontier in 1919 was exceptionally severe; temperatures in Peshawar averaged 3 degrees C (6 degrees F) above normal through June and July. Temperatures in tents were recorded as being in excess of 50 degrees C (125 degrees F) on several occasions; the heat is exacerbated by hot strong winds and dust storms. These conditions, of course, affected both sides, but were particularly severe for European troops. Disease as well was prevalent; cholera takes its toll from every force operating in the region, and in the summer, bowel complaints were common.[22]

The population of Afghanistan in 1919 was around 6,500,000. The true military strength of Afghanistan depends upon its armed population rather than its regular forces; the army was regarded as a force to reinforce and stiffen hordes of fanatical armed tribesmen, both within and without the border of Afghanistan itself. The tribesman, however, would rarely fight any great distance from their homes, and the British reckoned that the largest force of tribesman they were likely to encounter in the field would number no more than 20,000, and usually, the numbers would be considerably smaller. The regular Afghan army was formed of 78 infantry battalions, 21 cavalry regiments and 280 breech-loading artillery pieces. There were also a similar number of muzzle-loaded guns, but these were stationed on the Russian and Persian frontiers and need not concern us further. The effective strength was around 38,000 rifles, 8000 sabres and 4000 artillery gunners. Of these forces, 38 battalions of infantry, five of the cavalry regiments and 107 guns were stationed in eastern Afghanistan in the districts which bordered British India. The Kabul garrison then formed a strategic reserve, consisting of 20 infantry and pioneer battalions, seven cavalry regiments and 108 guns. These forces were generally better manned and equipped than the rest of the army.

The equipment and armament of the infantry battalions varied considerably. Less than half of the battalions had modern, small-bore repeating rifles; the remainder were armed with single-shot Martinis and sniders, many of which had originally been supplied by the British. Machine guns were the old four-barrelled Gardner variety, which were operated by turning a handle. A bayonet was issued, although troops were untrained in its use. For carriage of personal equipment leather pouches and belts were issued, but only the Kabul units had a khaki field service dress; units tended to campaign in local dress of a sheepskin coat with equipment worn over it and a round fur hat. Authorised battalion strengths varied between 1000 and 500, but when the war came no battalion had greater than 75 per cent of effectives. A number of battalions made up numbers by drafting local tribesmen. The cavalry regiments were mounted on sturdy ponies of about 14.2 hands; these were capable of great exertions. Cavalrymen were armed with a rifle and a sword; Kabul regiments were supposedly issued with lances, but these do not appear to have been carried. A cavalry regiment's strength varied between 600 and 300. They are best considered as mounted infantry or scouts, rather than shock troops. The field artillery lacked sufficient horses and the pack guns were carried by ponies which were poorly looked after. The field guns had a maximum range of 4150m, and the pack guns 3200m. The guns actually employed against the British in 1919 consisted of a 10cm Krupp field howitzer, Krupp 75mm pack (mountain) guns and some older seven-pound pack guns. There was a functioning logistic system, but it relied on camels rather than mechanised transport. Only black powder, and very limited quantities of smokeless powder, were manufactured in the country; cordite cartridges were usually imported from Europe via India. Overall, the Afghan regulars lacked training and mobility and could not be considered as world class troops; they were certainly not capable of defeating the British army by themselves. However, they were courageous, determined and their powers of endurance were considerable. But Amanullah would depend on the assistance of the border tribes on both sides of the Durand Line if his invasion was to be successful. Finally, the regular Afghan army was supplemented by about 10,000 militia, or tribal levies, known as *khassadars*. These wore no uniform and carried the ancient Snider rifles. They had no higher organisation than a company of about 100 strong; they were generally distributed in small parties on road protection, general police works, revenue and customs duties. Militarily they were probably less effective than the tribesmen.[23]

In contrast, the British, even in 1919, kept two armies in India, one in the north and the other in the south. Available for service on the North West Frontier were the 1st (Peshawar), 2nd (Rawalpindi), 4th (Quetta) and 16th (Lahore) Divisions, with 1 (Risalpur), 4 (Meerut) and 10 (Peshawar) Cavalry Brigades, in addition to the 12 (Baleli) Mounted Brigade. Additionally, specific units were designated for the defence of the North West Frontier; the main elements of these were the three independent brigades from Kohat, Bannu and Derajat. Each of the divisions was made up of three infantry brigades, each of which consisted of a British and three Indian infantry battalions, a squadron of Indian cavalry, a field and a mountain artillery brigade, which between them had two batteries of 18-pounder field guns, a battery of 4.5 inch howitzers and two batteries of 2.75 inch pack guns, and two companies of machine guns, each with 16 guns. In addition, the division had companies of sappers and miners, pioneers, signallers and an ammunition column, as well as other ancillary units. Each of the independent brigades consisted of three or four Indian infantry battalions, a regiment of Indian cavalry, a battery of mountain artillery and an armoured car battery. They had sufficient transport to make them mobile. These field army and independent brigade units were largely concentrated in cantonments on the Indian side of the administrative border; effectively, they were held as a striking force which would concentrate, in the event of hostilities, in order to strike the decisive blow. The tribal lands would be lightly held by irregular forces as an outpost zone. These forces were recruited locally to the region in which they operated and consisted of the various militias,[24] the Frontier Constabulary and some local levies. The militia were officered by selected officers from the Indian Army; like the regular army they were organised into battalions and companies. Each company had a strength of around 100, with the number of companies in the battalion varying from district to district. The militia wore the same uniform as the Indian Army and were armed with a low velocity .303 rifle with the short bayonet. The Frontier Constabulary had been raised in 1913 as armed[25] civil police and were also organised into battalions commanded by selected civil police officers. The local levies were employed by individual political officers to provide escorts of outpost garrisons. Although armed with Martini-Henry rifles they had little value as fighting troops.[26]

So, in 1919 British/Indian fighting troops totalled approximately 75,000 men, formed into 18 cavalry regiments, 73 infantry battalions, 29 batteries of artillery, nine armoured car companies and 13 companies or squadrons of machine guns, as well as engineers and signals. There was a supporting tail of two or even three times that number. The main issues for the British lay in the quality and locations of their troops. Through the course of the 1914–18 war, regular British battalions had been pulled from India to other theatres of war. They had been replaced with territorial army battalions, and 'duration of the war' conscripts, but in lesser numbers; by May 1919, large numbers of British soldiers were being moved to demobilisation camps between Bombay and Delhi to await repatriation to UK. Only eight regular British infantry battalions and two cavalry regiments had been retained in India throughout the war; although these remained stationed on the frontier, a considerable portion had, along with many of the Indian battalions, moved to the slightly cooler climate of the summer hill stations.[27] In order to support the requirement for manpower in theatres overseas from India, the Indian Army had expanded four-fold from its pre-war strength. There was still the numerical equivalent of the pre-war Indian Army available in India, but the quality had suffered considerably. Many of the new battalions had been raised in 1917 and 1918, and recruiting standards had been lowered considerably. There was a distinct shortage of experienced officers, with junior officers and non-commissioned officers largely wartime recruits themselves. They lacked knowledge and experience, and in the case of British officers, fluency in the Indian language. The pre-war Indian Army battalions were still overseas or in the process of repatriation through depots and taking long delayed leave.[28]

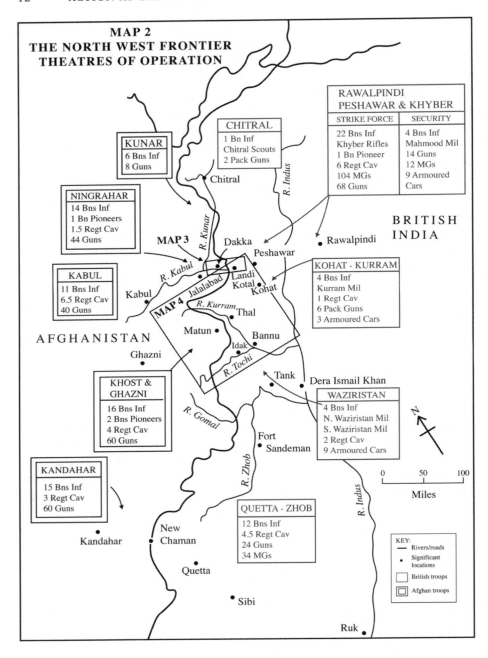

**MAP 2
THE NORTH WEST FRONTIER
THEATRES OF OPERATION**

RAWALPINDI
PESHAWAR & KHYBER

STRIKE FORCE	SECURITY
22 Bns Inf	4 Bns Inf
Khyber Rifles	Mahmood Mil
1 Bn Pioneer	14 Guns
6 Regt Cav	12 MGs
104 MGs	9 Armoured
68 Guns	Cars

CHITRAL
1 Bn Inf
Chitral Scouts
2 Pack Guns

• Chitral

KUNAR
6 Bns Inf
8 Guns

NINGRAHAR
14 Bns Inf
1 Bn Pioneers
1.5 Regt Cav
44 Guns

MAP 3

R. Kunar

Dakka

Peshawar

• Rawalpindi

BRITISH
INDIA

R. Indus

R. Kabul

KABUL
11 Bns Inf
6.5 Regt Cav
40 Guns

Kabul •

Jalalabad

Landi
Kotal

Kohat •

KOHAT - KURRAM
4 Bns Inf
Kurram Mil
1 Regt Cav
6 Pack Guns
3 Armoured Cars

MAP 4

R. Kurram

Thal •

AFGHANISTAN

Matun •

Bannu •

Idak •

R. Tochi

Ghazni
•

Tank •

Dera Ismail Khan
•

KHOST &
GHAZNI
16 Bns Inf
2 Bns Pioneers
4 Regt Cav
60 Guns

R. Gomal

WAZIRISTAN
4 Bns Inf
N. Waziristan Mil
S. Waziristan Mil
2 Regt Cav
9 Armoured Cars

N

Fort
Sandeman
•

R. Zhob

KANDAHAR
15 Bns Inf
3 Regt Cav
60 Guns

0   50   100

Miles

R. Indus

New
Chaman •

Kandahar
•

QUETTA - ZHOB
12 Bns Inf
4.5 Regt Cav
24 Guns
34 MGs

Quetta
•

KEY:
— Rivers/roads
• Significant
  locations
☐ British troops
☐ Afghan troops

Sibi •

Ruk •

If the British/Indian fighting forces had been organised to a well thought-through plan, the picture regarding the logistics of supporting the force was less satisfactory. There had been a steady drain on Indian resources since 1914 and stocks of electric and railway plant, which could only come from UK, had been reduced well below safe levels. Owing to the shortage of shipping, there was no means of re-stocking. Animal transport had been exploited to the maximum extent possible which had drained the reserves of animals available in India; there were no mules available. Ponies were being employed as draught animals in the field army, despite being inferior to mules in endurance and utility. There was also a shortage of camels, as many had been shipped overseas and the remainder had been savaged by *surra*. There was, however, a 60-day reserve of supplies for the field army; 50 per cent of this was held in stations to the west of the Indus. The remainder was in depots in Lahore, Bombay and Karachi.[29]

Airpower was the one aspect of the campaign which the British dominated completely. The Royal Flying Corps had arrived on the frontier, in the shape of 31 Squadron, in time to take part in the Mohmand campaign of February 1916. However, the development of the capabilities of air power in the demanding environment of the frontier was very much in its infancy, and in no way at the levels which had been achieved on the Western Front; the army remained suspicious of the value of airpower. This was partly due to the Indian theatre being well down the priority list for both men and machines; even after the war in Europe had ended, the majority of aircraft available in India were low powered, obsolete and worn out. In May 1919, the Royal Air Force aircraft available to support the frontier were the B.E.2cs of 31 Squadron, located at Risalpur, and a flight of the same from 114 Squadron, based at Quetta.[30] Also, due to be stationed at Risalpur was 20 Squadron, which in May was in the process of transferring to India from France, shipping from Marseille to Bombay; this was equipped with rather more modern Bristol Fighter aircraft.[31]

The official history summarises the British position at the start of May as:

> Independent tribal territory was either not held at all or lightly held by Pathan Militia. The line of the Administrative Border was garrisoned by armed police. A striking force of two divisions and two cavalry brigades was available for offensive action on the Khyber front, and one division and one mounted brigade for operations on the southern front. A defensive role was assigned to the troops in the Central area, and to the garrisons of Malakand and Chitral. A General Reserve of one division, two mobile brigades and one brigade of cavalry were ready for service wherever required. The units, however, were short of effectives and senior officers. Supplies were sufficient, but there was a shortage of transport.[32]

In the northern theatre, the Khyber was the route by which the Afghans initiated the war on 3 May 1919; they crossed the frontier at the western end of the pass to capture the town of Bagh. The British initially considered this a minor border infraction, but it was actually part of the wider invasion plan, which had been launched ahead of schedule. Amanullah had intended for it to coincide with an uprising that was being planned in Peshawar later in May. Bagh was strategically important to the British and Indians because it provided water to Landi Kotal, which at the time was garrisoned by just two companies of troops from the British Indian Army. The Afghan forces in the theatre were estimated as 14 battalions of infantry, a battalion of pioneers and a regiment plus of cavalry with 44 guns. Although the British could concentrate 23 infantry battalions, six regiments of cavalry and 11 artillery batteries at Peshawar, had Landi Kotal fallen it would have enabled the Afghans to control and close the western end of the Khyber. It would have been difficult to evict them and might well have brought about a rising of the border tribesmen. By the evening of 6 May, the Afghans had concentrated three battalions and a couple of guns at Bagh; five battalions of infantry, 200 cavalry and six guns were at Loe Dakka, some 10 miles back. But the Afghan commander, Muhammad Anwar Khan, had already missed his chance. Despite the risk of an uprising in Peshawar, General Charles Fowler, in temporary command of 1st (Peshawar) Division had already despatched 2nd Battalion Somerset Light Infantry to reinforce Landi Kotal, which they reached on 7 May. On the same day, Brigadier-General George Crocker was instructed to move forward with his 1 Infantry Brigade in order to subsequently strike back up to Bagh. The brigade reached Landi Kotal on 8 May. Crocker launched two of his battalions, 1/15th Sikhs and 1/11th Gurkha Rifles, straight into an attack on 9 May, but the majority of his brigade were held in covering positions and unable to support the advance. The Afghans reinforced their positions, the attack stalled short of Bagh and the attacking battalions dug in. However, the British had succeeded in regaining the Tangi Springs, thus restoring the water supply to Landi Kotal.[33]

Meanwhile, events in Peshawar were interrupting the flow of reinforcements into the Khyber. The Afghan postmaster in Peshawar, Ghulam Haidar, was conspiring with the Indian Revolutionary Committee, anticipating raising a mob of 8000, to attack the cantonment and civil lines, railway and radio stations, and to seize the city to incite a general uprising. This was due to take place on 8 May. Fortunately, the British Indian police had informants who gave them notice of the plan. As a result, on that day, troops coming up from Nowshera were de-trained at Peshawar, the city was speedily surrounded and sealed off, and an ultimatum issued that unless Haidar and the other ringleaders surrendered, then the water supply would be cut off. By sunset, Ghulam Haidar and 22 rebels had given themselves up; the threat of an uprising had been nipped out and Peshawar remained secure for the course of the war.[34]

Back at Landi Kotal, General Fowler arrived on the evening of 9 May, following the failed attack by Brigadier Crocker's 1 Infantry Brigade, and decided to take command of the situation in person. Freed from the task of securing Peshawar, 2 Infantry Brigade arrived in Landi Kotal on 10 May. Without waiting for further reinforcements from his 3 Infantry Brigade, Fowler effectively launched a divisional attack on 11 May on the Afghan positions at Bagh and on the Khargali Ridge. Covered by a single battalion, his striking force of the reinforced 2 Infantry Brigade, commanded by Major-General Skipton Hill Climo CB, DSO, succeeded in forcing the Afghans out of their positions and into retreat towards Loe Dakka. As they fell back, they were bombed and machine-gunned from the air by the aircraft of 31 Squadron. British casualties were eight killed and 31 wounded, while Afghan losses were estimated at about 100 killed and 300 wounded. The British also captured five guns and a machine gun.[35] The official history gives the reasons for success as 'the efficient co-operation of all arms; to the accurate shooting of the artillery and machine guns; and to the dash and energy of the infantry. This latter feature was the result of the careful and methodical training given to the 2 Infantry Brigade by its commander, Major-General Climo, who handled it during the action with skill and boldness.'[36]

Having successfully restored the integrity of British India, the next step for the British was to advance to Loe Dakka in order to open up the route to Jalalabad and Kabul beyond. Dakka also offered the British the space to camp with large formations of troops, space for a landing ground for the RAF and the ability to water horses in the Kabul river. On 12 May, Fowler was ordered to open up the route to Dakka in order for the 1 Cavalry Brigade and the 30th Lancers to pass through. Accordingly, on 13 May, General Climo, commanding a force drawn from both the 2 and 3 Infantry Brigades, picquetted the route and the cavalry force, under the command of Brigadier-General G. M. Baldwin[37] passed through to form a camp in the vicinity of Loe Dakka. The infantry picquets were then withdrawn back to Landi Kotal. Picquetting was a standard drill of frontier warfare and formed the basis of infantry tactics in mountain warfare. Essentially, small parties of troops, the 'picquet', secured high features above the pass through which the main force was due to pass, in order to prevent tribesmen or other opposition from interfering with the transit. A picquet generally consisted of an officer and six to 30 men; a section up to a platoon. They were supported by a covering party while they climbed to their position and then fortified themselves within a *sangar* built up from stone. Once the main force had passed below, the picquet was withdrawn to join the rearguard. This part of the operation, in particular, required speed, timing and a close following of procedure; it was tiring and used up manpower very quickly.[38]

Two battalions of Brigadier Crocker's 1 Infantry Brigade then moved up to Dakka on 14 May, to be followed the next day by the other two. Up to this stage, there had been no organised resistance from the Afghans. A further westward reconnaissance on 16 May by British cavalry, the 1st Kings Dragoon Guards, and 1/15th Sikhs, supported by guns and machine guns, ran headlong into an Afghan force of about 3000 regulars, in the process of counter-attacking to clear Loe Dakka. The reconnaissance force conducted a fighting withdrawal back to the camp at Dakka. The Afghans then succeeded in establishing themselves on the hills to the west of Loe Dakka, in positions from which they could keep the British camp under fire, which they continued to do through the night of 16/17 May. On the morning of 17 May, General Crocker launched all elements of his brigade into attacks to clear the Afghans away from Dakka; as at Bagh, he failed to concentrate his forces, and the attacks stalled by about 1000 hours. Fortunately for the British, the Afghans failed to take advantage, and shortly afterwards, reinforcements arrived at Dakka, in the shape of Major-General A. Skeen, with his brigade headquarters (3 Infantry Brigade) and two battalions, (1st Battalion Yorkshire Regiment and 2/1st Gurkha Rifles), as well as guns and a company from the Machine Gun Corps. Skeen took command of operations intending to regain the initiative, but under heavy fire from British howitzers, the Afghans were already starting to melt away.[39] British and Indian casualties on the northern, Khyber, front from 16–17 May totalled 32 killed and 246 wounded. Afghan casualties were estimated at about 200 killed and over 400 wounded; they also lost five of their seven Krupp guns.[40]

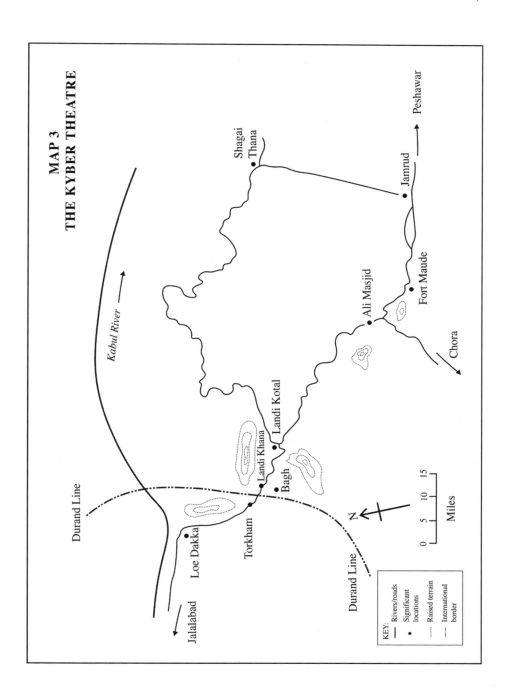

MAP 3
THE KYBER THEATRE

So, by the evening of 17 May, on the northern front, the British had successfully repulsed the Afghan incursion into British India, and in their own turn, advanced into Afghanistan and secured a foothold. The Khyber Pass was held, with troops from 1st Division, 1 Cavalry Brigade and 10 Cavalry Brigade spread throughout its length from Loe Dakka back to Peshawar, with further troops available at Nowshera and Risalpur.[41] There was no sign that the tribes were going to rise en-masse to support the Afghans, although life in Loe Dakka, in particular, was far from comfortable. The local tribesmen on the Afghan side of the border had no more cause to love the British than their fellows in British India. Sniping of the camp was a frequent occurrence, especially at night. As the British attempted to build up their forces at Dakka, temperatures were rising to sweltering, dust lay everywhere and every movement stirred it up in large clouds. To this was added the stench of rotting corpses. Rations were getting through, but until fresh supplies were secured and field kitchens and bakeries were set up, these consisted of biscuit and tinned mutton. The latter, which could not be eaten cold, tended to emerge from the tin in a liquid mess in the prevailing heat. It was then rendered down into curry or a stew. Landing grounds were constructed for the RAF, and the B.E.2cs of 31 Squadron provided reconnaissance in support of the camp, as well as bombing the Afghans and Jalalabad itself. The British continued to build up their forces and, more importantly, their stores, preparatory for an advance to Jalalabad and, if necessary, onto Kabul itself. Although they were severely hampered throughout by the shortage of motorised transport, by 26 May it was assessed they were ready to push forward again. The advance was planned for 1 June.[42] Before it could take place, however, events had moved on both the diplomatic front and in the central theatre of operations. These events will be covered in the next chapter. Before doing so, we will examine operations in the southern theatre.

The problems which faced Major-General Richard Wapshare in the southern theatre were somewhat different from those in the northern and central theatres. As described earlier in the chapter, although the passes from Kandahar to Quetta were the second major route between Afghanistan and British India, this was considered an unlikely invasion axis in 1919. There were no independent tribes which were likely to be incited into rising against the British, and the area was British Indian administered right up to the Durand Line. Additionally, General Wapshare's forces,[43] of 4th Division and 12 Mounted Brigade, were qualitatively superior and numerically similar to the

Afghan forces available in south-western Afghanistan, centred on Kandahar. British forces initially available in Baluchistan totalled around 10 battalions of infantry, three cavalry regiments, a machine-gun company and three gun batteries. Further forces were available in the Zhob, which also lay within Wapshare's responsibilities.[44] The Afghan forces were assessed as between eight and 16 battalions of infantry, one and five regiments of cavalry and 31 to 41 guns.[45] Wapshare favoured an offensive strategy, leaving Zhob unreinforced and concentrating his forces on the border at New Chaman, with a view to launching an attack to seize the great Afghan fortress of Spin Baldak and ultimately making a speedy advance onto Kandahar.[46]

Spin Baldak lay just over five miles north-west of New Chaman, astride the main track to Kandahar, and at the south-western edge of a ridge running south-west to north-east for about 925m The ridge rose about 60m above the plain and had three knolls which the Afghans had fortified with gun platforms (although there were no guns mounted or present in the fort), trenches, breastworks and towers. The fort itself was a square structure, with inner and outer walls, and had bastions at each corner. Each wall was about 230m long and 8m high. To the south and west were large walled gardens. The garrison was estimated, reasonably accurately, as being 500–600 regulars. The British plan of attack was simple. The cavalry would deploy to the north and north-west of the fort as cut offs. 57 Brigade was to attack along the ridge from the north-east. 11 Infantry Brigade was to advance up the track from New Chaman and capture the walled gardens. The advance was to be covered by artillery and machine-gun fire, and howitzers were to be used to breach the fort's walls. Once the ridge and walled gardens had been captured, further orders would be given for assaulting the actual fort.[47]

The howitzers arrived in New Chaman on 26 May and the attack was launched the next day, achieving surprise. It went more or less as planned, although the 57 Brigade attack, with 1/4 Royal West Kent in the lead, was held up and took much longer than planned. In contrast, 11 Brigade captured the gardens relatively quickly and the howitzers opened a couple breaches in the fort's wall. Wapshare ordered forward his reserve, 1st Battalion, Duke of Wellington's Regiment, initially in support of 57 Brigade, but the left-hand companies managed to get into Spin Baldak, where they were soon joined by 1/4 Gurkhas and 1/22 Punjabis from 11 Brigade. Over 200 of the garrison, many of whom were armed only with single-shot Martini-Henry rifles, were killed in the action and 186 were taken prisoner. The British, with 18 killed and 40 wounded, set about incorporating the fort into the defensive scheme for New Chaman. The capture of the fort greatly reduced the chance of an Afghan invasion into the southern theatre, although the Afghans were both shocked and humiliated by its capture and they showed every intention of attempting to retake it. Abdul Qudus, the Afghan Prime Minister and commander of the southern forces, moved forward in early June to Mel Karez, about 32 miles from New Chaman, with a force of a cavalry regiment, five infantry battalions, 10 guns and about 9000 tribesmen. He subsequently moved forward to Murgha Chaman, just five miles from Spin Baldak, and cut off the fort's water supply. However, by this time, events in the central, Kurram, theatre were dominating the strategic picture, so this will be the focus of Chapter 2.

CHAPTER 2

The War in the Kurram

Having described operations in May 1919 on the northern and southern flanks of the North West Frontier, in order to set the strategic picture of the conflict, this chapter will focus on the war in the central, or Kurram, theatre of operations, which included Badama Post. It will expand on the ground description of Chapter 1 and also provide a description of the Afghan forces, British forces in the area and of the reinforcement of the Kurram as hostilities commenced in mid-May. It will describe how Thal was besieged by Nadir Khan, to the absolute surprise of the British, and subsequently relieved by Brigadier-General Reginald Dyer. Events on the diplomatic side will also be covered as Khan's forces were pushed back over border and the armistice was declared. This chapter will conclude with a brief overview, which will be developed in a subsequent chapter, of the ongoing clashes and skirmishes in the central theatre of operations, which lead up to the action at Badama Post.

The Kurram valley, lies to the north north-east of Waziristan separating it from the Khyber and Peshawar. Thal, which in 1919 was the principal garrison town, lies at the base of the valley, which runs roughly north-west to south-east for about 65 miles. The name Kurram comes from the river which flows along the valley. The river drains the southern flanks of the snow-covered or 'white' mountains, the Safed Koh, locally known as the Spīn Ghar, before entering the Indus plains north of Bannu. The Safed Koh formed the natural border between Afghanistan and British India, although the Durand Line did run along them. In ancient times, the Kurram valley offered the most direct route to Kabul and Gardez. The route crossed a pass over 3400m (11,250ft) high, at Peiwar Kotal, about 15 miles west of Parachinar, which was blocked by snow for several months of the year. But once over Peiwar Kotal and Shutagardan Pass to Kushi it was just 44 miles along the Logar valley to Kabul, an easy route which avoided the Khyber. It was by this means that Major-General Sir Frederick Roberts had advanced on Kabul in the autumn of 1878 in the Second Afghan War. The Kurram valley was well irrigated and well populated by the Turis tribe, who differed from the neighbouring Pashtuns in being Shia, rather than Sunni, Muslims. The Kurram was crowded with small fortified villages, orchards and groves, to which a fine background was afforded by the dark pine forests and alpine snows of the Safed Koh. The beauty and climate of the valley attracted some of the Mughal emperors of Delhi, and Shah Jahan[1] planted a garden; the remains of which still exist.

At the northern end of the Kurram valley, Parachinar was the administrative centre for the Upper Kurram, and housed the headquarters of the Kurram Militia. The cantonment had been built by General Roberts in 1879. From Parachinar a track followed the Kurram river a little over 50 miles, initially south-east and then roughly south, to the town of Thal. This was the major town of the Kurram, the administrative centre for the Lower Kurram and the headquarters of British rule in the area. About 25 miles down the track from Parachinar, just south of where river and track both bent to the south, was the little village of Sadda, which contained a small fort, garrisoned by the Kurram Militia. Here the river was joined by the Khurmana river, flowing in from the north-east. From Sadda, a camel track followed the Khurmana a couple of miles up to the cluster of huts which formed the hamlet of Badama. Here again was a small post garrisoned by the militia. Track and river then continued a few miles north-east from Badama, up into the foothills of the Safed Koh, before both petered out. Continuing on down the Kurram from Sadda, about halfway along (15 miles) the track to Thal passed the tiny village of Alizai. Scattered through the Kurram were a number of other small posts which were garrisoned by the Kurram Militia. The most significant of these were probably Kharlachi, located south-west of Parachinar where the Kurram crossed from Afghanistan to India, and Lakka Tiga, about 10 miles cross country south-west of Sadda, again right on the Durand Line.[2]

Thal was vulnerable to attack from three directions; first from the Afghan province of Khost, which flanked the western bank of the Kurram skirting Waziristan, second from Kabul, straight across the pass at Peiwar Kotal and down the line of the Kurram past Parachinar and Sadda and third, from the North West Frontier tribes of the Afridis and Zaimukhts, who occupied the land to the east of the Kurram valley. The former tribe, in particular, had the potential to dominate the road running east from Thal to the important post of Kohat, which was then only a relatively easy 30 miles from Peshawar. Indeed, Thal could be described as being under threat from the south as well;

it was only 25 miles north of Bannu, the administrative capital of Waziristan, and the Tochi Wazirs, whose neighbourhood that was, were far more natural allies of the Afghans than the British. An Afghan advance from Khost could, therefore, be expected to attempt to link up with any rising of the Tochi Wazirs; in 1919, British intelligence sources were suggesting that this was exactly Amanullah's intention.[3]

Facing the British-Indian forces in the Kurram was the most compact and formidable of the three Afghan forces, if one excludes the Kabul-based reserve. It consisted of 16 battalions of regular infantry, two of pioneers, four regiments of cavalry and 60 guns. The main base was at Ghazni, but aside from a detachment on the Peiwar Kotal, the force had been moved forward to Matun. This last town was located in the Afghan province of Khost, just across the border from the Kurram. From Matun, the Kaitu river flowed south-east, through Spinwam on the Indian side of the border, to join the Kurram a few miles south of Thal. The Afghan commander was the young (aged just 36), energetic and aggressive Nadir Khan, former commander in chief of the Afghan Army. He would go on to become Amir of Afghanistan from 1929, through to his assassination in 1933. The forward position at Matun offered Nadir Khan a number of options. The first was to move north to cross the Peiwar Kotal or Kharlachi and then come down the Kurram valley to Thal. The second was to head due east, cross country, direct at Thal. Or, he could move south into the Tochi river valley and head for Bannu. If he took Bannu, then Khan could reasonably expect the Wazirs and Mahsuds to rise in his support. From Bannu, he could either head south toward Dera Ismail Khan on the Indus or north towards Thal. And if he was at Thal, whether directly or via Bannu, then the Afridis would probably support him. From Thal, as we have already seen, it was relatively straightforward to move on Kohat and then Peshawar. However, on 6 May 1919, as the war was kicking off on the Khyber, the only sign of enemy activity on the central front was the building of *sangars* at Peiwar Kotal, and it appeared that the Afghan agents had had little success in their efforts to incite the tribes of the Orakzais, the Wazirs and the Mahsuds. And the British had little idea of the exact whereabouts of Khan and his forces.[4]

The British commander of this central front (the Kohat Area and Lines of Communication, which included the Kurram) was Major-General Alexander Eustace, based in Kohat. He had at his disposal four battalions of infantry, a regiment of cavalry (the 37th Lancers), three armoured cars and a mountain battery, 28th Battery, together with the Kurram Militia. These forces were insufficient, particularly considering the paucity of transport, to risk a pre-emptive attack on the Afghan forces in Khost. In addition, the reliability of the Waziristan militia was doubtful, so General Eustace settled for remaining on the defensive, but remaining ready to meet any incursion over the Durand Line. In early May, he was reinforced by the arrival at Kohat of a further three battalions of infantry and 22 MMG. Of these, a battalion and the Motor Machine Gun Battery were immediately sent forward to reinforce the Kurram Militia at Parachinar, where 22 MMG arrived on 17 May. This meant about a third of the total force was based in the Upper Kurram, at Parachinar, and now came under the command of Brigadier-General Edward Fagan, with his 60 Infantry Brigade Headquarters from Ambula. Up until this point, the senior commander in the Upper Kurram had been Major Percy Dodd, 31st Lancers, commandant of the Kurram Militia, and it appeared that Parachinar, isolated from Thal up the Kurram, was the point of the valley most threatened. Percy Dodd reacted to initial reports of Nadir Khan's concentration at Matun by pushing forward picquets from the Kurram Militia to the border in the vicinity of Peiwar Kotal, Kharlachi and Lakka Tiga, to observe Afghan movements and try and identify the direction of Khan's main attack. Through early and mid-May, as various rumours reached him

Percy Charles Russell Dodd. Taken in 1913 on his promotion to the rank of Captain. Wearing the ribbon of his Durbar medal. (With permission of Percy Dodd's daughters)

of movements by Khan, Dodd pushed forward reinforcements of troops and guns, to these locations. As the rumours proved unfounded, he recovered the guns, in particular to Parachinar, so they could be held as a central reserve. And he was reinforced by 22 MMG on 17 May, and 3rd Guides Infantry Battalion on 22 May.[5]

Nadir Khan moved from Matun on 23 May, heading south-east, down the Kaitu, effectively threatening both Bannu and Thal. In the face of this threat, the Waziristan militia evacuated Spinwam border post on 24 May and other garrisons along the Upper river in north Waziristan. These were pulled back to Idak on the Tochi. A number of the militia deserted and the Wazirs rose and joined the Afghans. Nadir Kahn occupied Spinwam on 25 May with a force of 3000 Afghan infantry, two 10cm Krupp field howitzers and seven 7.5cm Krupp pack guns, as well as a large force of tribesmen, perhaps 9000, from Khost and Waziristan. Khan's movements caught the British by surprise; the route he used had been reported as being unfit for use by a large force. At Spinwam, Khan was equidistant from both Thal and Bannu and it was still not clear which he would move against. A small, all-arms column, a little under a battalion in strength was sent out from Bannu to watch the defile where the Kaitu joined the Kurram.[6] At the same time, from Kohat, General Eustace reinforced Thal with two battalions of infantry and a section of 23rd Mountain Battery; he then moved to Thal himself in order to take command in person. Although this left Kohat virtually defenceless, he could be reasonably confident that further reinforcements would arrive there from Peshawar and the Army Reserve. Once in Thal, Eustace set about improving both the inner and outer lines of defence.[7]

Thal is positioned at the meeting point of the Kurram, the Sangroba and the Ishkali. The Kurram flows in from the north-west and out to the south; at the time, it was between 75cm–1m deep. It is joined from the north-east, first by the Sangroba and then, about a mile to the south, by the Ishkalai. The main post, containing the fort, railway station and civil rest house, was situated on a broad plateau, about a mile across, between the Sangroba and the Ishkalai, and rising about 30m above them. Half a mile to the north of the post, across the Sangroba, was a militia fort and the village of Thal. The fort's water supply came from a well located by the Sangroba and was then pumped 300m to the fort. The road and rail links to Kohat left the post to the north-east, along the line of the Ishkalai, while the track to Parachinar followed the Kurram upstream to the north and north-west. The road towards Bannu followed the Kurram downstream towards the south.

Thal is dominated by high ground; to the Ishkalai a series of hill ridges run east to west, gaining height as they recede south from Thal. West of the Kurram is Khapianga, an isolated hill which rises 250m above the river. To the north-west is the peak of Khadimakh at 700m above the plateau, while to the east the ground rises gently to the watershed between the Kurram and the Miranzai.[8]

The uncertainty was ended on 27 May when Nadir Khan invested Thal; he set up camp at Yusaf Khel, on the Kurram, three miles upstream from Thal. His guns, which significantly out-ranged General Eustace's mountain guns, opened fire from here and from the slopes of Khapianga almost immediately, while Thal village was occupied by the Afghan infantry. Tribesmen took up positions on the lower slopes of Khadimakh and the hill ridges south of Thal. The RAF attempted to bomb the Afghan artillery positions but had only limited effect. Artillery fire hit the British petrol dump, rations in the railway station yard were set on fire and the wireless station was put out of action for a short while. The British abandoned the militia fort on the night of 28/29 May; it was occupied by the Afghans who were then in a position to threaten the water supply. The garrison dug large pits and lined them with tarpaulins to act as emergency reservoirs. The following night, 29/30 May, the Afghans attacked on the southern edge of the plateau. They were driven back by 1/109th Infantry and the mountain guns, but on the morning of 30 May, the Afghans managed to emplace a 7.5cm gun on the heights to the south of the fort. The artillery kept up its bombardment all day, seriously knocking about the fort and British gun emplacements. Nadir Khan had achieved a stunning strategic surprise; he had forced the evacuation of a significant portion of Waziristan, the garrison of the Upper Kurram was isolated and Thal, although not completely cut off, was now seriously threatened, with Afghan artillery inflicting considerable damage, food supplies running low and the water supply in danger.[9]

It was immediately obvious to the British that Thal had to be relieved quickly; had Thal fallen it would have been an immense blow to British prestige and the local tribes would have risen to support the Afghans. As it was, Nadir Khan's success put paid to the British intent, described in the previous chapter, to push forward towards Jalalabad from Dakka in the northern theatre and did much to reverse the effect of the Afghan defeats there. Reinforcements and transport were diverted from Peshawar and concentrated in Kohat, with the first units arriving on 28 May. Brigadier-General Reginald Dyer's 45 Infantry Brigade arrived on 29 May and 12 battalions of infantry, two batteries of field artillery, two machine-gun companies and a company of sappers and miners had arrived by 1 June. The relief column was formed from these troops and from those already in Kohat and concentrated initially in Togh, 33 miles west of Kohat. Under the command of Brigadier Dyer, the column consisted of about 3000 men from the four infantry battalions of Dyer's 45 Infantry Brigade, elements of two other infantry battalions, a squadron of 37th Lancers, guns from field, garrison and mountain artillery and an armoured car battery. To give the impression of a larger force of artillery, Dyer had trees lashed to some of his lorries to raise more dust. Despite many of the troops not having been fed or watered, and the heat of the day, the column set out for Thal on 31 May. Driven hard by Dyer, who marched at its head for much of the way, the column reached Darsamand, just nine miles from Thal, that afternoon and entrenched for the night. Heliograph and wireless communications were established with Thal. The column resumed its march at 0500 hours the following morning, and at the RAF landing ground, two miles short of Thal, Dyer met with General Eustace's staff officer, Major Guy Wylly, to receive a detailed description of the Afghan forces. He then launched his forces into the attack straight away.[10]

Brigadier Dyer deployed his guns and fire was opened against both the hills to the south of the Ishkalai and Thal village, to give the impression that both would be attacked together. An infantry attack was then mounted by 1/69th Punjabis and 3/150th Infantry on the tribesmen occupying the ridges in the south. This was covered by 1/25th London Regiment and 2/41st Dogras who pushed forward to a position just east of Thal fort. The accuracy of the artillery fire and the swiftness of the attack proved too much for the tribesmen. They broke and ran and, by 1600 hours on 1 June, the key ground to the south of Thal was held by the British. A section of 89th Battery, Royal Field Artillery (RFA) was then pushed forward to Thal fort to engage and silence the Afghan guns on the slopes of Khapianga. Thal was relieved and the following morning, 2 June, General Eustace handed command over to Dyer and returned to his own headquarters in Kohat. Brigadier Dyer now deployed a two-battalion attack to clear the lower slopes of Khadimakh, north-west of Thal. The infantry were supported by the RAF dropping bombs and machine gunning the tribesmen, and it was while this attack was in progress, Dyer received notification from Nadir Khan stating he had been ordered to suspend hostilities by the amir. Dyer is supposed to have replied, 'My guns will give an immediate reply, and a further reply will be given by the Divisional Commander, to whom this letter has been forwarded.' It was soon apparent that Nadir Kahn was in full retreat back into Afghanistan. Attempting to preserve his infantry, for the heat of summer was intense, Dyer pushed a column consisting of his armoured cars and a squadron from 37th Lancers up the left bank of the Kurram to harass the retreating Afghans; his artillery also shelled Khan's former camp at Yusaf Khel, until RAF reconnaissance reported that the Afghan headquarters had withdrawn three miles to the west. The following day, 3 June, a further column of a half squadron of 37th Lancers, a half company of 1/25th London Regiment (60 rifles with four Lewis guns), a section of 89th Battery, RFA and two armoured cars moved off from Thal at 0700 hours. They forded the Kurram at Pir Kasta and reached Yusaf Khel at 1100 hours. Here they found a scene of utter disorder; the camp had been abandoned in haste and was littered with ammunition and stores. The column was unable to carry these off and arrangements were made for camels to come out and recover them back to Thal on 4 June. However, before this could be enacted, the local villagers stripped the site and removed everything of value. Preparations were then put in hand to follow Khan back to Matun, but these were curtailed when Dyer received official notification of the armistice which came into force on 3 June 1919.[11] The British and Indian forces lost 12 dead and 82 wounded during the siege;[12] Afghan loses are not known.

The Afghans had missed what was probably their best opportunity of the war. Nadir Khan had surprised the British and kept their high command on the back foot. He had brought a superior force successfully to Thal, which had a lengthy perimeter, hastily prepared and inadequately defended by largely young and inexperienced troops. A determined infantry attack might well have overrun the garrison. Instead, Khan had tried to rely on his artillery to batter General Eustace into submission. Had Thal fallen then this would almost certainly have led to a general uprising of the tribes, and a secure route would have been opened from Afghanistan right through the North West Frontier to British India. Additionally, Brigadier Fagan and his troops would have been cut off from reinforcement at Parachinar in the Upper Kurram. However, once Khan had appeared in front of Thal, the British had reacted promptly. Major-General Eustace had moved to command at the threatened point and Brigadier-General Dyer had proven an aggressive and able commander. Dyer had driven himself and his troops hard when required but was measured and sensitive when the situation was less urgent. His troops had responded well, and he had proven himself as a tactician. He will be remembered for Amritsar; he deserves to be better remembered for his success at Thal that undoubtedly saved the British from serious embarrassment.[13]

As indicated in the first chapter, even as military events were unfolding on the Khyber, at Spin Baldak and in the central theatres, activity was continuing on the diplomatic line. As early as 10 May, after the failure of the Peshawar uprising, but before the British had successfully regained control of Bagh, it appeared that Amanullah was starting to regret the invasion. He wrote to the viceroy on this date complaining about the arrest of Ghulam Haidar, the Afghan postmaster in Peshawar. The amir also stated he had moved troops to the frontier in order to prevent the disturbances in India from spreading into Afghanistan, and he regretted that the British would not formally recognise the independence of Afghanistan. The British were having none of it and responded by using the RAF to drop propaganda leaflets, claiming that the Afghan forces had been defeated, the British were assembling a vast army and attempting to divide the amir from his people.[14] Following the successful British attacks to restore the Khyber, the Afghans had opened unofficial negotiations on 15 May for an end to the conflict via the Afghan envoy in India, Sardar Abdur Rahman Khan. These negotiations continued throughout May, whilst the British made preparations to move forward from Loe Dakka and as Nadir Khan laid siege to Thal, encouraged in part by the RAF successfully bombing Kabul on 24 May. Then, on 31 May, even as Brigadier Dyer was marching to the relief of Thal, the amir formally asked for an armistice.[15]

This request was welcomed by the British side. Having been surprised by Nadir Khan at Thal, and despite the success of the attack on Spin Baldak and of operations to restore the Khyber, the British were feeling the strain. Both the southern and central theatres were still threatened by regular Afghan forces gathered on the border. It was also obvious that an advance from Loe Dakka towards Jalalabad would require more transport than was immediately available, now that the reserves had been diverted to Kohat to relieve Thal. In all three theatres, although the tribes had not risen in the numbers that Amanullah had envisaged, the situation remained tense. In and around Dakka, the Afghan tribes remained actively hostile. This was a particular worry as it was recognised that advancing to Jalalabad could not be the strategic objective, and the lessons of history were that even securing Kabul might not prove decisive.[16] So, in a letter from the viceroy to the amir, dated 2 June, the British granted an armistice, which was to come into effect the following day. The essence was that the Afghan forces would withdraw, the British would remain in place, the RAF would have freedom of movement, but would not undertake attacks, and Amanullah would discourage the tribes from hostile action. The detail is given in the official history, quoting an extract from the viceroy's letter:

1. That you should at once withdraw all your troops from the frontier. No Afghan troops are to be located within 20 miles of the nearest British Force.
2. That the British troops should remain where they are in Afghan territory, with freedom to continue such military preparations and precautions as may be deemed necessary. The troops will, however, take no offensive action whatever, so long as the terms of the armistice are observed by your side.
3. British aircraft will not bomb or machine gun Afghan localities or forces so long as the armistice is observed, but they will have freedom of movement in the air to reconnoitre and observe the positions of Afghan forces in order to ensure against any concentration or collection of Afghan forces or tribesmen in contravention of the armistice.
4. Further, that you undertake that your people will not fire on or molest British aircraft and will return without delay, unhurt, any British aircraft and airmen who may have been forced to land in Afghan limits and use your utmost endeavour to ensure the safety of any British airman who may be forced to land in tribal territory.
5. That you should at once send urgent messages to the tribes both on your own side and on our side of the Durand frontier, into whose limits your troops have advanced, or who have been excited by your agents and proclamations, stating that you have asked the Government of India for a cessation of hostilities and that you will not countenance further aggressive action on their part against the British Government; and if they take such action it will be at their own risk and they will receive from you and find no asylum in Afghanistan, from which they will be ejected if they come.[17]

The acceptance of the armistice brought to an end the major operations by British and Indian soldiers against Afghan regular troops, during which period there had been relatively little trouble from the tribesmen, with the notable exception of Waziristan. It saw the start of what the official history describes as, 'Phase 3 – From the 3 June to 8 August. Cessation of hostilities on the part of the Afghan regulars, but general activity on the part of our border tribes.'[18] Moreover, even as Thal was under siege, the Upper Kurram and Parachinar were also under threat, from four separate groups of Afghan regulars and tribesmen located near Peiwar Kotal, Kharlachi, Ghoz Garhi and Lakka Tiga. The first was the largest of these groups, numbering some 2000–3000 regulars, with mountain guns, backed up by about 1500 tribesmen. The other groups were smaller, with greater proportions of tribesmen to regulars, but each numbered at least 1000 persons. Facing these threats, Brigadier Fagan had continued the strategy initiated by Major Dodd, namely that the Kurram Militia maintained overwatch on each of the enemy groups on the border, while the regular troops were kept in reserve at Parachinar, ready to react to any incursion by the Afghans or tribesmen. Following the reinforcement mentioned previously, the forces held at Parachinar now consisted of a squadron of 37th Lancers, 22 MMG,[19] two sections (four guns) from 28th Mountain Battery and the infantry battalions of 1/57th Frontier Rifles and 3rd (Queen Victoria's Own) Guides Infantry. Those militia, some 400 of them, not deployed to the border or to the chain of posts linking Parachinar and Thal down the Kurram Valley, were also held in Parachinar.[20]

The first Afghan move was made by the group close to Peiwar Kotal, who attempted to advance across the border on 26 May. They were beaten back by the Kurram Militia, who were initially reinforced with a section from 22 MMG, with a second section following the next day. The attacks, however, lacked coordination. The militia post at Kharlachi was attacked on 28 May; again reinforcements, this time of Lancers, a section of 22 MMG and mounted and dismounted infantry from the Kurram Militia, were sent from Parachinar. Again, the attack was beaten off and the reinforcing elements returned to Parachinar. The most serious attack occurred over the course 28–29 May, when the Afghan force in the vicinity of Lakka Tiga attempted to invade, supported by a number of Jaji tribesmen from the Afghan side of the border. This attack was probably attempting to link up with the Orakzais and Zaimukhts, whose tribal lands lay on the eastern side of the Kurram, in the vicinity of Sadda and Alizai. No reinforcements were released from Parachinar to meet this attack, but the 200 men of the Kurram Militia, despite being greatly outnumbered, moved out to attack the enemy. They were unable to inflict a decisive defeat, but by aggressive and skillful manoeuvring, they managed to check and block the invasion. This was particularly significant because on 29–30 May parties of Orakzais gathered in the Khurmana and attacked Badama Post. The Kurram Militia garrison of Badama, however, combined with that of Sadda and drove off the tribesmen, inflicting about 20 dead, for the loss of one of their own. Had the attack at Lakka Tiga succeeded, it would have linked up with the Orakzais at Sadda, and the Upper Kurram would have been cut off from Thal; again, such an event could have prompted a much more general uprising of the tribes.

Brigadier Fagan, Major Dodd and the commanding officers of the other major units in Parachinar were now, at the end of May, aware that Brigadier Dyer was marching to relieve Thal. Offensive action was, therefore, planned in the Upper Kurram, in the form of raids across the border at Peiwar Kotal and Kharlachi, which could be followed up by a column planned to harass Nadir Khan's forces as they retreated on Matun. The raid at Peiwar Kotal was abandoned as being impractical owing to a lengthy approach march, which would have to be made at night across very poor ground. The Kharlachi attack was carried out through the morning of 3 June, after the troops had moved into position overnight. It was completely successful; the Afghan post at Amir Thana was captured and the Afghans retreated, having taken about 60 casualties. British Indian loses were two killed and five wounded. As it transpired, Khan's retreat from Thal was so rapid, and as the armistice came into effect, the plan to harass Khan on his way back to Matun was then abandoned. Confirmation of the relief of Thal and the armistice were received in Parachinar on 3 June, and no further offensive action was taken against the Afghans, although a column was sent south from Parachinar to check and open the track to Thal.[21]

The Afghans, however, continued to make threatening moves, particularly in the area of Peiwar Kotal. Commencing on 5 June, they attacked at Teri and the Kurram Militia were again reinforced from Parachinar. The action continued through 6 June as the Afghans then threatened Shalozan. Further reinforcements of the Kurram Militia were made from Parachinar in the form of 57th Rifles, Frontier Force, and the Afghans withdrew back to Peiwar Kotal on 7 June. They made no move, however, to withdraw any further, although they were required to do by the armistice terms. That same day, Major-General William Beynon, now commanding the Kohat-Kurram Force, arrived in Parachinar and despatched a letter to the Afghan commander, Shah Mahmud, Nadir Khan's younger brother, demanding the withdrawal of Afghan troops. An apology for the attack on Teri was received a little later, and Mahmud stated he had only become aware of the armistice on 7 June. Meanwhile the British set about reorganising their troops within the central theatre. Parachinar was reinforced and two additional infantry battalions were incorporated into 60 Infantry Brigade. 65 Infantry Brigade was formed at Thal with four infantry battalions, and 47 Infantry Brigade made up the garrison at Kohat. Those troops not belonging to the Kohat-Kurram Force were gradually withdrawn and returned to their home stations.[22]

The actions north and west of Parachinar on 6–7 June were the last engagements between regular troops of the war. However, south of Thal, two punishment operations were conducted against the Wazirs by 65 Infantry Brigade. The first, a small column, conducted its operation 10 June and carried off large quantities of grain, *bhoosa* and building materials from Biland Khel. The other, both larger and of longer duration, left Thal on 16 July. By the time it returned on 20 July, it had burned 54 villages, destroying their towers. The tribesmen were very unsettled by the drawn-out negotiations, which took place at Rawalpindi. Following the armistice on 3 June, the formal peace treaty was not concluded until 8 August. During this period, the tribesmen came to believe that the amir was playing for time and intended to resume hostilities; they, therefore, saw little point in ceasing to make trouble and carried out a series of attacks against British posts in the Kurram until the peace was formally ratified at Rawalpindi.[23] One of the last of the actions was at Badama Post at the end of July; it is described in the official history:

On the 30th of July, a report was received that a large body of Orakzais and Zaimukhts were collecting in the Khurmana Valley to raid the Kurram, and to attack the posts of Badama and Sadda. Reinforcements of regular troops were sent to Sadda, whilst four aeroplanes flew over the Khurmana to locate the gathering. On their way back, the last machine was shot down at short range by a party concealed on the hill side, and the pilot and observer were both wounded. A race for the wrecked machine then took place between the tribesmen and the Militia from Badama. The Militia just won, and the wounded airmen, who had roughly dismantled their machine, were brought in. The engine was brought in intact the following morning by a party of Kurram Militia from Badama, assisted by a detachment of regular troops from Sadda.[24]

This was the action at Badama Post, although, as we shall see, the official history does not give a complete picture as to what actually happened at the post at the end of July. The first regular troops to arrive in Sadda as reinforcements were from 22 MMG. The next chapter will look at the background to the early use of motorcycles and motorcycle combinations in the British army, at the forming of the battery in the UK in 1915 and how they came to be in India. The chapter will also describe the background and lives of some of those men who made up the personnel of the battery.

CHAPTER 3

Military Motorcycling and Raising 22nd Battery Motor Machine Gun Service

In the late 19th century, the internal combustion engine arrived in Britain. Bicycle manufacturers and engineering pioneers, such as Frederick Simms, experimented with the fitting of engines into bicycle frames and thus the motorcycle was born. At first, the military showed little enthusiasm for such innovations, but the advent of the Boer War started to spark some interest in mechanised transport on both sides of the Atlantic. Initially, the interest was in steam traction engines for towing artillery, but as mechanical transport developed, so did War Office curiosity; the Mechanical Transport Committee was established in 1900, responsible for experimentation and reporting. The committee was responsible for every aspect of transport for the army's supply chain and included four sub-committees. These were Experiment and Motor, Royal Artillery, Royal Engineers and Army Service Corps. By 1907, enthusiastic reservists, including Lieutenant Albert Trapman, 26th Middlesex (Cyclist) Volunteers, were lobbying for the use of motorcycle despatch riders. They were supported by organisations such as the Auto Cycle Union and the popular press; the Mechanical Transport Committee did not share this enthusiasm, reporting in 1909, 'It is understood that Motor Cycles are not generally suited for Mechanical Transport Work.'[1] However, even by this date, lorries and motorcycles were officially being used for the first time on military manoeuvres. This led to the starting of the Motor Vehicle Subsidy Scheme; private vehicle owners were paid to provide their vehicles to the army in the event of a mobilisation.

It was 1910, though, which was to be the breakthrough year for military motorcycling, certainly within the United Kingdom. A large-scale cavalry exercise was held in August 1910, during which volunteer riders, still using their own vehicles, were employed as vehicle escorts, despatch riders and scouts. The exercise was considered a success, despite difficulties in getting sufficient numbers of motorcyclists, in demonstrating that officers could use motorcycles to supervise motor transport in a manner not possible with a bicycle or horse. It was following on from this experiment that Major-General Douglas Haig recommended the organisation of a signals squadron of cars and motorcycles[2] and the Mechanical Transport Committee recommended that all mechanical transport companies should be using motorcycles to aid communications. The War Office formed a special technical committee to investigate how the men might be recruited, but the Mechanical Transport Committee was still focusing on the use of motorcycles as communication agents and scouts, not looking at the transporting of troops and equipment. The 1910/11 report did hint that this might be a possibility in the future,[3] but it was not pursued until 1914, when the use of machine-gun carriers was first considered.

The Special Technical Committee was chaired by Brigadier-General Carleton, Director of Recruiting and Organisation. In addition to War Office personnel, a number of prominent civilians were members, including Mr F. Straight of the Auto-cycle Union and Reverend F. W. Hassard-Short of the Automobile Association. Published in December 1911, the report recommended standards for numbers of personnel, pay, equipment and mechanical inspections of motorcycles.[4] But actual progress in establishing military motorcyclists remained too slow for Albert Trapman and his fellow enthusiasts. Early in 1912, they set up the National Association of Cyclist Defenders (later to become the Legion of Cyclists); a group of patriotic motorcyclists ready to support the army in time of need and keen to act as a lobby group to encourage the War Office to implement the recommendations of Carleton's Special Technical Committee. Through 1912, the Legion grew to over 2000 members and organised three mass mobilisations of riders. This seemed to be effective; the 1912 annual September manoeuvres were supported by 255 motorcyclists, and afterwards, the Territorial Force motorcycle establishment was increased to 112 for Royal Engineers and 221 for cyclist battalions. Volunteers had to be aged between 17 and 36 and provide their own motorcycle for a term of four years, attending for 40 hours service in year one and then 10 hours in the following years. An annual camp allowance of £6 6s. per day was paid, along with 8s. petrol and insurance allowance on manoeuvres with a further 8s. if lodgings were not provided. Those in the cyclist battalions received a £1 per year cycle grant and damage was made good if sustained on duty. Finally, in July 1913, once the Territorial Reserve was formally established, Army Order 230 put the recommendations of the Carleton Committee in place by establishing three classes of reserve military motorcyclists. These were Class 1, Royal Engineer Despatch Riders for service at home or abroad, Class 2, Territorial Reserve Force Motorcyclists for service at home, and Class 3, Technical Reserve riders to act as a pool to replace vacancies or casualties in Class 1 or 2.[5]

Motorcycle despatch riders and armoured cars were used from the earliest days of the war. Even though the army had been slow to appreciate the value of both the motorcycle and the machine gun, with the war initially characterised by fluid warfare, it soon became apparent that highly mobile machine-gun units would be of considerable value. An early proponent of their use was Commander Charles Rumney Samson[6] of the Royal Naval Air Service, commanding the Eastchurch (Mobile) Squadron. As the war broke out, Samson took his squadron to France, in support of Allied ground forces along the French and Belgian frontiers. In late summer of 1914, with too few aircraft at his disposal, Samson exploited the privately owned motor cars a number of his men had brought to war and had them patrol the local countryside, mainly with the intent of providing security for the lines of communications and picking up aircrew who might be forced to land in hostile territory. One of his earliest patrols, comprising two cars, nine men and one machine gun, ambushed a German car near Cassel. Inspired by this success, Samson had two of his cars, a Mercedes and a Rolls-Royce, armoured. These vehicles had only partial protection, with a single machine gun firing backwards. Within a month, most of Samson's cars had been armed and some armoured. These were joined by further cars that had been armoured in Britain with hardened steel plates at naval workshops. Aggressive patrolling by Samson's improvised force in the area between Dunkirk and Antwerp did much to prevent German cavalry divisions from carrying out effective reconnaissance. With the help of Belgian Post Office employees reporting German movements by telephone, Samson was also able to probe into German occupied territory. Around Dunkirk, his force was able to make use of their mobility and machine guns to exploit open flanks, cover retreats, and race German forces to key terrain.[7]

Army Order 480, dated 12 November 1914 and sanctioned in February 1915, approved the addition to each division of a unit known as a Motor Machine Gun Battery. They were designated to be units of the Royal Field Artillery and were collectively known as the Motor Machine Gun Service, with the first Commanding Officer being Lieutenant Colonel R. W. Bradley DSO. One battery was allocated to the divisional artillery of each division of the British Expeditionary Force. A battery consisted of 18 motorcycle/sidecar combinations, carrying six Vickers machine guns, ammunition and spare parts, eight motorcycles without sidecars and two or three cars or trucks. Despite Triumph, Phelon & More and Douglas being the preferred suppliers of motorcycles for despatch riders, it appears that Royal Enfield and Scott were the main suppliers of motorcycles with sidecars as gun and ammunition carriers for the Motor Machine Gun Service. These, however, were soon replaced by the more robust Clyno combination, which was adopted as the standard machine from February 1915. From then onwards, Clynos were delivered to Kempton Park Racecourse in convoys of 20–25 each weekend, before being shipped out to France. 22 MMG, when it shipped to India the following year, was equipped with Clyno carriers and Triumphs for the solo riders, and it is likely that these machines would have been allocated to them during their training at Bisley. A battery was typically commanded by a captain or major, with a senior lieutenant or captain as his second in command and three subalterns (lieutenants and 2nd lieutenants) as section officers. There was a battery headquarters section and then three machine gun sections, each operating two guns and typically being formed of about 18 men. The men were found from volunteers or by special enlistment of men known to be actively interested in motorcycles, such as members of the cycle clubs previously referred to. The Coventry office of the enthusiasts' magazine *Motor Cycle* was listed as a recruiting office for the Motor Machine Gun Service.

Even as the Motor Machine Gun Service was being formed, however, the war was changing from relatively mobile warfare to the stalemate of the trench systems. It became increasingly difficult for the motor machine gun units to operate as a mobile force, and in many cases, they had to operate as conventional machine-gun sections. The batteries did perform useful service on several occasions, in particular in March 1915 during the battle of Neuve Chapelle, following which, in April 1915, the Motor Machine Gun Service received an official acknowledgement from British Expeditionary Force HQ of the 'invaluable' work it had rendered in the fighting line.[8] Through the summer and autumn of 1915, as the war stagnated further into a static deadlock of trench systems, it became ever clearer that the machine gun was the new queen of the battlefield and that defence was the dominant phase of warfare. Battalion machine-gun sections were grouped together to form dedicated machine-gun companies and, eventually, battalions, operating under the centralised tactical control of brigades and divisions. To provide an administrative and training framework, the Machine Gun Corps came into being in October 1915[9] and incorporated the Motor Machine Gun Service as the Machine Gun Corps (Motors). This was as the early Motor Machine Gun Service batteries were being withdrawn from France and redeployed into other theatres more suited to the use of motorcycles. Other batteries had their manpower utilised to provide crews for the newly formed tank units within the Heavy Section of the Machine Gun Corps.

What then was the background to 22 MMG being on the North West Frontier for the Third Afghan War? Conventional wisdom has it that the battery formed in India in April 1916.[10] On the evidence of service records, shipping records and photos, it seems more likely that they formed in England, at Bisley, in the summer of 1915. Bisley was where Motor Machine Gun Service training took place, and in training here, the battery was following in the footsteps of previous, lower-numbered Motor Machine Gun Service batteries, particularly 'Coventry's Own', 5th Battery Motor Machine Gun Service. Training, of course, was the preserve of the War Office and Bisley, on the heathlands of Surry, provided a major training area which was suitable for both motorcycles and machine guns. Ranges of up to 1100m were available to enable the guns to be fired. The troops were cross trained; they had all established already that they had an element of mechanical ability and riding skills. These skills were developed by riding, both cross country across the heathlands and by longer road runs down to places such as Eastbourne on the coast.

Gunners from 22 MMG on the beach in Eastbourne. Probably taken while the battery was training in late summer of 1915. Note the cap proudly displaying the MMGS badge. James Petrie Jamieson front right holding a pipe. (From J. P. Jamieson's album)

All were trained to use their primary weapon system – the Vickers machine gun. This cross training gave flexibility to the battery in employing its soldiers and resilience in the face of casualties. Accommodation at Bisley was initially rudimentary, but certainly by early 1916, the majority of soldiers undergoing training was housed in 70-man huts. To combat the cold of winter, they were equipped with three stoves, although some recruits report using as many as seven blankets. The standard of food appears to have varied; some letters home record the writers as being well fed. Others had different memories; Gunner Frederick Harold Rood served with 1st Armoured Motor Battery of the Machine Gun Corps, but as he had a service number of 1812, and enlisted in 1915, he was at Bisley at much the same time as the soldiers of 22 MMG. He recalls:

> Training at Bisley was keen and thorough, but the diet we got was not up to the standard of our training routine, and like most young soldiers I was always hungry. There was no such thing as supper; well not officially! But one day a quiet rumour floated around that anyone wanting supper could get this at Hut 7 at 9pm. Our pay of 1/- per day did not leave much scope for an evening meal outside camp, so my chum and I decided to look into this supper rumour. The price per head was a mere 3d (no change given) and the number limited to the first 300 arrivals. 'Just up our street', said my chum and we joined the crowd already assembled outside the specified hut at 8.45pm. Two quartermasters stood outside the closed doors of the hut taking the cash and counting the number in the queue. Directly the stipulated number had been reached the doors opened and in we filed. In anticipation of something good, we had brought along our own enamel plate, pint mug, and a knife. Each of us received a pint of cocoa, one thick slice of bread, a lump of cheese, and a lump of butter. All went down well and we did not grumble at the price. Supper over, we were ordered to depart by the rear doors and without noise. During the training period at Bisley my friend and I attended many of these unofficial supper sessions. We often wondered how much cash was collected from our ration, and if any charitable fund received any benefit![11]

Frustratingly, there are very few surviving records from the Machine Gun Corps, following a fire in their headquarters after the war, and official paperwork to detail exactly when 22 MMG formed does not appear to have survived. Nor has it been possible to establish whether the battery was always intended for service in India or why the decision was taken to deploy it out there. What is clear, however, is that the men of the Motor Machine Gun Service, or 'The Motors' as they were commonly known, thought themselves a breed apart. They had been recruited, or joined, because of their mechanical knowledge and skills; applications from chauffeurs and mechanics were particularly encouraged. The Coventry-based magazine *The Motor Cycle*, particularly through the editor Mr Geoffrey Smith, was the primary source of recruitment, and indeed selection, to the Motors. It was he who launched the initial campaign to recruit a battery from the Coventry area because it was the centre of Britain's fast-growing motor industry. This was the battery which was to become 5th Battery Motor Machine Gun Service. Initially, applicants were invited to *The Motor Cycle*'s office in Coventry, in order to undergo selection interviews and practical tests. The process attracted motorcycle and mechanical enthusiasts from around the country and from the overseas colonies, with potential recruits often making long journeys back to UK at their own expense. Those who had failed to get selected for pilot training or Royal Flying Corps applicants were also attracted and frequently had the required skills and knowledge. Formed in the autumn of 1914, 5th Battery Motor Machine Gun Service were in France by spring of 1915. The majority of the soldiers who ended up in 22 MMG were enlisted during the period from March through to July 1915. By this time, the supply of men from the Coventry area was diminishing and, still largely through *The Motor Cycle*, the Motor Machine Gun Service was casting the net wider around the country. A recruiting tour was conducted to Scotland; about a third of 22 Battery's men come from either Glasgow or Edinburgh and east coast Scotland. North-west England and London were also hot spots for battery recruits. Among the Scots

Gunner Walter Patrick. An enlistment photo in MMGS uniform, almost certainly from 1915. (Alex Bowell, from W. Patrick's album)

was James Petrie Jamieson. He does not appear to have qualified for the India General Service Medal 1908, with the North West Frontier clasp for the Third Afghan War of 1919, so he cannot have been present at Badama Post in July 1919. However, his grandson holds a large album of photos which cover his time and his comrades in India and have provided excellent reference material. From the album, it is clear that Jamieson was a member of 22nd Battery's Number 1 Section. It is also clear that Walter Patrick, born in the north west in 1894 was another member of Number 1 Section, and that he and Jamieson remained friends and kept in touch with each other after the war, at least until the late 1930s. Walter too cannot have been at Badama Post, but his descendants also hold many photos of his time in India.

As stated before, the men of the Motors thought themselves a breed apart. They had been recruited or volunteered as motorcycle machine gunners. They were less than happy to be incorporated into the Machine Gun Corps, even the branch of Machine Gun Corps (Motors), and they seem to have retained a high degree of loyalty to the Motor Machine Gun Service. They were proud of the unique cap badge of crossed Vickers machine guns surmounting the letters MMGS. They were reluctant to adopt the plain Machine Gun Corps cap badge, without letters underneath, or even the Machine Gun Corps (Motors) cap badge with its MGC (M) lettering. Whether in protest or otherwise, many broke off

Gunner Walter Patrick. In India, probably in 1916. (Alex Bowell, from W. Patrick's album)

the 'S' from the original cap badge and continued to wear it with the MMG letters. The battery also appears to have had cloth shoulder patches, with red 'Motor Machine Guns' lettering, when it was first formed. These appear from many photographs to have been recycled and used as helmet patches – fastened to the left-hand side of the soldiers' pith helmets. It is also telling that although its formal title should probably have been 22nd Battery, Machine Gun Corps (Motors), the battery is always referred to as 22nd Motor Machine Gun Battery. Even the battery war diary from the Third Afghan War uses this title.

There is some evidence that 22 MMG, in the autumn of 1915, either camped or at least conducted training runs down to Eastbourne and other destinations on the south coast. Certainly, the local Eastbourne press[12] makes much of a recruiting parade that was to take place in the town in early October 1915 and the fact that a battery (no number given) of the Motor Machine Gun Service was to take part. Sadly, the same press following the event describes it in detail but makes no mention of the presence of a motor machine gun battery; from which it is assumed the battery was pulled out of the parade at the last minute. The official battery photograph was taken in the autumn of 1915 at a training camp near Eastbourne.

22 MMG Battery photograph. Probably at Eastbourne, summer 1915. Cpl E. W. Macro thought to be the left hand, looking at the photo, seated figure. The officer in the centre of the seated row is thought to be Lieut Max Roescher. The photo is thought to have been taken before Maj Molony was appointed to the Battery. (From J. P. Jamieson's album)

It looks as if it was taken before the arrival of Major Alexander Weldon Molony as battery commanding officer because he cannot be identified in the image. The large officer in the centre of the seated row is probably Lieutenant Max Roescher, who spent some time in June and July 1915 as the assistant adjutant at Bisley but shipped to India with 22 MMG in February 1916 as Major Molony's second in command. He was with the battery during the Third Afghan War and briefly took over as the commanding officer, when Molony shipped home in October 1919. Max Roescher himself shipped home in December 1919 and was then discharged. Max was of German descent, his father was German, and he had the strong suspicions that he was sent to India in order to keep him away from the Western Front.[13] Certainly, after the war, he attempted to anglicise his name by changing it to Rosher; the National Archive holds two Medal Index Cards for him, one in each name.

Before proceeding overseas, motor machine gun batteries were also photographed for *The Motor Cycle* magazine. The photograph of 22nd Battery was published in *The Motor Cycle* of 23 March 1916. In the photograph, the battery can be seen with the CO, his driver and combination in the front, the three sections lined up behind and the support lorries of the Army Service Corps in the rear. The battery probably had about seven Army Service Corps personnel attached; they, in addition to a couple of medics, were very much part of the battery. Certainly, Driver John Girdwood ASC features in a number of photographs in the albums of two of 22nd Battery's soldiers – James Jamieson and Walter Patrick. As does Sergeant Alfred Fielder; more of him in a moment.

Before continuing, it is worth considering a little about the battery commanding officer, Major Molony. Although Molony was not present during the action at Badama Post, Bill Macro thought highly of him, and as the commander, he was the central figure of the battery and, as such, a key part of the story. It appears that after the war Molony contacted and tried to meet Bill, but Bill never responded; he was teaching by then and probably was too shy or thought it somehow not proper. Bill and others, including official documents, have him as Major Malony – he was in fact Alexander Weldon Molony. Born in Ireland on 5 June 1884 to Weldon Charles Molony and Eleanor Anne *née* Edwards,[14] Alexander was the eldest of three brothers, who all went in the army. Claude served with the Indian Army and was also to survive the war, but the youngest, Bertram was killed near Ypres in February 1915. Alexander's younger sister, Eileen, also married an army officer. Alexander was educated at Bedford College between 1895 and 1901, and in the 1901 Ireland Census, he is recorded as living with his parents on Upper Fitzwilliam Street in Dublin. Alexander commissioned into the 4th Leinsters in 1901[15] and then went to 1st Battalion Royal Dublin Fusiliers,[16] serving in

Officers of 1st Battalion Royal Dublin Fusiliers in early 1915 before embarkation at Avonmouth. Captain Alexander Molony is seated, third from right.

Malta, Egypt and India.[17] Life for a professional army officer before the war was good, offering travel and sport. Alexander was something of a tennis player, both on the amateur civilian circuit and on the military sports circuit.

When the war broke out in 1914, Molony appears to have still been serving with 1st Battalion in India. There is some evidence that he was posted back to the 2nd Battalion, who deployed to France with the British Expeditionary Force, but it seems more probable that this posting was cancelled and Molony returned to UK with the 1st Battalion in December 1914. Certainly, he was with the 1st Battalion when they embarked at Avonmouth for Egypt and subsequently Gallipoli; he appears in the photo of the battalion's officers.

So, he was with 1 Royal Dubs, as the battalion was known, when they were destroyed at V Beach at the Gallipoli landings on 25 April 1915. By this time, Molony was a captain, the second in command of W Company, onboard the SS *River Clyde*. This may be how he survived as the other companies of the Dublins went ashore from boats. He describes the experience as follows:

> The boats came in; they were met by a perfect tornado of fire, many men were killed and wounded. Wounded men were knocked into the water and drowned, but they kept on. Survivors jumped into the water in some cases up to their necks, and got ashore; but the slaughter was terrific. Most of the officers were killed or wounded. Colonel (Richard) Rooth, the C. O., was shot dead at the edge of the water; Major (Edwin) Featherstonhaugh, second-in-command, was mortally wounded in his boat; Captain (Arthur) Johnson (Y Company) was badly wounded while still in his boat; Captain (David) French, the biggest man in the Battalion, got ashore with a bullet through the arm; Captain (Denis) Anderson (X Company) was shot dead on the beach, and many others were wounded. The machine-gun detachment worked desperately to get their guns ashore, but they were nearly all killed or wounded; both the officers, Captain (George) Dunlop and Lieutenant (Reginald) Corbet, were killed. It was a terrible affair, and a few minutes of such fire decimated the Battalion. The people who got ashore established themselves on the beach as best they could under a bank which ran along the shore for some distance and was four to five feet high.[18]

Sergeant Alfred Fielder, ASC. Sergeant Fielder was the Battery Mechanic Sergeant. Here he is riding, in India, what was almost certainly the commanding officer's Clyno combination. His pre-war racing propeller mascot is just visible at the front of the motorcycle. (From JP Jamieson's album)

It must have been horrific, but it may also be that this experience shaped him and prepared him for command on the North West Frontier. Molony was wounded, either onboard the SS *River Clyde* or the following day once ashore. The wound was serious enough to cause his evacuation from Gallipoli in May to a hospital in Malta. In June, he was then transferred by hospital ship back to a UK hospital in Plymouth. He was subsequently granted two months' sick leave, and in October 1915,[19] he was attached to the Machine Gun Corps (Motors) and sent to command 22 MMG at Bisley.[20]

Alfred Fielder was one of the Army Service Corps personnel attached to 22 MMG and was the principal mechanic with the battery. His formal title was battery artificer sergeant mechanic; this was a key figure in a motorised unit. Fielder was also the CO's driver and well known on the pre-war motorcycle circuit as a trials' rider for New Hudson motorcycles. There is no evidence that Fielder was present in the action at Badama Post, indeed, it is highly likely that he was not because he does not appear to have been awarded the India General Service Medal 1908 and Afghanistan 1919 clasp, but he is included here for two reasons. First, to ensure the Army Service Corps are represented as integral members of the battery. And second because Fielder is an interesting character in his own right, and during the course of his service, he sent a number of letters back to UK which were published in *The Motor Cycle*. Alfred James Fielder, the son of Edward Benjamin Fielder and his wife Ann Elizabeth, was born in January 1891 in Lambeth and baptised on 12 April in Kennington.[21] Edward was also a London lad, while Ann was a northern lass, hailing from Manchester. Alfred was the second child and had a total of five brothers and four sisters. He enlisted 25 May 1915.[22] His papers give his profession as 'Motor Driver' and his height is recorded as being 5'9¾", with a chest of 37" and expansion of 3". He weighed in at 144lbs. One of his first letters to be published in *The Motor Cycle* describes the training at Bisley, probably before 22 MMG was formally formed:

> I have been in the Army now about six weeks, and like the open air life very much; in fact, it is a holiday, but we are being paid for it. The only thing I should like better is to be out in France with the boys, as no doubt we shall soon. I used to be a competition rider for the New Hudson Co., but some of the roads here are worse than in any trial.[23]

Shortly after this, on 28 August 1915,[24] Alfred married Florence Lilian Matthews at St James's, Holloway. While at Eastbourne, on 5 September, he was promoted to artificer sergeant. His rank was unpaid, although as an Army Service Corps soldier, he would have been receiving perhaps four times as much as his Motor Machine Gun Service counterparts.

Ernest William Macro was born 5 March 1896 in Stoke Newington, London. From his early days, Ernest was known as 'Bill'. He was the third child of William George Macro and his wife Adelaide née Broughton. William and Adelaide had married in July 1888, when William was aged 25 and Adelaide 24. Initially, certainly until after the 1891 census, they had lived with Adelaide's parents, Weldon and Louisa Broughton, in Tatsfield, Surrey, where Weldon was a land agent. Adelaide was the great-granddaughter of a Waterloo veteran, Trumpet Major William Weldon of the 13th Light Dragoons, but this is the only martial connection on this side of the family. William George Macro, like his father, also William, before him, worked for the Post Office throughout his adult life. The family were nonconformist congregationalist church goers. Bill's two elder sisters were Lily, born in 1890, and Olive, born 7 October 1891. Lily died just after the start of the war, tragically young, in October 1914, the day before her younger sister's 23rd birthday. Her death was not related to the war. Shortly after Bill's birth, his parents moved their family out of the Broughton family home to their own house in East Finchley, where, in due course, Bill won a scholarship to Finchley County School, his local grammar school. This was a mixed school and it is apparent from the school magazines that Bill was both sporty and intelligent, winning prizes for mathematics and representing the school in the 1st XI for football and the 1st VI for tennis. He was also a cricket player. Attending at the same school, although a couple of years below him, was Bill's wife to be, Avis Mary Prosser. Family stories[25] have it that Avis first noticed Bill when he came into her classroom, a little before the war, looking for a tennis partner; somewhat to her chagrin, she was not chosen. Her chance came a year or so later when Bill and a male friend were walking down a local road and encountered Avis coming in the opposite direction. Bill's friend asked to be introduced but Bill, claiming not to recognise Avis, crossed the road, introduced himself and departed with Avis, leaving his friend standing on the pavement.

Bill left school in the summer of either 1913 or 1914 and then went up to University College London. He enlisted in the army in 1915, when he was aged 19. By this time, he was 'walking out' with Avis, and throughout the war, he continued to write to her. His RAF service papers give his enlistment as 1 March 1915, however, if this is the case, he was not formally attested into the Motor Machine Gun Service until late June. This is recorded in *The Motor Cycle* and is supported by his service number of 1658; he was signed along with G F Bainbridge and W. Letheren (motor cyclists), H. Colwell and T. C. Pett (car drivers), and W. R. White and J. Henderson (artificers)[26] It was not entirely unusual for there to be a period of time between initial signing for the Motor Machine Gun Service and actual attestation and being taken on strength, but three to four months is longer than average. As it appears that none of those listed as signing with Bill ended up serving with him in 22 MMG, it is not known whether he knew them and was then separated, whether he had friends or knew others who had enlisted previously and then linked up with them in 22 MMG or whether he simply enlisted and was then posted to the battery without knowing those around him. Although his RAF service papers have survived, there is no trace of Bill's army service papers; they appear to have been either lost in the fire at Machine Gun Corps HQ at Shorncliffe in 1922 or when the World War I records were blitzed in 1940.

It is worth mentioning one other early member of 22 MMG, although he was not destined to sail to India with the rest of the battery. Instead, he was to travel to the battlefields of northern France as one of the very first tank commanders. Herbert George Pearsall, known as George, was born at Smethwick on 17 July 1888; the elder son of George and Mary Ellen Pearsall. Educated locally he trained as a teacher and won a scholarship to Cambridge. He attended Emmanuel College from 1907 to 1911 and then gained an appointment as a mathematics master at Batley Grammar School. He was acknowledged as a caring and thorough teacher, and he was also an active sportsman. When war broke out, George enlisted at Dewsbury on 6 April 1915 and joined the Motor Machine Gun Service at Bisley on 14 May. He was promoted corporal on 18 June and then sergeant on 14 August 1915 with 22 MMG. Whilst still on their unit strength, he applied for a commission on 1 January 1916, which was countersigned by Lieutenant Colonel Bradley on 8 January. After completing officer training at Cambridge, George Pearsall was commissioned into the Machine Gun Corps on 14 April 1916. He then joined D Company of Heavy Branch Machine Gun Corps, deployed to France with them and was commanding tank D11 *Die Hard* at Flers on 15 and 16 September 1916; the first occasion in which tanks were used in action. George earnt a Military Cross in the process. He remained with tanks for the remainder of the war, which he survived, only to die from Spanish influenza on 19 March 1919, shortly after his discharge.[27] George is the only person who is known to have left 22nd Battery before they deployed to India, but it is possible there were others who sought commissions or transfers. As we will see, there were to be others who did so once the battery had deployed to India.

We may not know exactly why 22 MMG was deployed to India, but we do know that the battery sailed from Devonport on 26 February 1916 on the SS *Beltana*. Five officers[28] are listed by name on the manifest,[29] along with, un-named, 68 NCOs and soldiers, and the battery's motorcycles, sidecars and lorries. It is likely that they were marched to Brookwood and then moved by train to Plymouth, although it is, of course, possible they self-deployed on their bikes and lorries. Certainly, 1st Armoured Motor Battery, with Gunner Fred Rood, were moved by train at night from Brookwood to Devonport.[30] 1st Armoured left the UK in January 1916, the month before 22nd Battery sailed, on the slightly smaller troopship *Huntsgreen*, and headed for British East Africa, but the experience must have been very similar. Rood continues:

> Early the following morning we filed on the troopship *Huntsgreen*. Our destination was somewhere out east but we did not know where. Hammocks were dished out and some of the crew showed us how to knot each hammock to the hooks running along the beams in the sleeping quarters below deck. It was a real work of art, for if one hammock got out of line it upset the whole lot. Next we were allocated to dining tables, 20 men to a table. Our troopship sailed at noon. A strong gale blowing in the English Channel kept everyone quiet. The storm got worse when we reached the Bay of Biscay. Giant waves, smashing against the ship, sounded like claps of thunder. The *Huntsgreen* pitched and rolled alarmingly. No-one

was allowed on deck. There were about two thousand troops on board, and everyone was sea-sick. I was ill for twenty-four hours, and most of the others in my section were sick for another twenty-four hours. When I recovered I began to feel hungry.[31]

Onboard the *Beltana*, James Jamieson records, on the back of one of his photos which shows troops on deck, that life jackets had to be worn while the ship cleared the danger area of the western approaches. This would almost certainly have been due to the threat from U-boats rather than the weather conditions. The officers travelled in first class, presumably in a degree of comfort, while the troops were accommodated in third class. The *Beltana* was Clyde built, by Caird & Co. of Greenock, and launched in 1912 for the P&O Branch Line. With a gross tonnage of 11,120, the ship was 160m long with a breadth of 19m and a draught of 10m; it was powered by 9000 IHP quadruple-expansion engines, which gave a speed of 14 knots. Before the war, *Beltana* had carried up to 550 passengers on the UK to Australia route via Cape of Good Hope.[32] Taken into war time service as a troopship, the vessel did many UK to India runs, normally via the Mediterranean and Suez Canal. *Beltana* resumed branch line duties after the war, but now via Suez, before being scrapped in 1933, after being sold to Japan as a whaling ship. Back in 1916, *Beltana* arrived in Bombay, India, on 20 March 1916.

H.M.A.T. Beltana. Taken during her wartime service; H.M.A.T. stands for His Majesty's Australian Troopship. 22 MMG shipped to India aboard this vessel, departing Devonport on 26 February 1916.

Onboard the *Beltana*. Lifejackets were worn at all times until the ship was clear of the Western Approaches, the danger area for U-boat attack. (From J. P. Jamieson's album)

CHAPTER 4

22nd Battery in India 1916 to 1919

Given the majority of 22 MMG soldiers had never been abroad, and that it is entirely possible that Major Molony was the only man of the battery to have previously been to India, the excitement and anticipation when the *Beltana* docked in Bombay must have been palpable. The heat, colours, smells, sights and sounds of India would have been as much an assault on the senses as they are today, and the contrast with wartime Britain would have been even more stark. India in 1916 was in many ways unaffected by the war; however, numbers of her soldiers, both from the British and Indian battalions, had been shipped to either Europe or the Middle East to take part in the war, but they had been replaced either by territorial battalions shipped out from UK or from increased recruiting to the Indian Army. There was no rationing, no blackout and no threat of violent death to the civilian population from German battleships appearing off the coast or from Zeppelin or Gotha aerial raids. The main threat to India was from a rising of the civil population, which German efforts were very focused on attempting to ferment. Bengal and Punjab remained sources of anticolonial activities. Revolutionary attacks in Bengal, associated increasingly with disturbances in Punjab, were significant enough to nearly paralyse the regional administration. Of these, a pan-Indian mutiny in the British Indian Army planned for February 1915 was the most prominent amongst a number of plots formulated between 1914 and 1917 by Indian nationalists in India, the United States and Germany. The planned February mutiny was ultimately thwarted when British intelligence infiltrated the Ghadarite movement, arresting key figures. Mutinies in smaller units and garrisons within India were also crushed.[1] Against this backdrop, the Defence of India Act 1915 was passed, limiting civil and political liberties. And in the succeeding months, the decision was taken to send 22 MMG to India.

Throughout 1915, the Germans, in addition to backing Indian nationalists indirectly, were fermenting their own Far Eastern strategy, designed to unleash a 'Holy War' that would sweep the British out of the Indian Empire. A key part of this strategy was infiltrating a diplomatic mission into Kabul, across British held Persia, to deliver German gold and gifts to the amir of Afghanistan, in order to persuade him to order his troops and tribesmen through the passes to invade British India. The mission was led by a Persian-speaking career diplomat, Captain Werner Otto von Hentig. The military commander was Captain Oskar von Niedermayer; a tough, ruthless and resourceful regular officer within the German army, with wide experience of the Middle and Far East, gained on behalf of German military intelligence. The two Germans, in addition to a number of other officers and non-commissioned officers, were accompanied by Raja Mahendra Pratap and Mohammed Barakatullah. Pratap was a minor Indian prince who hated the British and courted the Germans to try and drive them from India. Barakatullah was the leading Muslim revolutionary of the day who, due to his anti-British activities, had fled India before the war. He had offered his services to Germany as soon as the war had broken out.[2] Despite the difficulties, the mission crossed from Persia into Afghanistan in August 1915 and eventually reached Kabul in early October.[3] Here, however, although they were granted audiences with Habibullah, they never succeeded in gaining traction, although Habibullah managed to maintain the interest, without committing, until February 1916. At this point, the German elements of the mission gave up and retreated into Persia towards Turkey, leaving the Indians to form a 'Provisional Government of India' and continue to try and ferment unrest in India.[4]

Shortly after this, 22 MMG arrived in Bombay. In complete contrast to those of the battery that had never been abroad, there were also some who were extremely well travelled. Major Molony, of course, is the prime example, having served as a regular army officer in Malta, Egypt and, from 1911 to 1914, in India with 1st Battalion Royal Dublin Fusiliers. Amongst the soldiers were two brothers, Edward and Thomas Collins. The Collins parents and some of the family had emigrated to Canada before World War I. Edward Collins probably returned to the UK with Thomas to enlist in the Motor Machine Guns Service on 10 June 1915. The elder Collins brother, Charles, also returned from Canada and enlisted on the same day, into the Army Service Corps, attached to the Motor Machine Guns. Edward deployed to France, probably with Number 8 Light Amoured Motor Battery, in March 1916. He fell ill three months later, was returned to England in June and finally discharged in September 1917. But the younger brothers, Edward and Thomas, deployed to India with 22 MMG. Both served on the North West Frontier in 1919, but they were probably both in Number 1 Section and, hence, not likely to have been present at Badama Post. Thomas Collins later transferred to the Tank Corps, but both Edward and Thomas had been discharged by the end of 1920. The two younger Collins brothers then moved to Canada after the war working as mechanics and set up a motorcycle delivery service. In World War II, Thomas Collins served in Canada, training motorcycle despatch riders and then after the war as a civilian running a military vehicle repair depot. It may well be that there were others who travelled great distances to enlist; this was not unusual for the Motor Machine Gun Service.

Once the *Beltana* had docked, there would have been much work to do to get the troops off and also the motorcycles, transport and other equipment transferred onto the train that was to take the battery north to its ultimate destination of Rawalpindi. Doubtless, much of the heavy unloading would have been done by dockyard coolies, but there would have been the men's personal equipment to be transferred, and it is unlikely that any of the troops would have been willing to leave the transfer of the motorcycles in the hands of the Indians. Gunner John Travell Maton Gough, who was later to be the editor,

Gunner John Travell Maton Gough. With Barr & Stroud rangefinder and tripod. The instrument gave the exact range of any object up to 20,000 yards away. (Alex Bowell, enhanced by J. P. Jamieson)

with Sergeant J. R. Slater, of the 22nd Battery magazine, *Momagu*,[5] certainly indicates that there was little time in Bombay for sightseeing, 'On landing at Bombay we were met with the information that we had four days railway journey to Rawalpindi. We arrived safely, but before there was time to settle down we were called out for inspection, very shortly afterwards proceeding on a tour of the N. W. Frontier.'[6] However, there must have been some time for at least a few of the men to do a little exploring and absorb some of the sights and sounds of Bombay. For in the album belonging to Corporal J. P. Jamieson is a photo of a street vendor with the caption 'Our Cook, My first photo taken 8AM, breakfast.' Corporal Jamieson's grandson recalls that it was here that his grandfather learnt of that great Indian breakfast, the Bombay Oyster, a raw egg in a glass of vinegar, with a dash of Tabasco, swallowed whole. Apparently, JP remained a fan of the mixture even in his later years.[7]

As it still is today, the train was much the most common method of moving around India in the early 1900s. There were a number of potential routes and it is not known exactly what route was taken or whether the bikes and other motor transport were sent separately to the troops. However, the likelihood is that the vehicles would have been loaded onto rail flats which would have travelled as part of the same train as the men. The officers would have certainly travelled in first-class coaches. The soldiers would have been in no lower than second class and, given their status as white British troops, possibly in first class as well. Walter Patrick's photographs include a number of images taken on trains which might well be first class, although whether these are from an organised troop movement or from leave trips is not clear. However they travelled, the journey was long, taking about four days, and hot, but it would have doubtless been full of interest and exciting sights. Some 13 years later, a young officer, Frank Ingall, made a very similar journey to join his regiment for the first time, which he describes in *The Last of the Bengal Lancers*. Despite the elapsing of a decade, the experience would have been very similar for both the officers and soldiers of 22 MMG, although the soldiers would certainly have been rather more crowded than Ingall was:

> The distance between Bombay and Peshawar is over thirteen hundred miles, and in 1929 the train journey took about three days and two nights to complete. It was a fascinating journey, though, and a wonderful way to see the country for the first time. There were two main rail routes between Bombay and Delhi, the capital: one route, via Rutlam, was run by the Great Indian Peninsula (GIP) Railway; the other, via Baroda, by the Bombay, Baroda and Central Indian (BB & CI) Railway.[8]

It is not clear which route 22 MMG took north. However, as Bill Macro's album contains pictures captioned 'taken from B. B. & C. I. railway', it is perhaps likely that this was the route used, even if the photos may have been taken in 1919. Ingall continues:

From Delhi onto Peshawar it was the same train. On the Frontier Mail – all the trains had similar splendid names – I took the BB & CI route, along with three others of my group who were to be dropped off at different places en route; I was the only one going the whole way to Peshawar. We shared a four-berth compartment in a first-class carriage.

Indian trains of that era were drawn by huge locomotives, either coal- or wood-burning. Generally main-line trains were twelve or fourteen coaches long, with the third-class coaches immediately behind the engine, second-class behind them and the first-class coaches and restaurant car at the rear. The closer the engine the more the passengers suffered from smoke, smuts and cinders. And those old locomotives did spew cinders: one would find them in the bedding, the food, even in the drinking water. The bulk of passengers used the third-class, which had no bunks, just rows of hard benches, packed with humanity. Sometimes the overflow was such that people spilled out of the windows and stood on the running board or perched precariously on the roof of the lurching carriages. Whenever the train pulled in at a station there was always a frantic surge as people pushed forward, trying to enter the third-class coaches. Not that everyone paid; the Indian Railways did have ticket inspectors but in the scrum their job was well nigh impossible.

Second-class accommodation, chiefly patronized by middle-class Indians and Anglo-Indians, was a more spartan version of first-class, which consisted of two-berth and four-berth compartments, with a separate compartment for the personal servants of first-class passengers. The sahib log (basically white people) and the more affluent Indians travelled first-class. However, no matter how affluent, an Indian would never dream of sharing a compartment already occupied by a sahib if he could possibly avoid it …

Our four-berther on the Frontier Mail consisted of two lower and two upper bunks; by day the latter were hooked up to the roof and we all sat on the lower bunks. Each compartment had its own small bathroom with a tiny handbasin and a shower stall, both fed from a steel tank located on the roof. The water temperature depended on the air temperature outside: in summer it was scalding hot, in winter it was icy, and there was no way of regulating the system. The toilet consisted of an open vent directly above the permanent way …

… there were no air-conditioned coaches on the trains. Two small electric fans churned the turgid air overhead …

The carriage doors were heavy and could be locked from the inside. Three glazed windows on either side of the compartment were each covered with a framed wire gauze and a sliding wooden shutter. Theoretically all could be bolted shut but in fact they were very insecure; a smart bang on the outside caused the shutter, gauze and window each in turn to fall into its slot, enabling an intruder to enter the compartment. This was by no means uncommon, particularly at night when the occupants were asleep. Any noise the intruder made was covered by the constant rattle and clatter of the train. Professional thieves would wait in the darkness on station platforms and leap onto the running board as the train passed slowly through. As cunning as they were agile, they would stand on the running board until they were sure the occupants of a compartment were asleep, then open a window and quest with one hand for watch, wallet or handbag. Having made a haul they either climbed on to the roof or rode the buffers until the train slowed down at the next station when they would jump off and disappear into the night.

Major Alexander Molony. Believed to be taken in 1916 at Thal Fort. Major Molony, was the commanding officer of 22 MMG; he was attached to the Machine Gun Corps from the Royal Dublin Fusiliers. (From E. W. Macro's album)

Attock Fort. Built in the 1500's to protect the passage of the River Indus, the fort was, and still is, sandwiched between the river and the Grand Trunk Road, running from Rawalpindi to Peshawar. This photo appears to have been taken in March 1919, but the Battery would pass this way many times between 1916 and 1919. (From E. W. Macro's album)

Most of them were petty thieves and comparatively harmless, but sometimes the trains were worked by real thugs, armed and prepared to do murder if necessary.

... To pass the time, my three companions and I played endless games of bridge, vingt-et-un and piquet, in between watching the countryside pass and speculating on our future. And, every four hours or so, we were able to disembark when the train stopped at a major station. We would climb out onto the platform and wend our way, through hundreds of milling peasants trying to board the train, towards the restaurant car at the rear... The meals tended to be long and leisurely as we could not return to our compartment until the train stopped at the next station ...

And still the countryside slipped past. At first it all seemed the same, mile after mile of flat dusty brown plains with the occasional small hillock. By night the scene was dotted with endless tiny fires as families prepared their evening meal. I can still smell the aroma of burning cow dung to this day; it is strangely pleasant, quite unlike any other smell I have encountered. During the day we could see dozens of these cow dung patties drying out for use on the fire, either on the ground or on the walls of the mud huts. Decent sized trees are practically nonexistent over much of India, so dried cow dung is the only available fuel. Sometimes a new and enthusiastic civil servant would try to persuade the peasants to spread the dung on their fields, to improve the poor quality of the soil. But their attempts were in vain; cow dung was too precious as a fuel to be wasted like that.

Gradually, as the train headed ever north, the character of the countryside began to change and I saw more and more green fields where sugar cane, mustard and other crops were grown. This was the first sign that I was approaching the Punjab, for the fields were irrigated by man-made channels deriving their source from the great Punjabi rivers. The very name Punjab means 'Land of the Five Rivers': *panch* (five) and *ab* (water).[9]

Having arrived in Rawalpindi, 22 MMG moved into their new quarters of Cambridge Lines. These appear from photographs to be a solidly constructed Victorian cantonment barracks, which doubtless seemed relatively luxurious after the tents and accommodation huts in Bisley or the confines of the troop deck onboard the *Beltana*. At Rawalpindi, 22 MMG formed an element of the Divisional Troops (they belonged to, and were under the orders of, the divisional HQ, not one of its subordinate brigades) of the 2nd (Rawalpindi) Division. As such, their role was to form part of the response force should trouble break out on the North West Frontier; they could be sent quickly to the point of greatest need as a quick reaction force. In this role, it was important they were familiar with the whole of the frontier because, in time of crisis, they could find themselves being rushed to pretty much any point of it. So, the battery had little time to settle into their new accommodation. Almost as soon as they had arrived in Rawalpindi, they were deployed on a month-long familiarisation tour around the North West Frontier. Afterwards, Sgt Fielder, the battery sergeant mechanic, wrote to *The Motor Cycle*. A large section of his letter was reproduced in the issue of 13 July 1916 and is worth quoting here:

Attock Bridge over the River Indus. Sgt Macro's album records this was mined as the North West Frontier's last line of defence. (From E. W. Macro's album)

Remains of the Grand Trunk Road at Nicholson's Neck. The road is one of Asia's longest and oldest linking Delhi, Rawalpindi, Peshawar and Kabul. Alexander may well have had a hand in its construction, but the British maintained much of it as a military route during the colonial period. (From E. W. Macro's album)

We are very comfortable here, and, although rather hot, are getting used to it. We have just returned from a thousand mile patrol duty, and a brief description might interest you. We started from Pindi on April 5th for Nowshera, a distance of eighty miles, passing Fort Attock, near Hindus [sic], and Kabul [the junction of the rivers Indus and Kabul was at Attock] on the way and had a decent journey, except for the dust, which was awful. We stopped at Nowshera on the 6th. On the 7th we left for Chakdara Fort, up on the frontier, passing Mardan Malakan Forts, etc.; distance sixty miles. As this is up on the Himalaya Mountains, it was a fairly stiff climb. On the 8th we went field firing. The object of this was to put the fear of God into the native chief and tribesmen, which we fairly succeeded in doing, returning afterwards to Mardan; distance fifty miles. In the evening we went to see an Indian war dance, which is a very impressive affair.

The 9th, being Sunday, we spent tuning up our cycles. On the 10th we left for Peshawar in the pouring rain, and arrived covered with mud, etc.; distance forty five miles. On the 11th we went to Landikotal [sic] Fort, through the Khyber Pass, returning to Peshawar the same day; distance seventy-five miles. The road was very dangerous, being twisty and right at the edge of the cliffs. On the 12th we were inspected by the Chief Commissioner, who was very satisfied with our work. On the 13th we went to Chubcudda [I cannot determine where this might be] for field firing (this was where a big 'scrap' took place last August), returning afterwards to Peshawar; distance fifty miles. The 14th (day of rest) was spent overhauling the machines. On the 15th we were inspected by the General in Command before leaving for Kohat; distance forty miles. On the 17th we left Kohat for Thal, a nice journey; distance sixty-one miles. On the 18th we left for Parachinar, right up on the hills, where it was very cold at night, snow being on the hills just above; distance fifty-nine miles. On the 19th we went field firing on the Afghan frontier, afterwards returning to Thal; distance eighty miles. Here the natives held sports in our honour, and some of the performances were very good, especially their horsemanship.

On the 20th we left for Kohat, where we were inspected by the General in Command, afterwards going field firing; distance seventy miles. On the 22nd we left for Banu, a good journey, crossing several fords two feet deep; distance seventy-nine miles. On the 24th we left for Mirenshaw, over most awful roads; distance forty miles. One of the biggest frontier 'scraps' have occurred here. Quite a pleasant place to spend Bank Holiday in. On the 25th we left for Banu, a distance of forty miles, tuned up machines, etc. On the 26th we went field firing, and afterwards had a lecture by General Fane. On the 27th we returned to Kohat, a good journey; distance seventy-nine miles. On the 29th we returned to Peshawar, the hardest climb in the whole journey. On May 1st we left Peshawar for Pindi, a distance of 117 miles, in the pouring rain, and so ended a month's hard travelling.

Being the sergeant mechanic, in charge, I had a fairly busy time of it.[10]

The article is accompanied by a photograph captioned 'Sergeants of a M. M. G. S. Battery now in India' and identifying Kellett, Fielder, Ward, Whitfield and Barton. All are mounted on Triumph motorcycles, which, according to a sub-caption, 'Sgt. Fielder informs us, are giving every satisfaction.'[11]

When the battery returned to Rawalpindi in May the hot season would have been coming on fast. British troops would routinely leave their normal barracks on the plains during this season and move to what were referred to as summer

Nicholson's Neck monument. The obelisk, located just North of Rawalpindi, honours Brigadier-General John Nicholson, the Victorian 'Hero of Delhi'. Quite why the troops knew it as Nicholson's Neck is not clear, but the Battery would have seen it frequently as they left Rawalpindi for the Frontier. (From E. W. Macro's album)

Between Thal and Parachinar. Probably taken in 1916 the photo shows the Upper Kurram Valley. (From E. W. Macro's album)

or hill stations in the foothills of the Himalayas, in order to escape the worst of the heat and associated disease. 22 MMG was no exception, and at some stage in the summer of 1916, they moved to a tented/hutted camp at Kuldana near Murree in the Murree Hills. To this day, Murree remains a popular summer retreat in modern-day Pakistan. Thereafter, life for the battery settled into a routine of training and showing the flag, in order to impress, or intimidate, the 'natives', with the hot summer season generally being spent in the cooler hill stations and winter in camp at Rawalpindi. Life certainly was not unpleasant and there was time to take leave and travel to Calcutta or to see the Taj Mahal. However, the troops were not always appreciated, as Gunner Gough recorded:

> We have now been in country for almost two years, and our views [about being sent to India rather than France] have undergone a considerable change. Being accustomed to receiving the best treatment in Blighty, it felt very strange to be stationed in a country where the 'duration man' is not understood. No one realises that practically every man in Kitchener's Army has sacrificed an excellent civilian position in order to serve his country. We have heard of a park not a hundred miles from Calcutta where a notice once appeared to the effect that 'Dogs and soldiers are not allowed in here'. It is to the credit of the Territorials and 'duration' men that they are living down this prejudice.[12]

At least one of James Jamieson's photos shows the interior of barrack huts, complete with empty rifle racks, and carries the notation 'note the rifle racks!'; it is not hard to deduce that as the war progressed in Europe, with the great offensives of the Somme and Third Ypres, and as Indian troops were fully involved in the difficult campaign in Mesopotamia, and with no chance of home leave, there was a growing sense of isolation amongst the troops of 22 MMG, and even a sense that they were not doing their part. The original battery members were all volunteers, and all had done so in the full expectation of serving in France.

The chance to take leave though appears to have been available and appreciated. From his letters to *The Motor Cycle* it is known that Sergeant Fielder spent his Christmas leave of 1916 in Calcutta, although he also reports that troops were not well respected by civilians. James Jamieson's album also contains photographs of Calcutta, in particular of the memorial at the 'Black Hole'. So, it is a reasonable assumption that he too visited at least once. The Jamieson album also contains photographs of the Taj Mahal near Agra and identical images can be found in Walter Patrick's album; it is clear that both these soldiers travelled here. There are no photographs in Bill Macro's album that give any clues as to where he may have travelled to on leave, however, he does have photos that suggest the summer of 1917 was spent at a tented camp at Topa, which he captions as being 'Himalayan Foot Hills'. Topa lays in the

Near Parachinar in the Upper Kurram Valley. Probably taken in 1916. A Clyno combination climbs towards a group of tribesmen and soldiers, probably to conduct a firepower demonstration. A Triumph can be seen parked beside the track beyond the combination. (From E. W. Macro's album)

Near Parachinar, demonstrating the guns to the tribesmen. Probably taken in 1916. Sgt Macro identifies this as one of Number 1 Section's Vickers guns. (From E. W. Macro's album)

Murree Hills, close to both Murree town and Kuldana, about 50 miles (80km) north east of Rawalpindi. It is also clear from various albums that time was available to make up fishing and swimming parties; Bill Macro's letters home also mention fishing parties.

As the hard European winter of 1917 dragged into the new year of 1918, as the Russian revolution took them out of the war, as the Americans joined the war against Germany and as preparations were made in Europe to receive the German 'Spring Offensive' and then launch the decisive Allied counter-attack, the thoughts of members of 22 MMG started to turn towards whether they should be doing more. The Machine Gun Corps, having attracted and been selective over their applicants, always had a high percentage of soldiers who later took commissions. 22 MMG was no exception, and a number of its soldiers applied for commissions. Amongst these were Alexander Dowie and William Welsh. Both commissioned into the Highland Light Infantry, although this appears to be something of a wartime convenience because no Highland Light Infantry battalions were serving in India at the time. Others, with the technical background that had brought them into the Motors in the first place, got involved with the light armoured car batteries as experiments were made in India in the early forms of armoured cars. In due course, the light armoured motor batteries became the armoured car companies of the Tank Corps, and thus, some of those who had originally been members of the Motor Machine Gun Service eventually ended up in the Tank Corps. According to his service record, Max Roescher appears to have spent some time away from 22 MMG during the years 1916 through to 1918. At least some of this appears to have been in Dera Ismail Khan in Baluchistan with 7th Armoured Motor Battery, and according to his file, for the period February to July 1918, Max was acting as the commanding officer. However, once the war in Europe had ended, he returned to 22 MMG as preparations for demobilisation were being got underway. As part of those preparations, it appears that Max was due to take over from Alexander Molony, but then the Third Afghan War intervened. Max was mobilised on 11 May 1919 and appears to have again ended up as Alexander's second-in-command. Once the Afghan War had finished, however, Alexander returned to Europe ahead of Max, and for a short period from October 1919 to late December, or possibly early January 2020, Max was commanding 22 MMG. The end of his period in command appears to mark the formal disbanding of 22 MMG.[13]

Again, taking advantage of their technical skills, others, including some who perhaps had been rejected by the Royal Flying Corps initially, sought to transfer to the newly formed Royal Air Force. It is not clear whether Acting Sergeant Bill

Near Parachinar, demonstrating the guns to the tribesmen. Probably taken in 1916. Sgt Macro is bending forward over the Vickers gun. (From E. W. Macro's album)

Vickers gun in action near Bannu. This was probably another firepower demonstration for the tribesmen in 1916. (From E. W. Macro's album)

Macro had applied to the RFC before ending up in 22 MMG although it is not believed he did so, but in 1918, he was posted from India to Egypt to undergo pilot training. According to his RAF service documentation, he joined No 31 Training Squadron in Egypt in August 1918. Here, he was trained as a pilot on the B.E.2c aircraft type. His training was about complete in November 1918, just as the war in Europe ended. Bill, therefore, returned to Port Said, expecting to be returned to UK for demobilisation. However, despite having been away from home for three years, with no home leave for that period (unlike those on the Western Front), those who had served in India were considered to be at the back of the demobilisation list, compared to those who had fought on the Western Front. The troops in India had to be replaced with freshly conscripted 'regular' battalions, before the 'hostilities only' volunteer troops could be released. Bill Macro, therefore, returned to rejoin 22 MMG in Rawalpindi.

It was also during 1918 that 22 MMG suffered its only known casualties. Private/Driver William Arthur Cordwell was one of the battery's attached Army Service Corps personnel. He died on 5 April 1918 although the cause is unknown. Probably it was due to an illness or accident; it does not appear

Tribesman with peace offering. Taken in May 1916 during the 22 MMG familiarisation tour of the North West Frontier. (From both J. P. Jamieson's and E. W. Macro's albums)

The Sergeants' Mess, probably in 1917. Bill Macro, standing, left rear, leaning on the piano. A stark contrast to patrolling on the North West Frontier or life in the Western Front trenches. (From E. W. Macro's album)

Summer bungalow accommodation in Kuldana. Possibly summer 1916. J. P. Jamieson highlights the empty arms racks. (From J. P. Jamieson's album)

to have been due to enemy action. William had been born in Enfield, near London, on 8 February 1885 and was baptised a couple of months later on 26 April at St. Andrew. He was the son of John and Mary Ann, both from Essendon in Hertfordshire. His father was a labourer and supported, over the years, what we would now consider a large family. William had two elder brothers, two elder sisters as well as two younger sisters. In the 1911 census, William is shown as being a motor driver. He was single and living with his mother and two younger sisters – Florence and Maggie. In the last quarter of 1914, he married Mary Grace Chaffin, a widow, probably just before he joined up. Mary was paid William's widow's pension but is believed to have died in 1924. Less is known about the other casualty, 2420 Gunner Allan Gilmour, however, he was injured rather than died. He was probably a Scot and he appears to have been one of 22 MMG's later enlistments. He was enlisted on 13 September 1915. He was discharged in June 1918 and awarded Silver Wound Badge Number 418433, having fractured his left leg. This may have been as a result of a motorcycle accident but that is speculation. Nothing is known about his subsequent life. Allan Gilmour appears in his hospital bed being visited by his friends from the battery in James Jamieson's photograph album.

Gunner Alexander Dowie. On a Triumph 'Trusty H' in India, probably in 1916. Dowie commissioned in 1918 into the Highland Light Infantry and was subsequently on the Indian Army Reserve Officers list. He was almost certainly not present at Badama Post. (From J. P. Jamieson's album)

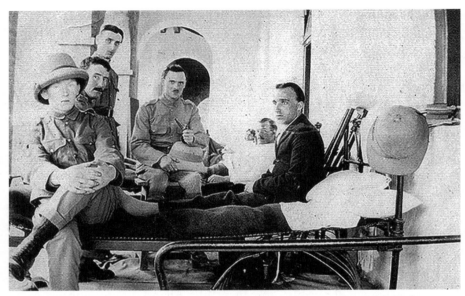

Gunner Allan Gilmour in his hospital bed, presumably following his accident. Probably late 1917 or early 1918 before his discharge in June 1918. JP Jamieson seated in the centre, holding his pipe with his helmet. (From J. P. Jamieson's album)

The fact that manpower had been drained away from the battery had caused a number of vacancies. Some additional soldiers, both from within the Machine Gun Corps and from other units appear to have been transferred in to the battery around this time, in order to fill some of these vacancies. These also resulted in promotions, so it is probably around this time that Bill Macro was made an acting sergeant – almost certainly without any additional pay because acting rank very rarely managed to attract the associated pay. In February 1919, Bill's album has pictures captioned 'Gondal 1919 M. G. C. Concentration and Demonstration camp'. It is possible that the purpose of the concentration was to conduct demonstrations as some form of handover to incoming troops and for the battery to proceed to demobilisation thereafter. Certainly, a number of the photographs are relatively light hearted and include pictures of the battery dogs, Billy and Peter, riding on a motorcycle combination. Gondal, which is located in Gujurat state, about midway between Bombay and Karachi, is also relatively close to Deolali, where a number of demobilisation camps were located. On the page opposite the photographs of the concentration, the album also has a series of photos of B.E.2c aircraft, also captioned as being at Gondal. So, it is likely that the concentration included the chance to conduct air–ground cooperation training, attempting to percolate the lessons of the Western Front out to the wider army and air force.

Whatever the intent for demobilisation of 22 MMG, events were moving in Afghanistan, with the assassination of Habibullah described in Chapter 1. At the same time, internal tensions within British India were on the rise. In both money and manpower, the cost of the war had been high. Casualty rates, increasing inflation, compounded by heavy taxation, the deadly 1918 flu pandemic and the disruption of trade all escalated human suffering in India. Indian nationalist sentiment from pre-war days was rejuvenated as moderate and extremist groups of the Indian National Congress unified. In 1916, the Congress had successfully established the Lucknow Pact; a temporary alliance with the All-India Muslim League. Towards the end of World War I, Britain's India policy began to change and political concessions were made. The first marker of these changes was the passage of the Montagu–Chelmsford Reforms in 1917. However, the Indian political movement deemed these reforms as insufficient. Mahatma Gandhi, recently returned to India, began emerging as an increasingly charismatic leader under whose leadership civil disobedience movements grew rapidly as an expression of political unrest. The 1915 Ghadar conspiracy, the continuing presence of Mahendra Pratap in Kabul and a still-active revolutionary movement, especially in Punjab and Bengal, as well as worsening civil unrest throughout India led, in 1918, to the appointment of a sedition committee chaired by Judge Sidney Rowlatt. It was tasked to evaluate German and Bolshevik links to the militant movement in India, especially in Punjab and Bengal. On the recommendations of the committee, the Rowlatt Act, an extension of the Defence of India Act 1915, was enforced in India to limit civil liberties.[14]

The Rowlatt Act was passed in 1919. It led to major political unrest throughout India. Gandhi's call for protest achieved an unprecedented response of furious protests. Particularly in Punjab, the situation deteriorated rapidly, with disruptions to the railways, telegraphs and other communications. The protests peaked in early April; in Amritsar, one of the principal cities in Punjab, over 5000 people gathered at Jallianwala Bagh – a walled public garden in the centre of the city. The situation deteriorated over the next few days. The Governor General of Punjab, Michael O'Dwyer, believed these were the early signs of a conspiracy for a coordinated uprising around May, on the lines of the 1857 Mutiny, to take place just when British troops would be moving to the hills for summer. Many other officers in the Indian Army believed such a result was possible and preparations were made accordingly.[15]

On 10 April 1919, there was a protest at the residence of the Deputy Commissioner of Amritsar. This was to demand the release of two popular leaders of the Indian Independence Movement, Satya Pal and Saifuddin Kitchlew, who had been arrested by the government and moved to a secret location. Both were proponents of Gandhi's movement. An army guard shot at the crowd, killing several protesters. Later that day, several banks and other government buildings, including the railway station, were attacked and set on fire. The violence continued to escalate, culminating in the deaths of at least five Europeans, including government employees and civilians. There was retaliatory shooting at crowds from the military several times during the day and between eight and 20 people were killed. The following day, Miss Marcella Sherwood, an English missionary, was caught by a mob, pulled to the ground by her hair, stripped naked, beaten, kicked and left for dead. She was rescued by some local Indians, who hid her from the mob and then smuggled her to the safety of Gobindgarh fort.[16] For the next two days Amritsar was quiet, but violence continued in other parts of the Punjab. Railway lines were cut, telegraph posts destroyed, government buildings burnt and more Europeans murdered. By 13 April, the British government had decided to put most of the Punjab under martial law. The legislation restricted a number of civil liberties, including freedom of assembly; gatherings of more than four people were banned.[17]

On the evening of 12 April, the leaders of the *hartal* in Amritsar held a meeting at which it was announced that a public protest meeting would be held the following afternoon in the Jallianwala Bagh. The meeting was to be chaired by a senior Congress Party leader, Lal Kanhyalal Bhatia, who was widely respected. A series of resolutions protesting against the Rowlatt Act, the recent actions of the British authorities and the detention of Satya Pal and Saifuddin Kitchlew were drawn up. On 13 April, the traditional festival of Baisakhi, Brigadier Dyer, who was the acting military commander for Amritsar and the surrounding area, spent the morning touring through the city with a number of the city officials. They announced the implementation of a pass system to enter or leave Amritsar, a curfew beginning at 2000 hours that night and a ban on all processions and public meetings of four or more persons. The proclamation was read and explained in English, Urdu, Hindi and Punjabi, but few paid it any heed. The local police received intelligence of the planned Jallianwala Bagh meeting through word of mouth and plainclothes detectives in the crowds. Dyer was informed of the meeting and returned to the barracks to decide how to deal with it.

Through the course of the afternoon, thousands of Sikhs, Muslims and Hindus gathered in the Jallianwala Bagh. Many had worshipped earlier at the Golden Temple and were passing through the Bagh on their way home. The Bagh was an open area of six to seven acres, about 200m by 200m in size, surrounded by walls roughly 3m high. It was overlooked by houses, three to four stories tall, many of which had balconies, and was accessed by five narrow passageways, most of which had gates which could be locked. In the centre was a *samadhi* (cremation site) and a large well partly filled with water. During the rainy season, the Bagh was planted with crops, but for the rest of the year, it served as a local meeting area and playground.[18]

A feature of the Baisakhi festival in Amritsar was a horse and cattle fair. As a result, Amritsar was full of farmers, traders and merchants in addition to the usual pilgrims. The fair was closed by the city police in the early afternoon and, subsequently, a large number of people drifted into the Jallianwala Bagh. Brigadier Dyer sent an aeroplane to overfly the Bagh and estimate the size of the crowd. He reported this at about 6000, but the Hunter Commission estimated a crowd of 10,000 to 20,000 had assembled by the time Dyer reached the Bagh at 1730 hours[19] an hour after the meeting had started, with 90 Sikh, Gurkha and Baluchi troops, and two armoured cars. The vehicles were unable to enter the Bagh through the narrow entrances, which were locked. The main entrance was now blocked by armed troops backed by the armoured cars. There was no attempt to warn the crowd to disperse or even, it appears, that the troops would open fire. Dyer ordered his troops to begin shooting toward the crowd. Firing continued for approximately 10 minutes. Ceasefire was ordered only when ammunition supplies were almost exhausted, after approximately 1650 rounds had been expended. Many people died in stampedes at the narrow gates or by jumping into the solitary well on the compound to escape the shooting. A plaque, placed at the site after independence, states that 120 bodies were removed from the well. The wounded could not be moved from where they had fallen because a curfew was declared and many more died during the night. The official British count of casualties was 379 dead with 1100 wounded.[20] The Indian National Congress estimate was that about 1000 were killed, with over 1500 injured.

22 MMG were not involved in the massacre. Given both the slowness of communication between London and Delhi, and the onset of the war with Afghanistan, there was no immediate follow up to this event. However,

in October 1919, the Secretary of State for India, Edwin Montagu, issued instructions for the government of India to conduct an inquiry into the events in Punjab. Formally entitled the Disorders Inquiry Committee, it was later more widely known as the Hunter Commission. The purpose of the commission was to investigate the causes of the disturbances in Bombay, Delhi and Punjab, and the measures taken to deal with them. The evidence taken by this enquiry includes a statement made by a Captain J. A. S. Ewing of the 19th Lancers. This makes it clear that 22 MMG were involved in the policing operations in Punjab after Amritsar. Ewing's statement describes how half squadrons from the 18th and 19th Lancers were operating in the Sialkot and Wazirabad area of Punjab on policing and patrol duties from 13 April. 22 MMG were certainly involved from 19 April as Ewing states 'Mobile column composed of half squadron 19th Lancers, two sections Motor Machine Gun Battery, under command of Major Maloney [sic], left Wazirabad for Lyallpur.' The patrols appear to have been effective because the following day Ewing reports 'Motor Machine Gun Battery proceeded to Jaranwala to make arrests there, and arrested 12 men.'[21]

Up until the end of April, the focus of operations was on policing and making arrests. The method used was to 'march to the village by night

Possibly the same column as the photo on p. 92, from the rear. Near Jung in 1917. (From E. W. Macro's album)

and surround it before dawn, then have out the *Lambardars* [landowners] and make them produce offenders, then hold a "*jirga*" [tribal gathering] and get as much information as possible regarding other miscreants in surrounding villages.'[22] But the greater range of 22 MMG, when compared to the cavalry, meant they were often employed on these strike and arrest operations while the cavalry undertook more local patrols. Ewing records on 29 April, 'Motor Machine Gun Battery went to a village 57 miles away to make two arrests, returning same evening, distance 114 miles.'[23] From May the focus appears to switch to 'showing the flag' rather than arrests; more *durbars* were held at the villages and demonstrations were given of the machine guns firing.[24]

The Punjab disturbances were the last events before the Afghan invasion initiated the Third Afghan war described in Chapter 1. From both Captain Ewing's report to the Disorders Inquiry Committee and from the Battery war diary, it is apparent that 22 MMG were back in Cambridge Lines in Rawalpindi sometime between 7 and 13 May. On 14 May, the battery left Rawalpindi by train at 0200 hours, arriving in Kohat at 1300 hours the same day. The following day, 15 May, all the baggage cars, with the guns

Gun in action probably near Peshawar. This was probably an 'official' photo, as several relatives have copies, and it was used in the 22 MMG Battery magazine *Momagu* . The photo gives a good indication of the belts, canteens and haversacks carried by the soldiers. Hobnails are clearly visible on the soles of their boots. (From J. P. Jamieson's album)

of Number 1 Section, formed a road convoy to move forward from Kohat to Parachinar, taking forward a supply of petrol for the motorcycles. This petrol convoy arrived back in Kohat, having successfully completed its mission at 1900 hours on 16 May; it had covered 232 miles in 28 hours, including halts. Battery headquarters, along with Number 2 and 3 sections, then left Kohat on the morning of 17 May and arrived in Parachinar that evening. Number 1 Section then left Kohat at 1630 hours on 19 May, arriving in Parachinar at 1100 hours 20 May, having overnighted at Thal. Thus, the battery was complete in Parachinar where, as we have already seen in Chapter 2, they were key elements of the defence plan, along with the Kurram Militia, of the Upper Kurram valley. A description of the Kurram Militia, its formation and its commander, Major Percy Dodd, will be given in the next chapter.

On the ranges near Abazai. (From E. W. Macro's album)

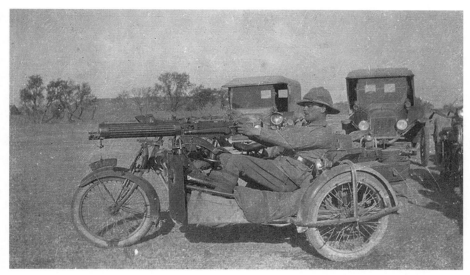

Gunner J. P. Jamieson demonstrating firing the gun while still mounted on the Clyno combination. This was good for a hasty engagement, but for stability, dismounting the gun onto its tripod was preferable. Two of the Battery's Ford cars/vans in the background. (From J. P. Jamieson's album)

Number 3 Section at Cambridge Lines, Rawalpindi. (From E. W. Macro's album)

CHAPTER 5

The Kurram Militia and Major Dodd

The purpose of this chapter is to give a feel for the character and make-up of the Kurram Militia because they played such a key role in the defence of the Kurram valley during the Third Afghan War. It will also provide background information on the Commandant, Major Percy Dodd, as he was the commander on the ground during the action at Badama Post. The other British officers of the militia, who almost certainly were not at Badama Post, will also be covered, as they too played important roles in the fighting in the Kurram valley. The chapter will also expand on the fighting by the Kurram Militia and 22 MMG in defence of the Upper Kurram. As recorded in Chapter 2, it was via the Kurram valley that General Roberts had advanced on Kabul during the Second Afghan War in the autumn of 1878. There was no intent during this expedition to occupy the valley permanently, however, the British soon realised the necessity and importance of holding it and securing it against both the Afghans and the tribes. In many ways, the Kurram Militia was typical of the local militias formed from the 'loyal' tribes on the North West Frontier. On the other hand, it was recruited from the Turis and Bangash tribes, who were largely made up of Shia Mohammedans. These were bitterly opposed to the orthodox Sunni tribes of the Wazirs, Chamkanni, Jajis and Mangals who surrounded the valley; thus, the Kurram Militia was one of the few militias which actively welcomed British presence on the North West Frontier, and it remained loyal throughout the Afghan invasion of 1919.

The British first formed the Turi Militia, recruited from the local inhabitants, in October 1892, possibly as a result of the efforts of Lieutenant G. O. Roos-Keppel,[1] although the first commander was Captain C. M. Dallas and he was succeeded by Captain E. W. S. K. Maconchey. The militia was initially based at Balish Khel near Sadda, but within a few months, the unit's headquarters were moved to Parachinar, and it was renamed the Kurram Militia. The militia was originally divided into two parts: the 1st Battalion as a mobile column, while the 2nd Battalion garrisoned the valley. This proved impracticable, and in 1902, the two battalions were amalgamated under a single commander and organized into two wings, each of three companies. The militia included two troops of mounted infantry and also had two obsolescent 10-pounder mountain guns, which could be carried on mules and camels. In 1894, the total strength of the militia was 948; by 1905, it had increased to 1475. They manned, on a semi-permanent basis, a number of posts and small forts scattered along the Kurram valley, principally from Sadda up to Parachinar and then on to the border with Afghanistan. The militia was not under military control but was tasked by political agents under the direction of the chief commissioner of the North West Frontier Province. The duties of the militia included garrisoning posts and picquetting roads; repulsing and pursuing raiders; guarding prisoners and government funds; escorting political agents; protecting road-making contractors; making border reconnaissance patrols; guiding visitors; obtaining political information; and arresting offenders.

The Kurram Militia first saw action during the Tirah Campaign in late 1897. By this stage, Roos-Keppel had returned to command, now in the rank of a captain.[2] On 1 September, Orakzais tribesmen attacked a militia post at Balish Khel, a little to the north of Sadda. The garrison held off the attackers for 24 hours, although 20 Kurram Militia men were killed, until the arrival of the flying column. Sadda itself, was attacked on 16 September by about 2000 Orakzais, but they were repulsed by a combined army and militia force. Subsequently, in late November and early December, a column of the Kurram Militia was sent in support of Brigadier-General Gaselee to undertake the punishment of the Chamkannis, Mamuzais, and Massozais. The Mamuzais and Massozais submitted immediately, but the Chamkannis offered resistance, and caused about 30 casualties among the British forces.[3]

In 1902, now under the command of Captain G. L. Carter, the Kurram Militia provided 200 men for the successful operations against Wazirs in Bannu, under the overall command of Major General Charles Egerton. Captain Carter was succeeded by Captain John Fortescue Finnis, and in 1904, when the Zazis from Zazi Maidan attacked in force, they were repulsed by a number of Kurram Militia under Lieutenant Boyle.

At the time of the Third Afghan War, the Kurram Militia was commanded by Major Percy Dodd, 31st Lancers, who had originally been attached in February 1916 as a wing commander and, subsequently, from January 1917 as the second in command. He held this position through much of 1917 and 1918, aside from a short period detached to the Mohmand Militia in

April/May 1917. How he was employed during the attachment is not clear, but this was the period of the Mohmand Blockade, and it is likely that Dodd would have taken a detachment of the Kurram Militia with him in order to reinforce the blockade line. In 1915, the Mohmands had announced *jihad* against the British and their *lashkars* invaded Peshawar district in April but were defeated. In October of 1915, another *lashkar* had come down from the hills. The Mohmand Blockade line was then instituted in late September 1916 and continued until July 1917. The line was made up of a series of blockhouses and barbed wire defences manned by the British and Indian Armies along the British border of Mohmand territory. It was lifted in July 1917 when the Mohmands finally submitted to British terms.[4]

Percy Dodd finally assumed command of the Kurram Militia in September 1918 and then held it until 26 November 1920.[5] Percy had been born on 15 November 1885 and baptised on 6 December at Allahabad Holy Trinity Church. His father, Charles, was a Lieutenant Colonel in the Bengal Staff Corps. His mother was Margaretta Anderson, a Canadian. She had married Charles on 19 August 1876 in Bombay. Percy was the fourth and last of Charles and Margaretta's children, having two elder sisters, Kathleen and May, and an elder brother, Arthur. Percy also had an elder half sister, Edith, as his father had been married previously to Christine Fagan, who died in India in 1872, when she was 29 years old, just two years after the birth of her daughter.

By 1891, Percy had been sent back to England and was living at the home of his widowed aunt Agnes, aged 53, of Asburnham Road, Bedford. Agnus (or possibly Harriet – she appears to have used them interchangeably) had been married to Charles Dodd's eldest brother, the Reverend Edward Sutton Dodd, who had died the previous year on 20 September 1890. Whether Percy was already back in the UK at this time is not known. Ashburnham Road was a large household; in addition to Agnes, there were her three sons and two daughters, and another nephew, Arthur Herbert Russell Dodd, who was Percy's older brother and who also joined the Indian Army. There were also two female staff. On the 1901 census, Percy is recorded as being a boarder at school, at 4 College Grounds, Great Malvern, Gloucester.[6]

It is not known what decided Percy on a military career, but given his family's strong military background, especially with the Indian Army, there was probably never much doubt in the matter. Early in 1902, probably in January, Percy followed his elder brother to Sandhurst. He was commissioned in December 1903 and is listed as being on general duty from 9 January to 9 March 1904. In fact, this involved travelling to India via France, in order to take up an attachment for regimental duty with 1st Battalion Somerset Light

Infantry. The initial attachment was short lived; Percy travelled back to Bombay in late June and by 2 July was sailing back to England on a medical certificate. The nature of the problem is not stated, but Percy remained at home for the rest of the summer and autumn before shipping back to India in November 1904, reaching Cawnpore on 18 December 1904 and rejoining 1st Battalion Somerset Light Infantry; doubtless he was the duty officer over Christmas that year. In August the following year (1905), Percy took up the appointment of double company officer in the 108th Infantry of the Indian Army; at much the same time, he completed a course of Urdu language training. He was gazetted as a lieutenant on 9 April 1906. From 20 March to 25 July 1906, Percy was employed on special duty in connection with the Minor Nawab of Radhanpur. In the time of the Raj, Radhanpur state was a princely state. The town of Radhanpur, in the Saurashtra region of Gujarat, was the capital and was surrounded by a loopholed wall; the town was formerly known for its export trade in rapeseed, grains and cotton. Its rulers belonged to a family of Babi tribe descent, although at the time of Percy's attachment, Sher Khan II was a minor, so British administrators were in charge of the regency of the state. The exact nature of the special duty is not known, but the commissioner wrote to the political agent at Palanpur asking that the commanding officer of the 108th Infantry thank Lieutenant Dodd for 'the efficiency with which he performed his duties'.[7]

At the end of 1906, Percy Dodd transferred to the 31st Duke of Connaught's Own (DCO) Lancers, a regiment which had its origin in the old Bombay Squadron of Cavalry, raised for service in the Second Anglo-Maratha War of 1804–5. The squadron was split to form the 1st and 2nd Regiments of the Bombay Light Cavalry in 1817. The 1st Bombay Light Cavalry served in the First Afghan War in 1839, when they fought in the Battle of Ghazni and took part in the march to Kabul. During the Second Sikh War of 1848–49 the regiment took part in the Siege of Multan, where they remained as the garrison for the remainder of the campaign. When the Indian Mutiny of 1857 erupted, the regiment was stationed at Nasirabad, where they were the only ones to remain loyal. Artillery and infantrymen urged the regiment to mutiny, but the *sowars* refused and, under their officers, charged in an attempt to take the guns. They failed to do so but successfully disengaged and took part in the campaign of pacification in central India. Burma was their next overseas posting in 1885, where they fought in the Third Anglo-Burmese War. The Duke of Connaught, then Commander-in-Chief of the Bombay army, became their Colonel-in-Chief in 1890. He still held the appointment in the 13th DCO Lancers, the successors to the 31st DCO Lancers, until his death in 1942. During the Kitchener reorganisation of the Indian Army of 1903, the Bombay cavalry had 30 added to their numbers and the 1st DCO Bombay Lancers became the 31st DCO Lancers.[8] Why Percy transferred from the infantry to the cavalry is not clear, but he served as a 31st Lancer, or a 13th Lancer, for the remainder of his military career. He completed an equitation course in Meerut, achieving a 'very good' result in March 1907. He was then employed as a squadron officer, with short spells as quartermaster in 1908 and 1909, and also in 1909, a short time as a squadron commander. Early in 1908, Percy received elementary Pashtu language training, also at Meerut. In 1909, he was then able to take his combined leave and was out of India from 4 March to 1 October.[9]

In July 1910, Percy was seconded away from his regiment to the South Waziristan Militia, initially as a reserve officer. He was, however, released, firstly to attend higher standard Pashtu training, at Dera Ismail Khan, and secondly to attend the 1911 Coronation Durbar in Delhi. The Delhi Durbar was an Indian imperial style mass assembly organised by the British at the Coronation Park to mark the succession of an Emperor or Empress of India. It was also known as the Imperial Durbar; it was held three times, in 1877, 1903, and 1911, but the 1911 Durbar was the only one that a sovereign, George V, attended. On 22 March 1911, a royal proclamation announced that the Durbar would be held in December to commemorate the coronation King George V and Queen Mary of Teck and allow their proclamation as Emperor and Empress of India. Practically every ruling prince and nobleman in India, plus thousands of landed gentry and other persons of note, attended to pay respects to their sovereigns. The official ceremonies lasted from 7–16 December, with the Durbar itself taking place on 12 December. The royal couple arrived at Coronation Park in their coronation robes, the King-Emperor wearing the Imperial Crown of India. They received homage from the native princes – including one woman, the Begum of Bhopal. Afterwards, the royal couple ascended to the domed royal pavilion, where the King-Emperor announced the move of India's capital from Calcutta to Delhi. The annulment of the partition of Bengal was also announced during the ceremony. The next day, the royal couple made an appearance at the balcony window of the Red Fort to receive half a million or more of the common people who had come to greet them. Then, on 14 December, the King-Emperor presided over a military parade of 50,000 troops. Delhi Durbar medals in silver were awarded to 26,800 officers and men of the British and Indian armies who participated in the 1911 event. Percy Dodd was among the 31st DCO Lancers' party of four British Officers and 11 Viceroy's Commissioned Officers[10] who attended, and the award of the medal is recorded in his service papers.[11]

Percy was appointed as a wing officer within the South Waziristan Militia in January 1913, in which month he was also promoted to the rank of captain. In late March, he was appointed as the adjutant, or chief staff officer, and, at the same time, quartermaster of the South Waziristan Militia. However, although this was a staff appointment, in the militia the adjutant and quartermaster also commanded the mounted infantry troops and Percy was soon in action. On 11 April 1913, he was in command of a party of the South Waziristan Militia which came into action against Mashud Waziri raiders near Girni, some miles to the west of Tank. Three of the raiders were killed and three captured, along with five rifles and five bandoliers. A copy of the Derajat Brigade orders from the following day is included in Percy's service papers, and this gives the details of the incident, including that one of the dead raiders was notorious and dangerous. One Naick (Corporal) from the militia was dangerously wounded. Percy was also wounded but the chief commissioner of the North West Frontier Province telegrammed the political agent in order that he might 'convey to Captain Dodd and his party congratulations from His Excellency The Viceroy on their smart piece of work'.[12]

When the Third Afghan War commenced, Percy had probably five, possibly six, other British Officers, under his command in the Kurram Militia.[13] The first two of these were Captain Frederick Champion, also 31st DCO Lancers, and Lieutenant Richard Percival Beamish, 21st Punjab Infantry. Frederick Walter Champion was born on 24 August 1893 in Surrey, the son of the English entomologist George Charles Champion. He later became a forester, working in British India and East Africa. In both the UK and India, he became famous in the 1920s as one of the first wildlife photographers and conservationists. Champion grew up in a family of nature lovers; his brother Sir Harry George Champion was also a forester, well known for classifying the forest types of India. Champion travelled to India in 1913 and served in the police department in East Bengal until 1916. He was commissioned into the British Indian Army Reserve of Officers (cavalry branch) on 21 August 1916 and was promoted temporarily to captain on 8 March 1917 and to Lieutenant on 21 August 1917. He saw service with the 31st Lancers and then he was appointed wing officer with the Kurram Militia on 8 March 1917. He retired a Lieutenant but was granted the rank of Captain on 1 May 1922. He ultimately died in 1970 in Scotland.[14] Richard Percival Beamish was born in Cork, Ireland, on 13 May 1895 to Anne Hosford and Samuel Charles Beamish. After his war service, he married Kathleen Margretta Constance 'Kay' McCaherty on 16 October 1935 in Belfast, Northern Ireland. He died on 9 September 1951 in Belfast. The other three British officers were Captain R. H. Wilson, 82nd Punjabs,

Lieutenant Arthur Evelyn Farwell of the 2/129 Baluchis and Lieutenant R. F. F. Carter, 15th Sikhs. Lieutenant Carter was officially appointed as a wing officer within the Khyber Rifles but was attached to the Kurram Militia. The Indian Army List of January 1919 also lists a lieutenant, temporary Captain, P. R. Higgs, 2nd Somerset Light Infantry, Indian Army Reserve of Officers, as serving with the Kurram Militia. However, his tenure was due to complete on 16 March 1919 and he is not mentioned in the Kurram Militia war diary; so it seems probable that Higgs was not present in the Kurram valley during the conflict. The war diary also lists a Lieutenant Guy as joining the Kurram Militia on 13 June 1919, so it is possible that he was a replacement for Higgs.

At some stage in the days before World War I, probably around 1910, a young man called Miru Mian joined the Kurram Militia. There is no way of knowing how old he was at the time, but it is assumed that he was in his mid-teens. His father's name is known; Miru Mian was the son of Mir Abdullah. Miru must have been a capable soldier because by the time of the Third Afghan War he was a lance daffadar, the equivalent of a corporal, and to achieve this rank, he must have first been an acting lance daffadar, the equivalent of a lance corporal. Given that he was a lance daffadar, a cavalry

A Subadar of the Kurram Militia in the early 1900s. From a watercolour by Major Alfred Crowdy Lovet. (NAM 1953-02-71-1 Courtesy of the Council of the National Army Museum)

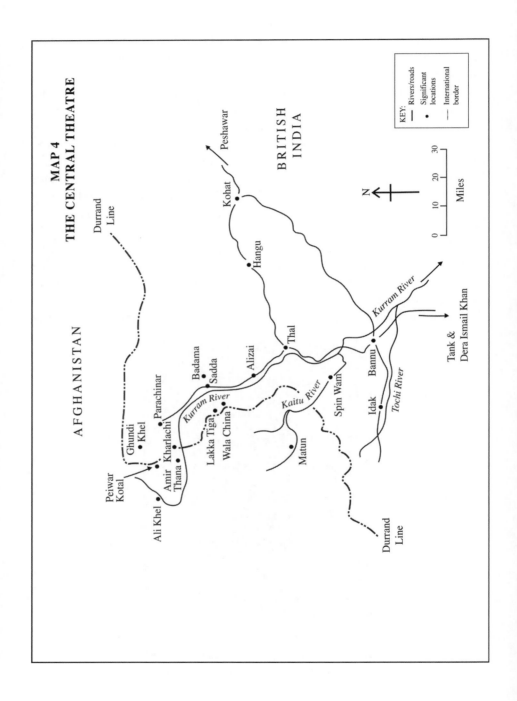

MAP 4
THE CENTRAL THEATRE

rank, rather than the infantry rank of naik, it is likely that Miru Mian was one of the militia's mounted infantry.

Even before the Afghans initiated their invasion down the Khyber, in the Upper Kurram, Percy Dodd had, via the political agent, Major Robert Heale,[15] picked up rumours of impending trouble with Afghan movements. Kurram Militia leave men were recalled and picquets were sent out to the border. On 2 May, Lieutenant Farwell and Subedar Ali Hassan, with 60 men, were despatched from Parachinar to Peiwar Kotal. At the same time, another picquet of 45 men, under a jemadar, an Indian junior Viceroy commissioned officer, was sent to secure the route of the Kurram river through Kharlachi. Both picquets were well equipped with medical stores, reserve rations and ammunition, tents and other stores, so that they could be used as secure bases in the event of trouble at either location. At first all was quiet, with nothing more serious being reported other than that Afghan villagers were building *sangars* on their side of the border. On 9 May, it was recorded in the Kurram Militia war diary that the general officer commanding (GOC) of the northern front had sanctioned 'to all Militias money allowance in lieu of Field service rations at the rate of 4 annas per man per diem'.[16] However, as reports, which later proved false, were coming in that Nadir Khan was moving towards Peiwar Kotal, on 14 May, Percy Dodd, with Captain Wilson and Lieutenant Beamish, marched a column of 400 infantry, 30 mounted infantry and his two guns up towards Peiwar and bivouaced nearby. The mounted infantry were sent up to Ali Mangal, to the north of Peiwar Kotal, while the guns were kept within the picquet and the infantry were billeted in the local villages. Meanwhile, Lieutenant Carter was left in Parachinar with 200 infantry and 60 mounted infantry to form a reserve.

Percy Dodd returned to Parachinar on 15 May as did the two Kurram Militia guns, followed a day later by Richard Beamish with 250 infantry. The situation on the border was increasingly tense and there are several instances recorded in the war diary of fire being exchanged between Afghans and the militia, as well as reports of tribesmen and troops gathering. However, the reinforcing forces were now arriving in Parachinar as described in Chapter 2. The Kurram Militia war diary specifically mentions the first arrival of 22 MMG on 16 May.[17] The diary also records the arrival and assumption of command of Brigadier-General Fagan and his staff on 22 May, the same day as 3rd Guides also reached Parachinar. On this day as well, Frederick Champion and Richard Beamish marched out of Parachinar with 200 infantry and 60 mounted infantry. The column reached Lakka Tiga the following day and moved on to Wali China. They encountered some opposition, killed three enemy and carried off 60 head of cattle; they also

Number 3 Section, near Morgah, Rawalpindi, January 1918. Probably a training exercise. (From E. W. Macro's album)

gathered intelligence that the Afghans were holding the border along the Durand Line. Percy Dodd was kept busy explaining the ground and the dispositions to Brigadier Fagan. On 24 May, they visited Peiwar Kotal and, on 25 May, the Lakka Tiga front, in order to inspect the positions.[18]

The first serious action in the Kurram took place near Peiwar Kotal, on 26 May, the day before Nadir Khan invested Thal. A sizeable force, probably a couple of thousand Afghan regulars and tribesmen, advanced across the border at dawn and came down the pass towards Chapri village to the north east of Peiwar. Under Captain Wilson's direction, the Kurram Militia, drove the invaders back into the hills, inflicting a number of casualties, including the mullah who had led the attack. Militia casualties were one man wounded in the stomach and one killed.[19] At 1500 hours Number 2 Section of 22 MMG was despatched from Parachinar to reinforce the militia near Peiwar Kotal. The next morning, 27 May, the Afghans attacked again; Number 2 Section moved out of their overnight bivouac at 0600 hours, which was around dawn, and carrying their guns and ammunition on mules, they got onto the hills and came into action at about 0900 hours. Supporting the Kurram Militia in keeping the Afghans at bay, the guns fired 3500 rounds at a range of 925–2000m (1000 to 2200 yards), before coming out of action at 1200 hours and returning to Parachinar, where they arrived at 1730 hours. Almost immediately, at 1810 hours, Bill Macro was sent out with Number 3 Section in order to replace them. Number 3 Section arrived at the Peiwar Kotal picquet at 2130 hours, by which time it would have been pitch dark.[20] The Kurram Militia war diary for the day records no casualties but does suggest that the enemy 'suffered fairly heavily'.

The same day, 27 May, reports arrived in Parachinar that Nadir Khan had moved on and besieged Thal. It was also reported that the village of Alizai, between Sadda and Thal, was threatened by a gathering of tribesmen and the garrison of 1/109th Infantry had been withdrawn into Thal. Number 1 Section of 22 MMG was sent with a party of 200 men from 3rd Guides and 10 *sowars* of the Kurram Militia, in lorries, to counter this threat. The column left Parachinar at 2130 hours and eventually arrived into Alizai at 0215 hours, no mean feat in the dark and on unmade, unlit tracks. The threat from the tribesmen never materialised and the guides and machine guns were withdrawn back to Parachinar. The defence of the Upper Kurram valley was left in the hands of the Kurram Militia manning their posts, with the regulars retained at Parachinar as a striking and reinforcing force.

The Afghans then attacked all along the frontier with the Upper Kurram on 28 May, although the attacks lacked coordination. In the Peiwar area, the militia came under attack from both shell and rifle fire. These attacks were driven off by effective fire from the Kurram Militia and the machine guns of Number 3 Section of 22 MMG. At the end of the day, Number 3 Section returned to camp having fired 8500 rounds.[21] Meanwhile, the post at Kharlachi was attacked again in force at 0600 hours.[22] Reinforcements for the 75 Kurram Militia in the shape of Number 2 Section of 22 MMG, two troops from 37th Lancers, 25 mounted and 50 dismounted infantry from the Kurram Militia, were sent from Parachinar, departing at 0845 hours. The machine guns of 22 MMG, under the command of Major Molony, arrived at Kharlachi first at around 0930 hours, and taking up gun positions in the fort, kept the Afghan attack at bay until the remainder of the reinforcement came up. In the early afternoon, the attack commenced against the Afghan *sangar* line with the machine guns giving covering fire. The Afghan forces were seen to retire and the attacking infantry reached within 175m (200 yards) of the *sangars* but were unable to take them.[23] In the Kurram Militia war diary, it is recorded, 'Enemy driven well back within his own limits. Kurram Militia Infantry reported to be not quite dashing enough but the general result was most satisfactory. A good day's fighting with good results. G. O. C. congratulates Kurram Militia on good work at Kharlachi.'[24] The results were that 29 Afghans were killed and

A Kurram Militia post in 1919. Somewhere in the Upper Kurram Valley, exact location unknown. The photo gives a sense of how Badama and Sadda Posts would have looked in 1919.

some rifles captured, while two Kurram Militia were killed and one slightly wounded. The cavalry and motor machine guns returned to Parachinar in the evening.

The most serious attack of 28 and 29 May, however, was in the vicinity of Lakka Tiga where Afghan regulars and Jaji tribesmen invaded and attempted to link up with the Orakzais and Zaimukhts in the vicinity of Sadda and Alizai. From Wala China and then to the north of Lakka Tiga, Captain Frederick Champion was patrolling in the vicinity of Shabak with 90 *sowars* but without encountering the enemy. Lieutenant Richard Beamish, however, with somewhere between 150 and 200 Kurram Militia troops moved out to attack some 3000 or more Afghans. The enemy were in strong positions and supported by guns, but despite this, only one Bhishti was reported as wounded. Beamish continued to manoeuvre against the Afghans across a front of about four miles through both 29 and 30 May. On the latter date, the Kurram Militia managed to capture some Afghan *sangars*, but the war diary records that little headway was made. Nevertheless, it was sufficient to check and block any Afghan attack, although the continuation of Frederick Champion's patrol just to the north must have helped to protect Beamish's flank. Incredibly, despite the overwhelming odds they faced, Beamish's force reported just one Kurram Militia killed and two wounded.[25] It was a skillful, aggressive and determined little operation, but unaccountably, neither Richard Beamish or Frederick Champion were decorated for it.

Meanwhile, on 29 May, the post at Badama reported increased sniping in the hills above the post. The following day, 30 May, and again on 31 May and 1 June, numbers of Orakzais, principally Massuzai, Alisherzai and Khoni Khel, under the leadership of Mullah Mahmud Akhinzada gathered in the Khurmana and attacked Sadda and Badama Posts. However, Subedar Gul Khan, the commander at Badama Post was not prepared to sit it out behind the walls of his post. Taking 60 men from his own garrison of 80, and collecting 40 men from Sadda, he boldly counter-attacked in conjunction with local villagers. This unexpected assault drove the tribesmen some 3 miles (5km) back into their hills, and when taken in conjunction with the blocking of the Afghan invasion at Lakka Tiga almost certainly prevented a general uprising of the tribes. The counter-attack killed at least 20 tribesmen at the cost of one dead from the Kurram Militia. The war diary records that the general congratulated Gul Khan on his 'gallant and most successful action'.[26]

With the exception of Badama, the Upper Kurram was generally quiet on 31 May and 1 June. In Parachinar, Brigadier Fagan and 60 Infantry Brigade HQ, in conjunction with Percy Dodd and the other commanding officers, planned to switch from defensive to offensive operations. News that Brigadier Dyer was marching to the relief of Thal arrived in Parachinar on 1 June, by which stage raids had already been planned to take place across the border at Peiwar Kotal and Kharlachi and order were issued on 31 May. The plan to raid Peiwar Kotal was eventually abandoned as impractical, although Number 1 Section of 22 MMG moved up to Peiwar on the afternoon of 1 June and was in action the following day, firing 250 rounds.[27] The raid at Kharlachi was conducted successfully; Percy Dodd was in command of the column that consisted of two troops from A Squadron 37th Lancers, Number 2 Section of 22 MMG, a section of guns from 28th Mountain Battery, a section of Stokes Mortars manned by 57th Rifles, A Company 3rd Guides, a troop of Kurram Militia mounted infantry and 100 Kurram Militia infantry. The column marched from Parachinar at 1830 hours on 2 June and was in position at Kharlachi by 0100 hours. The attack commenced at dawn with the shelling of the Afghan fort at Amir Thana. The guides were on the right of the attack and saw little action, except at the village of Kuz Istia. The Kurram Militia, however, advanced under covering fire from the machine guns, which were positioned on a hill some 350m (400 yards) to the west, surrounded the fort and attempted to scale the walls. This attempt was unsuccessful, but the 50-man garrison surrendered shortly after and the fort was burnt. The raid then pushed on to burn a further six border villages of the Jaji tribe. The column then withdrew to Parachinar, with the machine guns and artillery remaining until the last, ready to provide covering fire, although this was not required. Number 2 Section of 22 MMG fired 2000 rounds during the day and were back in Parachinar at 1800 hours.[28] The Kurram Militia recorded inflicting 60 dead on the Afghans. Militia casualties were one Indian killed and two wounded; additionally, Lieutenant Carter received a wound to his left shoulder.[29]

News of the relief of Thal was received in Parachinar 3 June. However, there were reports that the Afghans were still holding the road to Parachinar some six miles north of Thal. Headquarters 60 Brigade placed Alexander Molony, the officer commanding 22 MMG, in command of a small column to proceed south from Parachinar to check and open the track to Thal. The column was made up of Number 3 Section of 22 MMG, with Bill Macro, and 70 soldiers from 57th Rifles Frontier Force, who were transported in four motor lorries. It departed from Parachinar at 1130 hours and managed to drive right through to Thal without encountering any enemy. Although the road had been blocked

A column of two sections of 22nd Battery on the road, with a Ford lorry at the rear. Probably on the North West Frontier, near Jung, in 1917. (From E. W. Macro's album)

at a couple of locations, the obstructions were cleared away easily. Having reached Thal, the column returned to Parachinar that night, with Number 3 Section getting back into camp at 0015 hours.[30]

The news was received in Parachinar at 60 Infantry Brigade HQ that the amir had ceased hostilities and that British Indian forces were not to engage across the Afghan border, although punishment of tribes actively engaged against friendly forces was permitted. The Afghans, however, continued to make threatening moves, particularly in the area of Peiwar Kotal, where they resumed their attack on 5 June. The Kurram Militia outposts were driven back from the border and the post at Teri Mangal was threatened. Reinforcements, consisting of 100 infantry and 30 mounted infantry from the Kurram Militia, along with Number 1 Section of 22 MMG, were sent from Parachinar. These stabilised the situation, but the fighting continued all through the night and then into and through 6 June as the Afghans then threatened Shalozan. The Turi villagers were forced to abandon *sangars* they were holding on the flanks of the militia, meaning the militia were threatened with envelopment on their left flank. Number 1 Section of 22 MMG were relieved by Bill Macro and Number 3 Section, and a further reinforcement of the Kurram Militia was made from Parachinar with a company of 57th Rifles, Frontier Force. This enabled the Kurram Militia to attack from the south back onto the Teri Mangal ridge from which they had been driven the previous day. This secured the left flank, but the Afghans continued to press the right flank in the vicinity of the village of Shalozan. Through the course of the day, the Kurram Militia suffered one killed and four wounded. Brigadier Fagan now visited the front and determined that the remainder of the 57th Rifles should be sent up to reinforce the militia. On 7 June, the Afghans withdrew back over the Peiwar Kotal but made no move, however, to withdraw from the frontier as required by the armistice. The rest of the battalion of 57th Rifles now arrived in the Peiwar area and, on 8 June, they relieved the Kurram Militia to allow them to withdraw back to Parachinar for recuperation.[31]

The actions north and west of Parachinar on 6 and 7 June were the last engagements between regular troops of the war, and as Thal had been relieved, the British undertook the reorganisation of troops within the Kurram-Kohat Force. Troops not originally belonging to the force were gradually removed to other stations. As they did so, the pattern of life in the Kurram valley gradually returned to normal and the Kurram Militia resumed their normal manning of posts, whilst maintaining picquets on the border. The border remained tense as the Afghans refused to withdraw and the war diary through June and July records almost daily incidents of sniping across the border or concentrations of troops. The tribes remained extremely restless, with tensions building through July as the negotiations for a final peace treaty dragged on without resolution. On 23 July, the Kurram Militia war diary recorded a party of Massuzai coming down onto Badama post, but they were driven off with support from Sadda. And on 25 and 26 July, there was increased instances of cross-border sniping at Kharlachi and Peiwar Kotal.[32]

The previous chapters have set the scene of the overall campaign of the Third Afghan War and described the fighting in the central theatre and Kurram valley in particular. They have described the journey taken by the land forces involved at Badama Post, which brought them to that small action at the end of the war. The next chapter will once more go back in time, to 1915, in order paint the story of the air component of the action and its journey from the Great War to the Afghan War and ultimately to Badama Post.

CHAPTER 6

20 Squadron Royal Flying Corps: Formation to September 1917

20 Squadron Royal Flying Corps (RFC), subsequently Royal Air Force (RAF), was one of the most famous squadrons of World War I, despite flying two-seater fighter-bomber reconnaissance aircraft, rather than the more glamorous single-seat fighters. It was the single-seat fighters that tended to receive the public acclaim and caught newspaper attention for producing aces. However, 20 Squadron has some justification for claiming to be the highest scoring British squadron of the war, with a claim of 628 victories, of which over 460 were confirmed by senior officers. It was also the only RFC squadron to have a non-commissioned officer awarded a Victoria Cross, in the guise of Sergeant Thomas Mottershead. The squadron had shipped from Marseilles to India in May 1919, and by July were in the process of establishing a forward airbase at Parachinar. At this time, they were flying the Bristol Fighter F2B aircraft. This chapter will take us back to 1915, to the formation of 20 Squadron, in order to provide an overview of its wartime history and the path it took to be on the North West Frontier during the Third Afghan War and then involved in the action at Badama Post. Readers looking for a detailed account of 20 Squadron's World War I history should consult Robert A. Sellwood's excellent book *Winged Sabres.*

It is probable that, as a key commander in the Kurram valley, Major Dodd would have known, or at least made a reasonably informed guess, as he headed towards Badama Post, that the aircraft in trouble was from 20 Squadron. There is, however, no written evidence to support this, although it is clear that Dodd was subsequently told who the pilot was. It is much less likely that an acting sergeant machine-gun section commander like Bill Macro, even allowing for his relatively independent role, would have known the aircraft's squadron, and there is no evidence to suggest he discovered this information subsequently. For the modern historian, the assumption was that the aircraft would have come from 31 Squadron, which was the first and, for a long time, only British squadron in India. The other possible alternative appeared to be 114 Squadron, which by the time of the Third Afghan War was reinforcing 31 Squadron with a flight of aircraft based in Quetta. However, the newly formed RAF was fighting for its survival once the war had ended, and India went from being at the bottom of the priority list for aircraft to offering a prime target for RAF expansion in the new role of policing the empire. In November 1918, the Air Ministry proposed to the India Office that the number of squadrons in India would be increased from two squadrons to 12. Eventually, after the Third Afghan War, a total of eight squadrons was agreed for India.[1] Despite this, during the Third Afghan War, aircraft were sufficiently rare and expensive assets that it seemed certain that the loss of one on the North West Frontier, particularly to enemy, would trigger some form of record keeping. There is no record of 31 Squadron losing an aircraft in late July; however, the operational-level reports for the period back to RAF headquarters in the Middle East record that 20 Squadron, despite not being fully operational, lost a single aircraft on 30 July 1919, with both crew wounded. With the squadron established, 20 Squadron's operational record confirmed that this aircraft and crew were the squadron's first casualties in India and were lost near Badama on 29 July 1919.[2] The record also states that the pilot was Acting Captain G. Eastwood and his observer was 2nd Lieutenant D. M. Lapraik. The date must be an error as all other sources indicate that the aircraft was brought down on 30 July. These sources include the officers' casualty cards, both of which give the date of the incident as 30 July.

The squadron was formed initially on 1 September 1915 at Netheravon, as part of the RFC. The commanding officer responsible for forming it up, initial training and deployment out to France was Captain C. W. Wilson MC, who was one of the very first members of the RFC, having joined it even before the war commenced. He had flown over France during the initial German invasion and was promoted to major just before Christmas 1915. The squadron's first aircraft was the Royal Aircraft Factory Farman/Fighting Experimental No. 2 (F.E.2); a two-seater 'pusher' aircraft in which the pilot sat in front of the engine and propeller, with the observer-gunner sitting in front of him, in a separate cockpit right in the nose of the aircraft, armed with a Lewis gun. The first of the F.E.2Bs, which was affectionately known to its crews as the 'Fee', arrived at Netheravon shortly before Christmas and training on them started at once; in the summer of 1915, the Germans had introduced the Fokker Eindecker monoplane scout with a synchronised machine-gun firing forward through the propeller. The new machine was driving the RFC out of the skies of Flanders and France, interrupting its vital reconnaissance work and reinforcements, with better aircraft, were required urgently. The first F.E.2Bs had been attached to squadrons in ones and twos as individual reinforcements. However, the aircraft quickly proved itself to be robust and manoeuvrable, and a match for the Fokker in speed. With its effectiveness established, the RFC decided a squadron should be formed equipped solely with F.E.2Bs to take the fight to the Fokkers, clear them out of the sky in a sector and then revert to the primary role of reconnaissance. Thus, 20 Squadron was born. The mass of stores and equipment, spares, guns, ammunition, tents, medical supplies, rations and cooking equipment required to support a squadron in the field was assembled and moved by road to Clairmarais, near St Omer, France, in late January 1916. The squadron's eight F.E.2Bs were flown out on 24 January, along with four B.E.2cs which were exchanged for FEs held by other squadrons. By 29 January, 20 Squadron listed on its order of battle, in addition to the commanding officer, 11 officer pilots, 11 officer observers and an equipment officer, 2nd Lieutenant E. W. Wright. The ground support consisted of 99 non-commissioned officers and other ranks.[3]

The RFC at this time was in the process of adopting a brigade organisation, with each brigade attached to an army; 1 Brigade attached to the British First Army, 2 Brigade to British Second Army and so on. Each RFC brigade consisted of two wings; the first, a 'corps wing', was responsible for local tactical reconnaissance, air-to-ground cooperation and artillery observation, and the second, the 'army wing', was responsible for long-range reconnaissance, aerial combat and deep interdiction of ground targets by bombing. Each wing contained several squadrons and 20 Squadron was attached to 11 (Army) Wing, 2 Brigade RFC. As a fighter-reconnaissance squadron they would be expected to conduct all of the duties of an army wing. This was most usually done by means of an offensive patrol, or 'OP' for short, basically going out and looking for trouble, deep into German-held territory, and all the while, the observer would be recording, in detail, any activity or changes seen below. Frequently, an OP would fly as an escort to a dedicated reconnaissance aircraft, in which case it would fight in its defence. Sometimes, it would be tasked purely to fight, often as a counter to German aerial reconnaissance. Otherwise the OP might be tasked to bomb German airfields or railway movements. And there was always the chance that an OP would need to fight in order to return to the relative safety of British lines.

The first of 20 Squadron's combat missions beyond the enemy lines were flown on 3 February 1916. A patrol of three aircraft flew up to 15 Squadron's base at Droglant in order to provide an escort for that squadron's early morning patrol of B.E.2cs. After a couple of hours, all the aircraft returned safely without having met the enemy. A little later on the same morning, another three of 20 Squadron's aircraft went out on an OP. They all returned safely to Clairmarais, again without having found trouble. The first day of combat operations was something of an anti-climax, but this situation was short lived. On 5 February, Captain James Howett took off in 20 Squadron's solitary Martinsyde Scout aircraft[4] in response to a sighting of a German LVG reconnaissance aircraft over British lines. Howett successfully intercepted and engaged the intruder but ran out of ammunition for his solitary Lewis gun before he inflicted significant damage. Lewis gun ammunition was held in a drum of just 47 rounds and Captain Howett found himself unable to change ammunition drums and retain control of his aircraft. The LVG escaped, but the squadron's first victory came just two days later on 7 February. Two of 20 Squadron's Fees were escorting a B.E.2c reconnaissance flight over Roulers, 10 miles to the north east of Ypres and well behind German lines. Roulers was a nodal point of the German transport and resupply system, so was a frequent target for British reconnaissance in the Ypres sector. F.E.2B, serial number A6331, was flown by 2nd Lieutenant Reid with Lieutenant Frank Billinge as his observer. The aircraft were attacked by two Fokker monoplanes and four unidentified biplanes. One of the Fokkers attacked the B.E.2c, and as it passed in front and below A6331, Billinge opened fire; this caused the Fokker to sideslip away, trailing smoke from its engine. The second Fokker attacked A6331 unsuccessfully and the Germans then broke off the attack. Reid and Billinge were credited with an 'Out of Control' victory.[5] Frank Billinge was also to claim 20 Squadron's second victory, on 13 February, this time crewing on A6336, with 2nd Lieutenant Kirton in the pilot's cockpit, during an hour-long running fight between Courtrai, Menin, Halluin and Mouscron.[6]

The enemy was not the only difficulty facing 20 Squadron; the weather was frequently vile. In the early hours of 15 February, a gale overturned the squadron's hangars, wrecking three aircraft and seriously damaging five lorries.[7] Two further victories were recorded in February, one of them to 2nd Lieutenants L. Heywood and Hilary Francis Champion. However, sadly, it was not long before the squadron started to take casualties. On 29 February 2nd Lieutenants Newbold and Champion were flying a reconnaissance of German airfields. Two of their three escorting F.E.2Bs were forced to drop out with engine trouble and the reconnaissance mission was subsequently attacked by a lone Fokker. The remaining escort drove off the attacking aircraft but not before it had managed to damage the engine of Newbold's machine, forcing it down. Champion managed to destroy his maps and notes as well as dismantle his gun and scatter the parts before they landed in a field right next to some German infantry who promptly took both men prisoner.[8] Champion, however, eventually managed to escape and reported back to RFC Headquarters on 23 April 1916[9] although he did not return to the squadron. By this time, 20 Squadron were becoming battle hardened, scoring further victories, losing more aircraft to enemy action and starting to receive replacements and reinforcements as officers were posted to other squadrons or were wounded (which group included Frank Billinge), shot down or captured. They also had new commanding officer.

Major Wilson was transferred back to Home Establishment in the UK on 21 March 1916. He was replaced by Major G. J. Malcolm, formerly of the Royal Field Artillery.[10] Like Wilson, Major Malcolm had transferred to the Royal Flying Corps in 1914 and had been in action over France and Belgium in the earliest months of the war, including claiming one of the first enemy aircraft to be shot down when his observer had opened fire with a rifle. Major Malcolm had been born in Canada, and his arrival seemed to start a lengthy list of Canadian officers who served with 20 Squadron. Major Malcolm was, perhaps, fortunate to still be flying; just a year before he took command of 20 Squadron, his engine had failed while he was at 150 feet (40 metres) over the airfield at Bailleul. Without height to regain control, his aircraft had come down hard, and Malcolm's ribs, jaw and skull had all been fractured in the accident. He was rendered unconscious for four days, and this posting marked his return to combat duties.[11]

Flying in the first half of May was limited by poor weather conditions, but on 16 May, 20 Squadron suffered their first pilot fatality. 2nd Lieutenant Trafford Jones, a Canadian who had joined the squadron at the same time as Major Malcolm, was killed when his F.E.2B was badly shot up over Ypres. His observer, Captain Forbes, was also hit in his lung and shoulder but, incredibly, managed to reach back into the pilot's cockpit behind him, take control of the stick and then bring the battered Fee into a landing on the British side of the lines. Forbes was awarded the squadron's first decoration, the Military Cross, for this feat.[12] Major Malcolm was proud of his squadron and this is recorded in his letters home; he believed he commanded the best squadron in the RFC, due to the performance of the officers and men. They had taken the fight to the Germans and made them pay heavily for the casualties the squadron had suffered. Next to their fighting skills, they were extremely capable at taking high-quality aerial photographs over enemy lines. And they were all looking forward to receiving new, more powerful, F.E.2Ds to replace the F.E.2Bs.[13] The first of these new machines arrived in 20 Squadron on 2 June 1916, and the squadron had been fully re-equipped by the end of the month. As well as having a more powerful 250hp Rolls-Royce engine, the F.E.2D carried a heavier armament of three Lewis guns. In addition to the forward firing moveable gun which the F.E.2B also carried, the observer had a second gun mounted at the rear of the cockpit which could be fired backwards over the aircraft's upper wing. The third gun was fixed along the axis of the plane and was fired forward by the pilot using a Bowden cable on the control lever, although in extremis this gun too was re-mountable by the observer.[14] The squadron was to need all its hard-won battle experience as well as its improved aircraft; the Battle of the Somme was about to begin.

On the evening of 30 June 1916, Major Malcolm gathered his officers together and briefed them on their part in the forthcoming offensive. The intent was to mount continuous patrols from British-held Armentieres to German-held Lille and, by doing so, keep the German squadrons in the Ypres sector so busy that they were unable to reinforce and support the defence against the Somme offensive.[15] 20 Squadron's part in this plan on 1 July was to send five aircraft in support of six RE5 aircraft from 21 Squadron conducting a bombing raid on St Sauver. Before a link up was made, the 20 Squadron aircraft became involved in a running fight with at least 20 Fokkers. As a result of the encounter, 20 Squadron claimed two Fokkers shot down over German lines and at least a further two damaged without loss to themselves,[16] although one pilot, Lieutenant F. J. Tyrell, was wounded and a couple of the Fees were somewhat shot up.[17] The following days continued in a similar vein and the remainder of the month was also noteworthy for the arrival of a number of replacements. Among these replacements, on 8 March, was a new sergeant pilot called James McCudden. Having started his RFC service as an air mechanic, he had proved himself as an observer before undergoing pilot training. He was to spend two months flying as a pilot with 20 Squadron, without scoring a victory, before being posted to 29 Squadron, a single-seat scout squadron equipped with DH2s, on 7 August 1916. McCudden would go on to be one of the most celebrated British aces, achieving over 50 combat victories before being killed in an accident in 1918.[18]

The day after Sergeant McCudden's arrival, 20 Squadron suffered another loss. The commanding officer, Major Malcolm, was killed in another accident, along with Lieutenant Geoffrey Chancellor, who was flying with him to collect another new F.E.2D from the depot. As they took off from Clairmarais, the aircraft in which they were flying suffered an engine failure just after take-off, crashed into woods and burst into flames, killing both officers. Malcolm's replacement arrived the following day on 10 July. He was Major William

Mansfield DSO, born in 1886, who had originally been commissioned into the Shropshire Light Infantry in 1909 and was another of the early RFC pilots. He had attended the Central Flying School in January 1914 and been flying from the first days of the war.[19]

The 'No. 20 Squadron Operations Record Book' held in the National Archive at Kew is devoid of entries from 1 July 1916 until 19 January 1917. However, this should not be taken as an indicator that the squadron was in anyway inactive. Indeed, the reverse is true for there is a table contained in the record which shows the squadron claimed a total of 16 enemy machines destroyed and 13 driven down out of control in the course of 1916.[20] During this period, the squadron first started to have its aircrew achieving ace status. The first ace, with five victories, within the squadron was Captain G. R. M. Reid, but his first three successes were scored with 25 Squadron before being posted to 20 Squadron. His fifth kill was on 31 July 1916, thus making him an ace, but only two of this count was scored with 20 Squadron, and within the squadron, there were four others who had reached the tally of two victories. Captain Reid's namesake, Lieutenant Guy Reid was the first to achieve ace status based solely on victories achieved while with the squadron. He achieved this status on 5 September when flying over Passchendaele in F.E.2D serial number A19 and encountered a pair of Fokker biplanes escorting as two-seater. The Germans dove into the attack, but Reid's observer, 2nd Lieutenant Golding got in a good burst over the top of his wing resulting in the Fokker diving away with smoke pouring from the engine.[21]

As September passed into October in autumn 1916, it was becoming clear that 20 Squadron and the RFC were slowly establishing an ascendency over the Fokkers, but the Germans were working hard to replace them with newer, faster and better designed aircraft. Initially these were Halberstadt and Fokker D series biplane scouts. Not only were these faster and better than RFC aircraft, they were also being produced in greater numbers and German organisation was improving. Instead of being attached to reconnaissance units in ones and twos, the new scouts were now being grouped into fighter squadrons; Jagstaffeln or Jastas as they came to be known. Jasta 8 was formed at Rumbeke near Roulers on 12 September 1916, and this was followed shortly afterwards by Jasta 18. Initially, Jasta 8 was equipped with Halberstadt scouts, while Jasta 18 was equipped right from first formation with the even more deadly new Albatros D1 scout. As 1916 slipped into 1917, Jasta 8 and Jasta 18 were to become 20 Squadron's most implacable opponents in the skies over Flanders.[22]

However, the RFC was very much an early 'learning organisation'. In mid-August, Major Mansfield was requested by his headquarters to report on the fighting techniques used by 20 Squadron. He commented on the advantages of the 'X' formation adopted by 20 Squadron in which a machine dedicated to reconnaissance flew in the centre of a formation of four aircraft dedicated to its protection, two ahead and two behind. In this way, each pilot and observer could watch every other machine, each aircraft was in a position to protect the others and be protected in turn, and the formation leader was able to easily keep the speed adjusted to that of the slowest aircraft. This last was essential in order to ensure no aircraft dropped behind and thus became isolated and an easy target. Mansfield also observed that the Fokkers were becoming increasingly reluctant to attack the F.E.2s; a measure of the fact that the Fokkers and, to a certain extent, the Halberstadts were simply not a match for the F.E.2Ds. However, this was certainly not the case with the new Albatros scouts, which were clearly more capable than the Fees. And Major Mansfield was also at pains to highlight that pilot training could be improved. The 'X' Formation was deliberately designed to give new pilots a safe formation in which to learn on the job; more practice at formation flying was an area in which training could be improved before new pilots arrived at a squadron. 20 Squadron went to considerable effort to familiarise new pilots with formation flying and the local area before they allowed them to fly across the enemy lines. Mansfield also commented on the lack of aircraft recognition training, notably for enemy aircraft. This was particularly important so that the appropriate angle of attack could be determined; a forward-firing aircraft was best attacked from above and behind, while a rearward-firing aircraft found an attack from ahead and above most difficult to deal with.[23] As 1916 drew to a close, the obsolescence of the F.E.2D was starting to show as the Germans were introducing the Albatros D1 scout, which was faster and slightly more manoeuvrable and had a higher ceiling. Major General Trenchard, commander of the RFC in France, was prompted to write to the War Office, complaining about the poor quality of British aircraft and, in an ominous portent of 'Bloody April', forecasting an inability for the British to maintain control of the air in spring 1917 if specific measures were not taken. These measures included engine upgrades for all DH2, F.E.8 and Sopwith aircraft and the provision of five squadrons of F.E.2Ds with their more powerful engines. Additionally, to add to the difficulties 20 Squadron was facing, many of the squadron's more experienced and battle-hardened crews, both pilots and observers, were transferred to reinforce other units or to Home Establishment in order to train new pilots. The replacements were most frequently fresh out of training.[24]

One new pilot arriving in the squadron in autumn 1916 did not fall into the category of inexperienced. Sergeant Thomas Mottershead DCM had been flying F.E.2Bs with 25 Squadron; he was another non-commissioned officer who had undergone pilot training after initially serving as an air mechanic. He had been born in Widnes, Cheshire, on 17 January 1892 and was one of the nine children, six boys and three girls, of Thomas and Lucy. Educated at Simms Cross school and later at the Widnes Technical school, he was apprenticed as a fitter and turner at the Widnes Alkali Works on leaving school and studied engineering in his spare time. In February 1914, Tom, as he was usually known, married Lillian Bree and before his death the couple had a son Sydney. Tom had worked at the Cammel Laird shipyard in Birkenhead but in summer 1914 took a new job at Portsmouth Naval Dockyard. War broke out a few days later and he enlisted in the Royal Flying Corps on 10 August. In April 1916, having been accepted for pilot training, he was promoted to sergeant and started flying training at the Central Flying School, Upavon, in May. He obtained his 1st Class Flying Certificate on 9 June and was posted to 25 Squadron at Auchel on 6 July 1916; he was soon in action.[25] Mottershead was awarded the DCM after shooting down a Fokker during the Somme battles and possibly for an attack on an enemy airfield.[26] The latter story lacks confirmation but runs along the lines that Tom and his friend Sergeant Sydney Attwater, who followed him to 20 Squadron, made a pact to keep the attack from their officers, landed on a German airfield and then taxied across it while their observers machine-gunned the hangers and then took off and returned to British lines before the Germans were able to exact any retribution. That the story emerged suggests there is at least some truth in it, although Tom Mottershead's DCM was probably for his victory over the Fokker rather than the attack on the airfield.

Late in the morning of 7 January 1917, Mottershead deployed on an OP over Ploegsteert Wood near Ypres with Lieutenant William Edward Gower as his observer. The pair were accompanied by 2nd Lieutenant Marsh with Air Mechanic Lee flying as his observer. They were attacked by several Albatros from Jasta 8, including one flown by Sergeant Walter Gottsch, who hit Mottershead and Gowers's F.E.2D, serial number A39, in the fuel tank and set it alight. As aircrew were not equipped with parachutes at this stage, for Mottershead the obvious course of action would have been to put his aircraft on the ground and abandon it as quickly as possible, which in this case was behind enemy lines. Instead, despite the flames enveloping his engine, he chose to make for British lines to try and avoid being made a prisoner of war. Gower may have been wounded as it is unclear whether his injuries were suffered in the combat, subsequent crash or a combination of both. However, as his pilot struggled to keep the control of the F.E.2D, despite his clothing starting to catch fire, Gower did what he could to help with the primitive fire extinguisher until that was empty. Mottershead got the aircraft back across British lines and, although he could have crash-landed immediately continued until he found a clear area to land, even circling to check it was safe. He then brought the aircraft into touchdown, but as he did so, the badly burnt undercarriage collapsed and the machine cartwheeled. Gower was thrown clear of the crash but Mottershead was trapped in the burning wreckage until he was pulled clear by Gower and nearby soldiers. Mottershead was rushed to a casualty clearing station and then to field hospital. He was visited there by Sydney Attwater on 11 January and was attempting to remain cheerful despite being in considerable pain; Attwater later left an account of the visit with the Imperial War Museum.[27] Mottershead died the following morning, 12 January, and was subsequently buried at Bailleul with, unusually for a non-commissioned officer, full military honours. The whole of 20 Squadron were paraded by Major Malcolm to pay their respects.

The London Gazette announced the award of a posthumous Victoria Cross to Sergeant Thomas Mottershead in the edition of 9 February 1917:

> For most conspicuous bravery, endurance and skill, when attacked at an altitude of 9,000 feet; the petrol tank was pierced and the machine set on fire. Enveloped in flames, which his Observer, Lt. Gower was unable to subdue, this very gallant soldier succeeded in bringing his aeroplane back to our lines, and though he made a successful landing, the machine collapsed on touching the ground, pinning him beneath wreckage from which he was subsequently rescued. Though suffering extreme torture from burns, Sjt. Mottershead showed the most conspicuous presence of mind in the careful selection of a landing place, and his wonderful endurance and fortitude undoubtedly saved the life of his Observer. He has since succumbed to his injuries.[28]

He was the only non-commissioned member of the RFC, RNAS or RAF to be awarded the VC in the course of the war. George V presented the medal to the widowed Lillian on 2 June 1917 in an open-air investiture in Hyde Park. Lillian was accompanied by William Gower who was awarded the MC for his actions during the incident. Gower had been born on 4 April 1891, attended Derby Grammar School and was subsequently employed by the Midland Railway Company. He volunteered in August 1914 and, on 16 January 1915, he was commissioned as a 2nd lieutenant in the Sherwood Foresters (Notts & Derby) Regiment. 2nd Lieutenant Gower embarked for France some months later and, after enduring several months with his battalion defending the trenches around Ploegsteert Wood, applied to join the Royal Flying Corps. He was successful and on completion of an observer's course in aerial photography, observation, map reading and gunnery skills in late December 1916 was posted to 20 Squadron, where he flew with Tom Mottershead two or perhaps three times before the 7 January mission.[29] Gower was hospitalised after the incident and was struck off 20 Squadron's books on 26 March 1917. He continued to suffer ill health but was employed as a photography equipment officer for the RAF in the Middle East for which he was mentioned in despatches in May 1919. Gower was then discharged at the end of 1919 but was mentally scared by the incident.

The 'No. 20 Squadron Operations Record Book' also has almost nothing to say about the period of March and April 1917, simply recording that the squadron moved to St Marie Cappel[30] in the middle of April; somewhat surprisingly because this was 'Bloody April' and the Battle of Arras. In fact, the squadron had been busy assisting RFC preparations for the coming army offensive at Arras; preliminary air operations were reconnaissance missions to gather information and bombing missions to disrupt and dislocate the German lines of communication. At the end of March, the reconnaissance area of responsibility of the Second Army was extended further north and south in order to relieve the pressure on squadrons to the south. Throughout the first three months of 1917, the weather was as much an adversary as the Germans, frequently bringing wind, rain and low cloud, which frequently prevented flying. During these months, 20 Squadron claimed 11 victories at the cost of 26 casualties; eight dead, seven captured and 11 wounded or injured, and perhaps 13 aircraft destroyed. However, the exchange rate was not as favourable as it first appeared; of the 11 victories, only four were claimed as destroyed or crashed rather than an 'Out of Control' which could frequently have lived to fight another day. Worse, the British were yet to discover, that in nearly every case of the crashed or destroyed aircraft, the German pilots had survived uninjured.[31]

A full-scale air offensive was planned for 1 April 1917, in order to establish local air supremacy over Arras and to obtain up-to-date photographs of the German defences. Bad weather intervened again, and it was not until 5 April that the air offensive got properly started. Once it did, 20 Squadron played a full role throughout the month, conducting reconnaissance, bomber and protective missions and frequently coming into battles with squadrons of the German Albatros scout fighters. By the time April slipped into May, they had lost a further seven men dead, nine injured and four taken prisoner of war. In exchange, they claimed nine combat victories. 20 Squadron was lucky compared to many squadrons; across the RFC and RNAS some 319 men were lost – 75 per cent were on the German side of the lines as the fliers strove to take the fight to the enemy despite their inferior aircraft.[32] The ground offensive at Arras achieved only limited success. British Army attention was switched to Messines and the Ypres Salient.

May and June of 1917 continued in much the same vein for 20 Squadron, with more frenetic fighting as the squadron battled for air supremacy ahead of the five-month long campaign of Third Ypres. The main role of the squadron, and the other fighter squadrons of the RFC, continued to be maintaining the secrecy of British preparations by preventing, or at least seriously impeding, German aerial reconnaissance. This meant keeping German aircraft east of their own balloon line and also keeping their fighters from interfering with British reconnaissance and bombing missions, so that the artillery-spotting aircraft could carry out their work unimpeded over German lines. For 20 Squadron, the reality of this role meant continuing their normal three tasks of conducting offensive patrols, reconnaissance and bombing missions. The two sides were roughly evenly matched in numbers as the RFC fielded around 400 aircraft on this battlefront, of which 170 were single-seat scouts. The problem for the RFC was that, with the exception of the Sopwith Triplane, its machines were outmatched by the German's improved Albatros DIII and DV scouts. The RFC was also facing some of Germany's finest airmen in this campaign and, in addition to its inferior aircraft, was hampered in that it was constantly having to replace battle casualties with new pilots and observers.[33] Both normally came to the squadron with minimal training; the pilots fresh out of flying school and they had to acquire combat experience, support their more experienced comrades and complete their own jobs. The first few missions were key; if they got through those then the odds on their survival increased dramatically. However, through these two months there were some variations to routines. In early May, the squadron started bombing targets at night, frequently with single machines; the first occasion being 6 May when Captain H. L. Satchell and 2nd Lieutenant H. Todd bombed the Hellenes railway workshops at Lille, while Captain Donald Charles Cunnell and 2nd Lieutenant H. R. Wilkinson attacked the nearby La Madelaine station. This last attack left two railway sheds ablaze.[34] The second change was to increase the size of the Ops, partly to provide a safer environment for new pilots and observers to gain combat experience. Increasingly, the patrols were sent out at eight machines strong. Nonetheless, it was a tough couple of months; over 40 victories were claimed by 20 Squadron, including at least three German aces – Karl Schafer, Ernst Weissner and Alfred Ulmer. However, 11 pilots and observers were killed and nine had been wounded. Several others had come down on the German side of the lines and been taken prisoner.

There was no let-up in activity in July 1917, although the month was particularly noteworthy for three events. The first took place on Friday 6 July when six 20 Squadron F.E.2Ds, led in A6512 by Captain Cunnell with 2nd Lieutenant Albert Edward Woodbridge as his observer, headed for Houthem on a bombing mission. Cunnell had been born in December 1893 at Norwich, the son of Charles Donald Cunnell and educated at Gresham's School. An architect by profession, he had served with Norfolk Officer Training Corps for two years, enlisted as private in September 1914 and was promoted to sergeant shortly afterwards. He was commissioned into the Hampshire Regiment in November 1915 and served in France before transferring to the RFC, being appointed as a flying officer on 24 November 1916. By July 1917, he was a flight commander with the temporary rank of captain. As the Fees arrived over Houthem, they were spotted by Rittmeister Manfred von Richtofen, Germany's most celebrated air ace, the 'Red Barron', who was leading most of his 'circus' of around 30 Albatros fighters. Von Richtofen promptly led in to attack the British aircraft, later recalling that he was amused that they had opened fire at such an extreme range. However, almost immediately von Richtofen was hit in the head and lost consciousness; he recovered just in time to land near some German soldiers in the vicinity of Wervicq. He was rushed to hospital for medical treatment and was out of action for several weeks. It was the only time he was wounded in action, and even when he returned to duty, he continued to suffer severe headaches for the rest of his life. The British authorities credited Woodbridge with the victory, although given all the Fees opened fire at much the same time, and it is possible the bullet may have struck von Richtofen from behind, it is impossible to be certain who actually inflicted the wound.[35] Woodbridge survived the war and described the incident as follows:

> Cunnell handled the old FE for all he was worth, banking him from one side to the other, ducking dives from above and missing head-on collisions by bare margins of feet. The air was full of whizzing machines, and the noise from the full-out motors and the crackling machine guns was more than deafening ... Cunnell and I fired into four of the Albatroses from as close as thirty yards, and I saw my tracers go right into their bodies. Those four went down ... Some of them were on fire – just balls of smoke and flame – a nasty sight to see. Two of them came at us head-on, and the first one was Richthofen. There wasn't a thing on that machine that wasn't red, and how he could fly! I opened fire with the front Lewis and so did Cunnell with the side gun. Cunnell held the FE on her course and so did the pilot of the all-red scout. With our combined speeds, we approached each other at 250 miles per hour ... I kept a steady stream of lead pouring into the nose of that machine. Then the Albatros pointed her nose down suddenly and passed under us. Cunnell banked and turned. We saw the all-red plane slip into a spin. It turned over and over, round and round, completely out of control. His motor was going full on, so I figured I had at least wounded him. As his head was the only part that wasn't protected by his motor, I thought that's where he was hit.[36]

Despite the loss of von Richtofen, the Germans continued to press the British aircraft with repeated attacks at close quarters as they fought their way back towards British lines. Eventually, they were joined by four Sopwith Triplanes from B Flight 10 Naval Squadron, led by the Canadian ace Raymond Collishaw. All the British aircraft managed to land safely, although two were unable to make it to St Marie Cappel, due to battle damage. The only British casualty was 20 Squadron observer Lieutenant Stuart Trotter, who was wounded and died at 53 Casualty Clearing Station.[37] Douglas Cunnell was killed just five days later. A little after 1700 hours on 12 July, he was leading another OP of four aircraft over Menin and, with his observer Lieutenant Albert Bill, shot down an Albatros out of control. Immediately afterwards Cunnel was hit and killed by shrapnel from German anti-aircraft fire. Albert Bill, an Australian ex-civil engineer, somehow managed to take over the controls of B1863 and get it back over British lines before crash landing. He was, however, injured in the process.

The second notable day was Tuesday 17 July. Little of the RFC's aerial artillery observation work could have been accomplished without the fighter squadrons maintaining control of the air. 20 Squadron FEs, tasked with both fighting and reconnaissance, saw every bit as much action as the single-seater squadrons. The difference was that the FEs were too slow and cumbersome to escape from a one-sided fight and had to slug it out as best they could, whereas the faster scouts had the option to remain above an action or break it off if they chose. That said, the Germans never found the robust F.E.2D an easy proposition. The day began when a mid-morning OP of eight aircraft, led by Lieutenant Arthur Norbury Solly, originally of the Manchester Regiment, took on five Albatros to the east of Polygon Wood. The charge of FEs broke up the enemy formation, but not before one was shot down by 2nd Lieutenants Durrand and Thompson in A6548. Seven more Albatros then joined the melee, but support was on hand from Nieuports from 1 Squadron. Lieutenant D. Y. Hay and 2nd Lieutenant M. Tod shot down an Albatros over Sanctuary Wood. Three-quarters of an hour later there was another bout as 20 Squadron Fees were joined by further aircraft from 23 Squadron and B Flight of Naval 10 Squadron. Lieutenant Cecil Roy Richards, an Australian who had served in Gallipoli and France with the medical corps, was flying with 2nd Lieutenant A. E. Wear in A6448. The pair got behind an Albatros and claimed an out of control. Minutes later they engaged another Albatros which subsequently crashed near Gheluvelt. Cecil Richards was up again flying A6448, this time with Sergeant John J. Cowell, an Irishman, originally a Royal Engineer, manning the guns in the front cockpit, as they took part in another eight aircraft OP in the evening, led by Captain Stevens. Again, the OP became embroiled in a dogfight, which lasted over an hour, swirling around the skies from Menin to Polygon Wood, as the 20 Squadron FEs were joined by Nieuports from 1 Squadron, Sopwith Triplanes from Naval 10 Squadron, 32 Squadron's DH5s, 56 Squadron's SE5s and Sopwith Camels from 70 Squadron. They found themselves facing the Germans from Jastas 6, 8, 11 and 36. Cecil Richards and John Cowell accounted for three of the seven victories claimed by 20 Squadron.[38] Richards was awarded the Military Cross for this and previous fights, which was announced immediately and gazetted in September, 'for conspicuous gallantry and devotion to duty when on offensive patrols in attacking and shooting down hostile machines. On one occasion he shot down four in one day, displaying great dash and offensive spirit.'[39] He survived the war to return to Australia in 1919, but his luck had deserted him on 19 August 1917, when he was wounded and shot down at Quesnoy, east of Arras and well behind the enemy front line. He was taken prisoner of war. John Cowell was awarded the Distinguished Conduct Medal, for previous actions, on this very day (17 July), 'For conspicuous gallantry whilst assisting an aerial gunner during bomb raids. He showed remarkable skill and judgment in the eight combats in which he has been engaged, and on several occasions has shot down hostile aircraft.'[40] For his actions with Richards, he was awarded a bar to his Military Medal.[41] He went on to train as a pilot, returning to 20 Squadron to score one more victory, bringing his tally to 16, before he was killed in action on 30 July 1918, shot down by Friedrich Ritter von Röth of Jasta 16.[42] Nor was Albert Wear destined to survive; the son of a Middlesex clergyman, an accountant by profession, credited with nine combat victories as an observer, he was killed on 11 September 1917. In one of the first 20 Squadron Bristol Fighter flights, his pilot, Sergeant William Roberts, a pre-war motor fitter in London, stalled and spun into the ground at the start of a formation practice flight. Roberts also died in the accident.[43]

The third notable day in the month was 27 July, although the weather was cloudy and there was little activity until it cleared in the evening. The previous days had seen 20 Squadron engaged in mass dogfights involving 30 or more aircraft. The British 'brass' were concerned, and 20 Squadron provided aircraft to act as bait in order to draw the Germans into an ambush. As the squadron operational history puts it: 'East of YPRES, No 20 Squadron had a formation acting as "bait" for the whole Army Wing, which for three quarters of an hour kept up a running fight with superior numbers of the enemy until the arrival of the British scouts. Of the 30 enemy machines brought down on this date, the squadron accounted for nine, no machines being lost.'[44] The bait formation was eight of 20 Squadron's Fees which circled over Menin until they attracted attention and then slowly headed back towards the lines, drawing the Germans with them to the area above Polygon Wood. Here, a large formation of British and French scouts were waiting, at altitude, in ambush for them. All eight of the 20 Squadron bait aircraft had a tough time of it, but none more so than 2nd Lieutenants G. T. W. Burkett and T. A. M. S. Lewis flying A6512. Engine trouble had caused them to lag behind the other aircraft and, as a result, they had been singled out for particular German attention. Both officers were wounded, Lewis so seriously by an incendiary bullet that his leg had to be amputated, but they succeeded in bringing down two of their attackers and still managed to get their battered aircraft back to British lines and safely on the ground at Bailleul. Burkett and Lewis were both awarded the Military Cross for this action. Burkett's citation stated, 'For conspicuous gallantry and devotion to duty. With his patrol he engaged a superior force of enemy machines, and although wounded early in the engagement, continued to fight. He brought down two hostile machines and drove off two more whilst returning to our lines with his own machine badly damaged. In spite of this, however, he succeeded in making a good landing. He displayed splendid dash and coolness under very trying circumstances.'[45] Lewis's citation read, 'For conspicuous gallantry and devotion to duty. Whilst acting as Observer his patrol engaged a superior force of enemy scouts. His Pilot was wounded, but they continued to fight, destroying one enemy machine. He was then severely wounded, but continued to work his gun lying on his back. By this means they were able to destroy a second enemy machine. Afterwards, when returning to our lines with their machine badly damaged, he and his Pilot drove off two machines which were pursuing them, having displayed the greatest gallantry and presence of mind.'[46] The story, however, has a happy ending; Burkett was visited in hospital by Lewis's sister, Charlotte, and the couple subsequently married. Meanwhile, the FEs which made it successfully to Polygon Wood were also having a hard time of it. In fighting which lasted for about an hour and a half and at heights from 13,000ft to 7000ft, (4000m to 2150m), 20 Squadron crews claimed a further 11 enemy aircraft either destroyed or out of control. The most successful crew were 2nd Lieutenant Reginald Milburn Makepeace and Private Stanley Pilbrow with an Albatros DIII destroyed in flames and two more driven down out of control over Polygon Wood. Additionally, Captain Harry Luchford and Lieutenant Henry

Waddington claimed a double victory.[47] The squadron received a congratulatory signal from General Trenchard; 'Congratulate you on your magnificent fight tonight aaa. The whole of the 9th Wing are enthusiastic about it aaa.[48]' So the month ended with the squadron claiming to have accounted for about 53 enemy machines through the course of the month, a total only surpassed in May and September 1918.[49] It also marked the squadron's total score moving passed the 200 mark.[50]

August was marked by atrocious weather as the British struggled to make progress in the Third Ypres battle. 20 Squadron flew in support whenever conditions allowed. The most significant event, however, came when the first Bristol Fighter F2B reached the squadron on 10 August. The event, however, was marred by tragedy when Captain Arthur Solly and Lieutenant Donald Hay, an Old Wellingtonian aged 24 years, took the machine, A7108, up for a test on the morning of 11 August. As the pair looped the loop at 8000ft (2500m) above St Marie Cappel, the wings folded back and tore away from the aircraft, which crashed to the ground killing both men.[51] It later transpired that the inter-plane struts had been hollowed out to save weight and so were unable to withstand the stresses of certain manoeuvres. Despite the less than promising start, deliveries of the new aircraft type continued and training on them began. In the meantime, the air fight over the Ypres Salient continued on the F.E.2Ds, and there is little doubt that some of the squadron's casualties were due, at least in part, to the fact the F.E.2D was just too old and slow to compete with the newest German scouts. By September, half the squadron were re-equipped with Bristol Fighters, and on the morning of 3 September, Major Mansfield sent out a mixed patrol of four Bristol Fighters escorting four F.E.2Ds on a photo-reconnaissance task. The Bristol Fighters were led by Captain E. H. Johnston and Lieutenant J. A. Hone in A7215, while Captain F. D. Stevens and Lieutenant W. C. Cambray were in charge of the Fees in A6516. The patrol was a success; the Bristol Fighters flew behind and above the Fees, and when the latter were attacked by a swarm of 10 to 15 Albatros scouts, the former came diving down to join the fray. The ensuing battle saw 20 Squadron gain its first Bristol Fighter victory when Lieutenants Makepeace and Waddington shot down an Albatros in flames, and all the squadron's aircraft returned safely; the F.E.2Ds with their vital photographs of an enemy battery.[52] Mixed patrols continued from then until the last 20 Squadron F.E.2D patrols took place on 20 September in support of fresh attacks by the Second Army around the Menin Road. The last F.E.2D was then returned to Number 1 Aircraft Depot at St Omer the following day. Over the 21 months that 20

Squadron had been in France, its F.E.2s had served it well. Though the squadron had suffered heavy losses, they had continually pushed the fight into German held territory and gained intelligence, which had saved British lives on the ground. Although slow and ungainly, the Fees had held their own as fighter aircraft as well, inflicting casualties on the enemy; despite frequently being out numbered, they had retained control of the air and prevented the Germans from gaining similar intelligence of British dispositions by air reconnaissance.[53]

CHAPTER 7

20 Squadron Royal Flying Corps and Royal Air Force: Third Ypres to India

The Bristol F2 Fighter was a two-seat biplane fighter and reconnaissance aircraft which was one of the most important and successful British designs to serve during World War I. In 1915, the RFC had identified a need to replace their Royal Aircraft Factory B. E.2cs with an emphasis on self-defence capabilities. Designed by a team led by Frank Barnwell, who had experience as a frontline RFC pilot, the prototype Bristol Type 12 F2A was first flown on 9 September 1916 at Filton, fitted with a newly available 190hp Rolls-Royce Falcon I in-line engine. Bristol had already received an order for 50 aircraft by the time the second prototype flew on 25 October, this time fitted with a Hispano-Suiza power unit. The type was a tractor engine, twin cockpit biplane, with pilot and observer sitting back to back; the pilot forward and the observer to the rear. The latter was equipped with a Scarfe-mounted machine gun in his cockpit. A forward-firing Vickers gun was mounted on the fuselage centreline, inside the engine cowling. The type was ordered into service with two prototypes and 50 production F2A being built, before construction was switched to the Type 14 F2B; the aircraft that became the definitive Bristol Fighter, frequently known by its crews as a 'Brisfit' or, even more simply, as a 'Biff'. When production was switched to the F2B, it became the subject of 'contract manufacture' across the aircraft industry with the first 150 or so fitted with either the Falcon I or Falcon II engine. The remainder received the Falcon III engine; this meant they could achieve a top speed of around 123mph which could reach 10,000ft (3000m) about three minutes faster. It had a ceiling of about 18,000ft (5500m). The F2B featured a fully covered lower-wing centre section and downward sloped longerons in front of the cockpit to improve the pilot's view when landing. Despite being a two-seater, it was an agile dog-fighter and was superior to many of its single-seater opposition.[1]

For 20 Squadron, the Brisfit was a stark contrast to its previous Fees. The high cockpit walls and tractor engine gave additional protection to both crew members, particularly the observer compared to his exposed and precarious perch at the very nose of an FE. The forward-firing Vickers gave the pilot considerably more firepower than before, while Scarfe mounting meant the observer could traverse the Lewis gun easily in any direction. The observer also had a basic seat and a control column to give him a chance of bringing the aircraft down to the ground if the pilot was incapacitated.[2] 20 Squadron crews now had to learn to fight in their new mounts. Keeping tight formations or flying in defensive circles became a thing of the past because the Bristol Fighter's speed and manoeuvrability gave greater scope for crews to use their initiative in a fight. Indeed, the most successful crews were those who learnt to fight the Bristol Fighter as a single-seat scout, but one that could fire backwards as well as forwards. The fighting roles of the crew in the F.E.2, where the observer did most of the shooting, were reversed in the Bristol Fighter. The pilot now had to learn to use his gun most effectively in the initial attack and then break away in a manner that allowed his rear cockpit observer to exploit the situation. The full potential of the new aircraft started to become clear on 23 September. A late afternoon patrol of 20 Squadron Bristol Fighters fought seven Albatros scouts over Lille and, in the fading light, the British formation was broken apart. The British leader, Captain Johnston, trailed the scouts by himself, dived on them to make a surprise attack and shot one down. The F.E.2D would have been too slow to carry out such an action.[3] The Brisfit was able to climb faster and higher than the Albatros and, at altitude, was able to turn more tightly. So, an outnumbered but high-flying Bristol Fighter patrol, unless caught off guard, was able to stay above an enemy and choose whether to engage or not.[4]

The new aircraft had arrived in the nick of time for 20 Squadron. The Germans were also introducing a new fighter, the Fokker Triplane Dr. I, and the first two protypes were delivered to the front in late August 1917. Designated as the Fokker F. I, these first two aircraft were flown by Manfred von Richtofen and Werner Voss. 20 Squadron encountered the latter on 6 September while still flying their F.E.2Ds, in a patrol of four, and immediately lost B1895 with Lieutenant Pilkington and Air Mechanic 2nd Class H. F. Matthews. Another burst left a second Fee struggling to get back to its lines, after which the Germans departed the scene.[5] The Fokker triplane completely outclassed the F.E.2D. The production variant, the Fokker Dr. I, was introduced into service in October 1917 with Jastas 4, 6, 10 and 11 of 'Richthofen's Circus'. However, although exceptionally manouevrable, partly because of its poor directional stability, the Dr. I could not match the Bristol Fighter in straight-line speed or ceiling.

Weather conditions which had blighted much of the Third Ypres offensive continued to cause problems for both the ground offensive and those tasked with supporting them in the air. It was now clear to Sir Douglas Haig and the other British commanders that a breakthrough was highly unlikely, and indeed, little progress would be achieved before the onset of winter. The goal became to extend the line of captured ridges to the point at which they could be defended from German counter-attacks. The ruined village of Passchendael became the key, and in order to reach it the offensive was renewed on 4 October despite the weather. Although the wind, rain and low clouds made flying almost impossible, a special reconnaissance of four 20 Squadron Bristol Fighters was sent out to report on the advance and German counter-attacks. Flying at just 500ft (150m), the F2Bs spotted about 2000 enemy troops marching west towards the lines. A call for fire was put in immediately by wireless, and the enemy column was swiftly broken apart by shells from the heavy guns of the ANZAC Corps. Whenever the weather did allow flying, the Germans would put up aircraft in an attempt to deny British air reconnaissance. Air fighting continued to be tough, and losses remained heavy, although 20 Squadron continued to extract a high price from their opponents.[6]

Another change came on 15 October. The Commanding Officer, Major Mansfield, was transferred to Home Establishment, and on a temporary basis, Captain E. H. Johnston assumed command.[7] The appointment was soon made permanent and Johnston, a South African who had enlisted in 2nd Imperial Light Horse in November 1914 for the German Southwest Africa Campaign, was promoted to temporary major.[8] Late October and, indeed, early November brought more arrivals, both as replacements of killed and injured, and to replace those like Major Mansfield who were posted back to Home Establishment, either to act as trainers or because they had been medically boarded as unfit for further front-line service. This time also saw more decorations for officers within the squadron, Captain H. G. E. Luchford, Lieutenant V. R. S. White and 2nd Lieutenant R. F. Hill were all awarded bars to their Military Crosses.[9] Sadly, Luchford, a 23-year-old flight commander, with 24 victories, was shot down and killed near Becelaere just a few weeks later on 2 December. On the ground, on 6 November, the Canadian Corps launched the attacks which finally captured Passchendaele village and the ridge beyond it; Field Marshal Haig had finally achieved his initial objectives, and the Ypres Salient was no longer overlooked by Germans holding the high ground. The casualty lists since the initiation of the battle with the blowing of the massive mines on

Messines Ridge in June was appalling, but there is little doubt that it would have been even worse if it had not been for the contribution of the RFC and 20 Squadron.

For 20 Squadron, December 1917, after a tough start, saw shorter days and alternating periods of poor and good weather. This brought a reduction in flying hours, which helped the squadron avoid heavy losses. It also allowed the squadron to have a period of relatively peaceful routine; this allowed the experienced crews to take leave, while the new pilots and observers were able to settle into life with an operational squadron and bring their skills up to scratch in a comparatively benign environment. This was just as well as there was to be no let-up in activity in 1918.

Meanwhile, on 8 December 1917, a young Scotsman left Ayr, having enlisted into the RFC as an air mechanic, and travelled to Eastchurch to undergo his training. Having been born at Mounthill, Blantyre, Lanarkshire, on 6 December 1899 he had just passed his 18th birthday. David McGeachie Lapraik was the second son and last child of Hugh and Fanny Allan. Hugh was a colliery surface manager, having been a plate layer previously. His wife, Fanny, gave her maiden name, McGeachie, to David as his middle name. Being in his late 50s, David's father, Hugh, was too old to serve and working in the colliery was a reserved occupation. How his three daughters, David's elder sisters Marion, Jessie and Fanny, were affected is not known. All were old enough to have been married by the time the war broke out. However, David's elder brother John Hugh, an assistant ironmonger, reached his 18th birthday in about September or October 1915, was enlisted 20 February 1916 and attested on 12 May into the Argyll and Sutherland Highlanders. John, though, was not a healthy young man; he was just under 5'3" (1.6m) in height and, when medically examined, was found to have defective vision and problems with his left arm and wrist. He was discharged as 'Not likely to become an Efficient Soldier' on 12 August 1916.[10] There were no such issues for David, who at 5ft 8 inches (1.73m) was considerably taller than his brother, and we leave him undergoing his mechanic training at Eastchurch. He was still at this location when the RAF was formed, on 1 April 1918, and David was transferred from the RFC into the new organisation.

The collapse of Russia on the Eastern Front in late 1917 had released large numbers of German troops who were being moved rapidly west, with the intention of making a big offensive before the Americans were able to build up their forces in support of French and British troops. The Allied leadership was, of course, well aware of this but not the timing or location of the impending onslaught. The air forces had a vital role in attempting to determine this, and right from the start of the year, 20 Squadron were in the thick of it, with almost daily air combats through the year. By the end of January 1918, it was becoming clearer that the German offensive would most likely be aimed primarily against British rather than French forces and General Trenchard issued a memorandum on 'The Employment of the Royal Flying Corps in Defence'.[11] In this, he emphasised the vital importance of observation from the air in order to detect where the enemy's attack would come from. Aircraft were also to interdict the enemy troops whenever possible by bombing or strafing and control of the air was to be maintained by attacking enemy aircraft whenever they were encountered. In short, the RFC was to remain on the offensive, even if the rest of the Army was temporarily on the defensive.[12] Casualties and victory claims for 20 Squadron continued to mount through January, February and into March.

The storm broke on 21 March when the Germans launched Operation *Michael*, as their spring offensive was codenamed, out of dense fog and mist, preceded by a lightening bombardment, directly against the junction of the British Third and Fifth Armies, across the old Somme battlefields. The British were soon in retreat and threw every available aircraft into desperate strafing of the advancing attack. 20 Squadron were instructed to support this as many pilots in the Somme area were flying five or more ground attack missions per day – if they survived. However, as there was also evidence that the Germans might launch a second offensive north of the Ypres Salient, 20 Squadron were split in two directions, sending a flight south each morning to assist 10 Wing. The 'No. 20 Squadron Operations Record Book' states, 'In March and April 1918, during the German offensive, the squadron took part in low bombing and shooting up of enemy troops and transport. At daylight each morning machines were flown to the Aerodrome at Bruay from which operations were carried out, the machines returning to St. Marie Cappel at dusk.'[13] These aircraft were in action from 26 March and, thereafter, almost continuously until Operation *Michael* was brought to a halt on 5 April. This was difficult and dangerous work; the German breakthrough had returned a measure of fluidity to the battlefield and troops were frequently at close quarters in fast-changing situations. The aircraft had to come low to the ground in order to identify friend from foe and, in doing so, exposed themselves to intense ground fire in addition to ceding their height advantage to the German fighters who would be circling and awaiting the opportunity to pounce. It was here that 20 Squadron first started to learn and put into practice the close cooperation with ground units that they would take with them to the mountains of the North West Frontier. Each Bristol Fighter carried four 25lb bombs in addition to its small-arms ammunition, so could inflict considerable damage if deployed effectively. The danger, however, was soon highlighted. In the early afternoon of 26 March, Lieutenant R. D. Leigh-Pemberton was wounded by ground fire and forced to land near Albert, fortunately still behind British lines at that stage. His Bristol Fighter, B1196, was wrecked, but his observer Captain Norman W. Taylor was fortunately unhurt. The flight leaders Captains Robert Kirby Kirkman (pilot) and John Herbert Hedley (observer) were flying B1156 the following day, strafing troops and transport near Bray sur Somme, when they were pounced on by an Albatros. John Hedley engaged the German scout, reporting after the war that he had thought he had brought it down, but was unable to prevent the Bristol Fighter's fuel tanks and engine from being machine gunned. The engine cut out and Robert Kirkman brought the aircraft into land just metres from the German infantry, whom the pair had been bombing and machine gunning just moments before. The Germans promptly opened fire and were only persuaded to cease when Kirkman and Hedley surrendered themselves. This was a loss of experience that 20 Squadron could ill afford; Kirkman was credited with eight victories and Hedley 11, in both cases all with 20 Squadron and only two of the victories shared between them.[14] Both spent the rest of the war in captivity. Hedley subsequently emigrated to the United States and went on the lecture circuit telling of his military experiences. Here, he was given the nickname 'The Luckiest Man Alive' by Floyd Gibbons, war correspondent of the *Chicago Tribune* during World War I. Hedley claimed that while in action with German fighters in early 1918, his pilot, Lieutenant Reginald Makepeace, had put their Brisfit into an abrupt nosedive, causing Hedley to fall out, with the rapid descent continuing for several hundred feet. However, when Makepeace pulled up, Hedley purportedly grabbed the tail and climbed back into his seat.[15]

On 1 April 1918, the RAF came into being, the world's first independent air force, as the RFC and the Royal Naval Air Service were brought together as one service, with its own command structure and entirely independent from the army and the royal navy. Just as Operation *Michael* was called off by General Erich Ludendorff on 5 April, the Germans switched their effort back to the north and launched Operation *Georgette* on 9 April. The Germans secretly massed 36 divisions in Flanders, east of the French town of Armentières. Less than 20 miles away was the vital Allied rail hub of Hazebrouck. The plan involved capturing the three low but prominent hills of Mount Kemmel, Mont des Cats and Mount Cassel, which rise out of the Flanders plains. Mount Cassel overlooked the aerodrome at St Marie Cappel, so 20 Squadron lay directly in the path of the offensive. More than 2250 German guns opened fire on some 25 miles of British front held by just 12 divisions. After four and a half hours of bombardment, the German infantry advanced, overwhelming much of the lightly held British front and advancing over three miles in the first few hours. The next day the village of Messines, taken at great cost the previous year, was lost, despite a counter-attack by the South African Brigade. By 11 April, the situation seemed desperate. German units were just a few miles from Hazebrouck, and it was realised that St Marie Cappel was within range of German artillery. Because of this, on 13 April, 20 Squadron moved back to the west to the aerodrome at Boisdinghem.[16] The execution of the move was not a success; it took place in gathering darkness and few of the pilots had flown at night. None of the aircraft had night-flying aides. At least three of the Brisfits were severely damaged and two pilots were injured. Many of the aircraft diverted away from Boisdinghem and it took several days for 20 Squadron to regroup as a fighting unit.[17]

However, the tide was turning. Allied reinforcements were arriving and the 1st Australian Division took up positions in the forest of Nieppe to block further German advances towards Hazebrouck. In response, the Germans turned their attacks on Mount Kemmel; a dominating geographical feature in West Flanders. On 15 April, the British were forced to reduce their line in the Ypres Salient, giving up virtually all of the gains made during the Third Battle of Ypres the previous year but crucially holding on to Ypres itself. On 17 April, Captains T. P. Middleton and F. Godfrey claimed a pair of Albatros DVs; one destroyed and one out of control. The squadron had a six-aircraft OP out again on 21 April, which was engaged by nine Albatros scouts. Captain D. G. Cooke and 2nd Lieutenant H. G. Crowe claimed one out of control, as did Captain D. Latimer and Lieutenant T. C. Noel. Mount Kemmel fell on 25 April, but it was the last German success of Operation *Georgette*. Captain Wilfred Beaver and Corporal Malcolm Brown Mather gained revenge of a kind by shooting down in flames an Albatros when they attacked five of the scouts in the area of Ploegsteert Wood.[18] However, fighting continued for several more days until German commanders finally called off the *Georgette* offensive on 29 April. Wilfred Beaver had been born in Gloucestershire, emigrated to Canada in 1914 and returned to fight with the Canadian Expeditionary Force. He returned to Canada after the war but relocated south into the States and became an American citizen. During World War II, he received a Bronze Star for outstanding leadership as group executive officer of the 447th Bomb Group; a B-17 group stationed in England under the 3rd Air Force.[19] Malcolm Mather was a Scot and this was the last of his eight victories.[20]

May 1918 was a spectacular month for 20 Squadron. Most days were busy and involved air-to-air combat. On 19 May, the squadron claimed seven enemy aircraft destroyed and one driven down out of control; on 31 May, they claimed eight destroyed and a further out of control. In the course of the month, they claimed no less than 75 combat victories, although they were credited with 56, of which 48 were considered as destroyed. The actual count is unlikely to be as high as this, but in addition, they had dropped 451 of their 112lb bombs, expended 99,790 rounds of small-arms ammunition and, perhaps most importantly, exposed 970 photographic plates. To do so, they had flown some 1165 hours.[21] The pattern continued through June and July, but the German efforts to force a final victory on the ground before an American intervention were increasingly weakened. In the air, the relentless Allied air offensive, carried out with increasing numbers of new and effective aircraft and squadrons, was slowly stripping away the previous advantage of the German Air Service. Increasingly in air combat, the Allied aircraft outnumbered their opponents. Additionally, Allied pilots and observers were benefitting from longer and better training programs.[22] Slowly but surely, the Allies were winning control of the air. The fighting units such as 20 Squadron, whilst taking losses, were preventing the Germans from interfering with the vital work of the bombers, reconnaissance aircraft and artillery observers in providing support to the army. In June and July, the squadron claimed 65 combat victories. But the Germans continued to exact a heavy price. During those months, the squadron lost 14 dead, six captured and three wounded or injured.[23]

Back in Britain, still at Eastchurch, Air Mechanic David Lapraik was benefiting from the improved training programmes for observers. Having been taught basic ground-crew skills and mechanics, the trainee observers were now trained in aerial gunnery, including the mechanism, stripping, care and cleaning of the Lewis gun, generally at the gunnery school at Hythe. There was firing practice both on the ground and in the air and David Lapraik would have been taught how to use the ring sight in order to try and hit a small, fast-moving target whilst his own aircraft was also manoeuvring at high speed. His further training would have included map reading and reconnaissance skills so that he could recognise fortifications and barbed-wire entanglements from above and interpret how shadows could conceal or betray an enemy depending on the time of day. This would have included instruction of what, and in how much detail, he should record in notes. He had to learn photography skills so that he could take accurate photos from several thousand feet and change awkward camera plates with frozen fingers, all while his pilot threw the aircraft around to avoid German anti-aircraft fire. David would have spent a little time at the Wireless Telegraphy school at Brooklands, learning how to use the primitive wireless sets and the basics of artillery fire observation and registration. Most importantly, he would have been instructed in the art of air tactics, the likely arcs of enemy attack and the importance of maintaining all-round observation, even whilst conducting his other tasks. On completion of training, trainee observer-gunners had to conduct two cross-country flights of between 20 and 40 miles. They were given maps on which to mark any points of interest, such as trains or road transport. On their return, they were then tested on the features of the ground they had flown over.[24] At some point in this training, David Lapraik applied to be an officer. He commenced his officer training with the No. 2 Officer Training Training Wing on 20 July and was granted a temporary commission, as a 2nd Lieutenant Reconnaissance Observer, on 26 September 1918. David was then posted to the British Expeditionary Force on 29 September and to 20 Squadron on 1 October 1918.[25]

2nd Lieutenant D. M. Lapriak. Probably taken in 1918 after commissioning and before he shipped to France, and eventually India.

In France, in August 1918, the Germans were now on the defensive, while the British planned a major offensive at Amiens. A number of the German air units from the Flanders area were moved south towards this area and, as a result, 20 Squadron increasingly found themselves flying unopposed OPs and reconnaissance missions. The focus of the squadron shifted further towards supporting troops on the ground. On 11 August, the squadron put up a force of 16 Bristol Fighters, nearly the entire squadron, in order to conduct a raid on the railway station and sidings at Courtrai. They were escorted by aircraft from four other squadrons. Each Bristol Fighter carried one 112lb bomb, which was dropped on trains and rolling stock at heights of between 400ft and 1000ft (100–300m). Additionally, about 9000 rounds of small-arms ammunition were fired by the squadron in strafing ground targets. On the return trip, the patrol leader, Captain Horace Percy Lale, flying E2467 with 2nd Lieutenant John Hills, engaged and destroyed an enemy kite balloon. At the rear of the formation, Lieutenant E. W. Sweeney and 2nd Lieutenant C. G. Boothroyd flying C987 did the same a short time later,[26] as did one of the 29 Squadron SE5As.[27] The first serious air fight of the month came on 14 August when Horace Lale, this time flying with 2nd Lieutenant F. J. Ralph, led an OP of nine aircraft which met a mixed German formation of Fokker DVIIs and Pfalz scouts over Dadizeele. 20 Squadron claimed six victories but lost C987 with pilot Lieutenant David Esplin Smith killed. Smith was originally from Dundee but had emigrated to the USA before the war. Smith's observer, John Hills, survived the crash but was taken prisoner.[28]

The month continued in a similar vein until 26 August. The squadrons which had been directly supporting the Amiens offensive had been hard hit while supporting the ground troops. Particularly so in the case of 48 Squadron, and 20 Squadron was now transferred from 2 Brigade RAF to 5 Brigade in order to replace them. This involved leaving Boisdinghem and moving to the aerodrome at Vignacourt.[29] OPs flown in the morning of 4 September reported large-scale German motor transport movements heading east. Subsequent OPs in the evening reported many fires on the German side of the lines. The Germans were retreating again, back to the positions they had held in early 1917 on the Hindenburg Line.[30] Over the course of the month, the British Fourth Army followed them up and 20 Squadron moved forward on 16 September to the old German airfield of Suzanne[31] and, again, on 24 September to Proyart.[32] This was a prelude to the next big ground attack when, on 29 September, the Fourth Army launched a major assault on the Hindenburg Line between Bellenglise and Vendhuille. Continual reconnaissance of the enemy lines and rear areas was always required, and 20 Squadron continued to assist the effort to provide this.[33]

The British attack on the land continued into October and the Germans were finally forced to evacuate Vendhuille and withdraw over the St Quentin Canal. The Hindenburg Line was finally broken and the German army was now in full retreat from disaster. Even in the north around Ypres, the British were able to advance as the Germans retired in front of them, knowing that no reinforcements would be sent from the south. While the ground troops advanced, 20 Squadron continued to conduct OPs with the primary purpose of protecting British aircraft carrying out reconnaissance patrols and ground strafing.[34] It was at this time that David Lapraik joined the squadron, just in time for it to move forward again, to the airfield at Moislains, on 7 October 1918.[35] This was to support the next phase of the ground attack, stretching from Cambrai to north of St Quentin, but events were moving fast across the front; the following day the allied troops were entering Le Cateau. Even as they did so, the weather closed in and, for the following two weeks, low cloud and heavy rain restricted operational flying. This provided something of a respite for 20 Squadron, as well as a chance for David Lapraik to ease himself into the realities of putting his training into practice with an operational squadron.[36]

The squadron was next involved in serious fighting on 23 October, when it was tasked with bombing the railway junction at Aulnoye. The 15 aircraft were again led by Horace Lale, this time with Lieutenant Clement Boothroyd as his observer. As Boothroyd was taking photos of the effects of the attack, a similar number of Fokkers were spotted barring the route back to British lines and a fight soon developed. In the course of this fight, David Lapriak claimed what is believed to be his first and only victory. Lapraik's pilot was Lieutenant Alan Christopher Temple Perkins MC and the pair were attacked by one of the Fokkers. David Lapraik, however, kept up a steady and accurate fire and the German aircraft eventually spun away and crashed west of Aulnoye. In addition to this victory, 20 Squadron claimed a further four Fokkers shot down. However, one of the Bristol Fighters was shot down with the loss of both pilot and observer killed and two of the others collided. Of the pair involved in the collision, one was landed safely by its pilot, Captain Tom Traill, when his observer, Captain Leslie Burbridge, climbed onto the wing of the aircraft to counter balance it. Traill went on to become an air vice marshall following World War II, while Burbridge was awarded the Distinguished Flying Cross for his actions. However, the other aircraft crashed and its pilot, Lieutenant Francis Goodearle, was killed and the observer, Lieutenant A. M. McBride, injured.[37]

On 25 October, 20 Squadron made its final move of the war to Iris Farm, still following up the retreat of the German army.[38] The German Air Service was flung into battle in an ever-increasing desperate manner. Although now heavily outnumbered, the Jastas were now grouped into massed formations of 50 or more aircraft in order to briefly achieve control of the air over a particularly critical section of the battlefield. Massed air battles were the norm and the RAF were engaged in more air-to-air combat on 30 October 1918 than on any other day of the war. 20 Squadron was fully involved, as always, and the day bought further victories, without loss,[39] including two more for Horace Lale and Clement Boothroyd, their 22nd and 23rd and 11th and 12th respectively.[40] The squadron saw further fighting on 1 November, but this time there was a price; F6116 failed to return and Lieutenants Philip Segrave and James Kidd were both killed.[41] Victories and losses continued right until the very end of the war. On 10 November, a patrol of eight 20 Squadron Bristol Fighters engaged seven Fokker DVIIs attacking British DH9s over Charleroi. Four victories were claimed, but the squadron returned missing two aircraft. F6195 went down with its crew of 2nd Lieutenants Alexander McHardy and William Rodger dead. Also shot down, probably by Lieutenant Hans von

Number 20 Squadron taken in France 13 Nov 1919 just after the end of the war. David Lapraik's signature is visible on the left hand side of the photo, but he has not been firmly identified.

Freden, commanding officer of Jasta 50, for his 20th and last victory, was F4421. The observer, Sergeant Richard Dodds, was severely wounded and died almost immediately. The pilot, Lieutenant Edmund Arnold Courtney Britton, was captured but suffered probably one of the shortest captivities in the history of warfare. Nicknamed 'Babs', due to his short stature and youthful looks, he escaped, with the aid of some locals who disguised him in women's clothes, and swiftly returned to British lines.[42] He would subsequently deploy with the squadron to India in 1919.

So, the war came to an end on 11 November 1918. None of the 24 officers who had deployed to France with 20 Squadron in early 1916 were still serving with it. All told, more than 600 men had flown with the squadron over the course of 33 months and they had suffered a casualty rate of around 50 per cent. Some 128 had been killed while flying with the squadron, a similar number wounded and about 60 were taken prisoner of war.[43] However, along with its fellows, the squadron had never lost control of the sky over the Western Front, and it was one of the highest scoring and most decorated squadrons. It had played its role throughout, saving the lives of many British and Allied ground soldiers through providing vital intelligence and was destined to continue to do so. Meanwhile, despite the Armistice coming into effect, flying continued. Aircrew and ground staff were kept as busy as they had been during the war; constant patrols were required in order to ensure the Germans were keeping to the terms of the Armistice. The end of the war did not bring an end to either movements or to danger. On 16 November, the squadron, once again, came under the orders of 22 Wing, and on 23 December, they moved from Iris Farm to Ossogne.[44] Flying accidents and the influenza epidemic continued to extract a toll as the squadron waited to hear their fate within the post-war RAF.

For the still temporary RAF, against the background of British defence cuts, the wait was for nearly nine months just to see if it would be retained by the cabinet. 6500 officers, all holding temporary commissions or seconded from the army and navy, applied for permanent commissions. The cabinet sanctioned a maximum of 1500 and the air ministry offered 1065 to the applicants, publishing the first list on 1 August 1919, 75 per cent of them were short-term – between two and five years. The service was reduced in strength to 35,500. The primary task, certainly overseas, was policing the British Empire from the air. It was argued that the use of air power would prove to be a more cost-effective way of controlling large areas than by using conventional land forces. 20 Squadron, however, did not have to wait as long for their fate to be clarified. Although many of the aircrew, particularly the longer serving 'Duration of the War' enlistments, returned to civilian life in the United Kingdom, the squadron was transferred to IX Brigade in March 1919 and warned for operations in India. A new commanding officer, Major John Cannan Russell, formerly a Royal Engineer, was appointed on 26 April 1919.[45] The squadron was transferred to 52 Wing serving in the Middle East, and the first party of personnel sailed from Marseilles onboard SS *Malwa* on 14 May 1919. The remainder sailed on the SS *Syria* the following day.[46] Both ships were from the Peninsula and Oriental Steam Navigation Company having been requisition as troopships by the British government. According to the 'No. 20 Squadron Operations Record Book', the squadron's transport and aircraft then followed on the SS *Clan Striart*[47], although this must be a mistake in the record; there is no Striart clan and the Clan Line have never had a ship with this name. The ship was almost certainly Clan Line's SS *Clan Stuart*, the third and last ship of the company to carry this name, which had been built in 1916. She was eventually sunk in a collision off Start Point in 1940.

A number of 20 Squadron members who sailed to India in May 1919 had been with the squadron at the end of the fighting in France. These included Horace Lale, Clement Boothroyd, Edmund Britton and David Lapraik. However, plenty had not. The 'No. 20 Squadron Operations Record Book' lists those officers deploying to India, in addition to the commanding officer, as 40 officer pilots and observers, an armaments officer, Captain G. H. Salaman and two administration officers, Lieutenant D. R. Mullan and 2nd Lieutenant E. Bryant.[48] Among those who had not been with the squadron as the Armistice came into force was a Captain G. Eastwood. Although his RAF service papers list his date of birth as 22 May 1897,[49] it is almost certain George Eastwood was born exactly a year earlier in 1896. He was born in Alfreton, Derbyshire, the eldest son of railway worker, William Eastwood, and his wife, Sarah Ann, *née* Whitaker. He was baptised in nearby Ashover on 15 July 1896. By the time of the 1901 census, George Eastwood had been joined in the family by a sister, Dorothy Marjorie, born in 1897, and a younger brother born on 9 June 1900 and named William like his father. The 1901 census[50] records that the Eastwood family were living at Westhouses; a settlement which had been founded in the 1870s. The Midland Railway, which later became part of the London, Midland and Scottish Railway, was the main employer and landowner. Many roads such as Allport Terrace, Bolden Terrace and Pettifer Terrace were named after Midland Railway directors, and the school was also built and maintained by the company. The majority of the houses were two up and two down, with an outside toilet in the backyard. On the same page of the census, and the adjacent pages, the breadwinners of every household are employed by the railway. By 1911, the family had moved north to Sheffield and are recorded as living at 37 Blayton Road,[51] although William senior was still working for the railway, he is now listed as an engine driver. Aged just short of 15, George is recorded as being an apprentice sign writer. His younger siblings were still at school. George joined the army in 1916, whether conscripted or through choice is not clear, but his army officer's record held in the National Archives,[52] indicates that he commissioned directly into the RFC, as a temporary 2nd lieutenant on probation from the General List on 7 July 1916 for duty with the RFC, probably at the Central Flying School at Upavon. A note on his file states that George had 'passed for school on main paper' and that he should sent to Cambridge; this would probably be No 31 Training Squadron at Wyton. His appointment as a Flying Officer RFC was confirmed on 13 December 1916. What is not clear from either George's army or RAF Officers papers is how he spent 1917 and 1918, but it does not appear that he went to France or any other overseas duty. The lack of a medal index card for him supports this theory, and his air officer's file[53] suggests that he spent time at the Farnborough School for Wireless Operators from 31 March 1917. It is also possible that George was selected, or managed to get himself selected, as an instructor at one of the schools during this period, but there is insufficient detail in his files to be certain. However, it is certain that he was transferred from the RFC to the RAF when the latter formed on 1 April 1918. He was also promoted to lieutenant (temporary) from 7 January 1918 and then appointed acting captain from 1 October 1918. Finally, on 15 April 1919, George was appointed to join the British Expeditionary Force in France, so presumably sailed to India with the rest of 20 Squadron on either the SS *Malwa* or SS *Syria*.

As soon as 20 Squadron arrived in India, probably into Bombay, the men moved directly to Risalpur, where they arrived on 19 June 1919.[54] The main fighting of the Third Afghan War, as covered in previous chapters, was over by this time, but the squadron still represented the first significant reinforcement to the RAF in India; at this stage Nos 31 and 114 Squadrons were still the only squadrons available to provide air support to the ground troops. Given the distances and climate, as well as the tired nature of the existing aircraft, it is likely that 20 Squadron's arrival had been eagerly anticipated. However, as 20 Squadron's personnel had travelled ahead of their aircraft, a period of three or four weeks was to elapse before they could get involved in the action. The frustration of the aircrew at this enforced delay is also easy to imagine. In the interim, unacclimatised, they suffered cruelly in the heat and disease of Risalpur. A sergeant and two mechanics died from heat stroke. During this period, Major Russell was detached from the squadron to temporarily command 5 Wing at Peshawar, so Captain Horace Lale acted as commanding officer of the squadron.[55]

The Bristol Fighters started to arrive in Risalpur early in July. Work to assemble them started immediately. The first aircraft to be ready was F4446 on 14 July. The same day it was test flown by Horace Lale, with Lieutenant S. P. de M. Bucknall as his observer; this was the first flight of a Bristol Fighter in India.[56] As soon as the aircraft were ready, the squadron started moving forward to Parachinar. This was to be able to support the ground troops, and the Kurram Militia in particular, in policing both the frontiers and tribes of the Kurram valley as the regular reinforcing troops were withdrawn from the theatre following the June armistice. The move forward, however, was slow and not just because of the time taken to assemble aircraft. Even once the aircraft had been assembled and flown forward to Parachinar, the stores required to support them still had to moved up. The closest rail head was Thal, 56 miles (90km), at least a full day's journey from Parachinar. When at Thal, the stores then needed to be convoyed forward to Thal by lorry, at a time when there was still considerable unrest amongst the tribespeople of the Kurram. A small party of the squadron's ground staff were positioned at Thal, with several lorries, for just this purpose. And the effort continued to be hampered by a large number of men sick in hospital, following the ravages of heat and disease in Risalpur.[57] Nevertheless, by the end of July 1919, the squadron had established a forward operating base at Parachinar, with slightly less than one flight's strength of aircraft, probably four. The war diary from the headquarters of 60 Infantry Brigade records the 20 Squadron strength in Parachinar at the end of July as 29 British Officers and 62 British of other ranks. The scene was now set, with all the major actors in place, for the action at Badama Post.

CHAPTER 8

Action at Badama Post – 29 and 30 July 1919

In the previous chapters, the strategic background to the Third Afghan War and its conduct at the operational level have been described. The backgrounds to the units of the principal actors, namely the Kurram Militia, 20 Squadron RAF and 22 MMG, in the action at Badama Post have also been explained. Towards the end of July 1919, the situation in the Upper Kurram valley, in the vicinity of Parachinar, could best be described as quiet but tense. The Afghan

A Motor Machine Gun Battery on the North West Frontier in 1919, from an album compiled by W. K. Fraser-Tytler, later Ambassador at Kabul. 3rd, 15th, 19th and 22nd Batteries Motor Machine Guns were all in India during 1919. The location, is not known, but this is almost certainly 22 Battery, identified by Sgt Fielder's propeller mascot being visible on the commanding officer's combination, to the front left of the photo. (NAM 1953-02-31-175 Courtesy of the Council of the National Army Museum)

invasion had been pushed back across the Durand Line and the territorial integrity of the tribal territories of the North West Frontier had been restored. Despite some unrest, particularly in the area of Badama, there had been no serious rising by the tribes, although they remained extremely restless. Tension with the tribes had been building through July as the negotiations for a final peace treaty were delayed in starting. Although the armistice with the Afghans was in effect, it had not been fully honoured by them, and Afghan troops remained in positions close to the border, rather than withdrawing as required. Throughout June and July, there had been almost daily incidents of sniping across the border. This chapter, and the two which follow, will describe one of the last actions of the Third Afghan War, which took place around Badama Post, when one of 20 Squadron's Bristol Fighters was shot down.

How, and exactly when, the news of a further gathering of tribesmen in the vicinity of Badama reached Parachinar is not entirely clear. The official history[1] and Sergeant Macro's report[2] indicate that it was on 30 July, but neither indicate how the news was received. After the siege of Thal had been lifted, the telegraph had been re-established, so it was probably by this means that the messages were passed. However, the war diary of 22 MMG[3] is quite clear that Number 3 Section departed Parachinar at 2015 hours on 29 July and spent the night at Sadda Fort. The war diary of the Kurram Militia also records that a report of a tribal gathering was received from Badama on 29 July and that Major Dodd, a section of motor machine guns and 50 Kurram Militia mounted infantry headed for Badama; however, no time is given.[4] The most reliable source is probably the war diary of 60 Infantry Brigade HQ which, for 28 July, states that 'Tribal Lashkar consisting of Ali Khels, Mishtais, Musazais, Mamozais, Alisherais and Afridis reported collecting in Musarai Country.'[5] The detail of the entry, which includes that fact the *lashkar* was under the command, once again, of Mullah Mahmud Akhinzada and that they intended to attack Badama, Sadda or Sultan Kot suggests that the intelligence was probably processed into the brigade headquarters by the political agent Major Robert Heale. The reports were taken seriously because the Brigade war diary also records that aeroplane reconnaissance had failed to locate the *lashkar* but had been fired on in the Khurmana valley.

The following day, 29 July 1919, the 60 Infantry Brigade HQ war diary states that the report of the *lashkar* gathering was confirmed; presumably, this was by the report referred to in the Kurram Militia war diary, which was received from Badama Post. This report from Badama also gives the numbers of the gathering as 1500.[6] The brigade diary, however, continues to provide more detail and states the *lashkar* were 'Expected to attack Posts and menace convoy.' It then confirms that a mobile column was warned and ready, and that Major

Dodd was in command of a reinforcement of 50 mounted infantry and two machine guns for Sadda Post.[7] From the various war diaries, it is possible to conclude that the bald statement of the official history is not entirely accurate, 'On the 30th of July, a report was received that a large body of Orakzais and Zaimukhts were collecting in the Khurmana valley to raid the Kurram, and to attack the posts of Badama and Sadda.'[8] Equally, it appears likely that Sergeant Bill Macro was referencing the official history when he states, again slightly erroneously, 'On July 30th 1919 a report was received in Parachinar by Major Malony [sic], OC 22nd Battery, MMG, that large numbers of tribesmen were collecting in the Khurmana valley for the purpose of attacking a convoy expected to pass along the Thal-Parachinar Rd.'[9] Piecing together these diaries with the official history and Sergeant Macro's account, it is possible to make some sensible deductions to describe events in more detail.

The long delay from the 3 June armistice without a formal peace treaty was the main cause of the restlessness amongst the tribesmen. They came to believe that the amir would resume hostilities and, therefore, continued to ferment trouble wherever possible. Despite his defeat in the late May attack on the posts at Badama and Sadda, Mullah Mahmud Akhinzada saw the withdrawal of British troops and the return to more normal operations by the Kurram Militia as a sign of weakness. The Orakzais had already made two unsuccessful attempts to interfere with the railway between Thal and Kohat. Additionally, on the night of 21/22 July, a party of 400 tribesman had attacked the frontier constabulary post at Shinawari, 18 miles (29km) north-west of Hangu; the tribesmen had dispersed when relief columns had marched from Hangu. Mullah Mahmund Akhinzada would also have seen the potential for rich pickings in the increased number of slow-moving convoys between Thal and Parachinar, particularly as 20 Squadron attempted to establish their forward operating base in the latter. A successful attack on a convoy or a small post offered the prime opportunity for tribesmen to acquire modern rifles, which were the most valuable commodity on the frontier. An assembly of even 1500 tribesmen, which may well be a conservative estimate, would have considerably outnumbered the garrisons at Sadda and Badama Posts, which stood at about 50 and 80 militiamen respectively, even if the garrisons did have the advantage of fighting from a defensive position. When news of the assembly reached Parachinar, it would not have come as any particular surprise to Robert Heale or Percy Dodd that the mullah was looking to make another attack. However, accurately locating the *lashkar* in the wilderness of the North West Frontier, and then successfully dispersing it, was another matter. Although 20 Squadron aircraft were tasked to locate the gathering on 28 July, it may well have been that this did not happen until the afternoon of that day. The gathering darkness would not have aided their attempts, even when they were fired on. It is also entirely possible that the airmen did not realise they had been engaged until they returned to their landing strip and realised the aircraft had been hit. Without an accurate location, there was little headquarters could do other than warn troops to be ready to support a post, escort convoys that might be threatened and continue to attempt to locate the gathering. It is likely that a *gasht* would have been deployed, in daylight, from Badama, in order to conduct a ground reconnaissance and locate the tribesmen. The success of this *gasht* allowed Badama Post to confirm on 29 July the numbers of tribesmen and their location at Masul, in the Khurmana valley, above Badama.

Once the tribesmen had been located, preparations to deal with the gathering were accelerated. The mobile column, which was to consist largely of regular Indian troops from 3rd Guides Infantry, was warned to be ready to move. As transport was at a premium, they would have to march to reach the action if required. In the meantime, the most urgent requirement was to reinforce the posts at Sadda and Badama, which were the most immediately threatened points. As Commandant of the Kurram Militia, and the man with the best knowledge of the ground and routine responsibility for its security, it was entirely logical that Percy Dodd should have moved to the threatened point. Moreover, he had the mounted infantry of the Kurram Militia at his disposal to give him greater mobility than infantry without motor transport. Percy Dodd deployed from Parachinar to Badama Post, with 50 of his mounted infantry, on 29 July. This deployment probably took place in daylight and would have been a matter of routine for the militiamen; it was how they normally operated. Other than checking weapons, ammunition and water, there would have been little to do by way of preparation; they would have moved out almost immediately and probably arrived at Badama before last light. It is likely that Lance Daffadar Miru Mian was amongst this party of mounted infantry.

The deployment of 50 additional rifles, however, would have seemed an inadequate response to support the militia posts given the size of the tribal gathering. And there was another highly mobile asset, which packed a considerable punch, in the shape of 22 MMG, readily available to support the threatened areas. Its mobility also meant, as had been demonstrated on the border in the previous months, that it could be readily redeployed should the threat not materialise as expected. 60 Infantry Brigade HQ, therefore, ordered Major Molony to provide a section of two machine guns, one third of his total firepower, to proceed to Badama in support of the Kurram Militia. Whether Percy Dodd specifically requested this or whether it was ordered anyway by the headquarters is not clear; however, given they were well used to using the machine guns and had routinely mixed them into mobile columns, it is likely the headquarters ordered the guns deployment. Had they not done so, then Percy Dodd would certainly have asked for them; he had seen how effective they were on the border. The deployment of the MMG section would have occasioned rather more excitement than the militia deployment; none of the three sections of 22 MMG had deployed from camp in Parachinar for all of July and much of June as well. In his report, Bill Macro records that the commanding officer of 22 MMG chose Number 3 Section for the task, 'Major Malony [sic] detailed Sgt Macro to take No 3 Section, 22 Battery MMG and patrol the road from Parachinar to Sadda, and there to rendezvous with Major Dodd to exchange information.'[10] Although the account does not mention it, this instruction would have initiated a rush of activity to prepare for the deployment. The motorcycles and sidecar combinations would have been uncovered, the fuel checked and spare fuel loaded. The two Vickers machine guns would have been mounted on their sidecars. Ammunition and spare ammunition would have been issued and stowed. The two Ford lorries would also have been prepared. As the man in charge of the section, Bill Macro would have provided a briefing to all the 18 or 20 men who were deploying, passing on all the relevant details that he had

Parachinar late May/early June 1919. 22nd Battery motorcycles and combinations sheeted to the rear, in front of the lorries. Three 1914 pattern Rolls Royce cars to the left. These are not Indian pattern so may be ex 13th Light Armoured Motor Battery vehicles which arrived in India in 1919 from Mesopotamia. The car front and centre is a Hotchkiss belonging to 1st Armoured Motor Battery converted back from armoured car to tender. (The Tank Museum Limited)

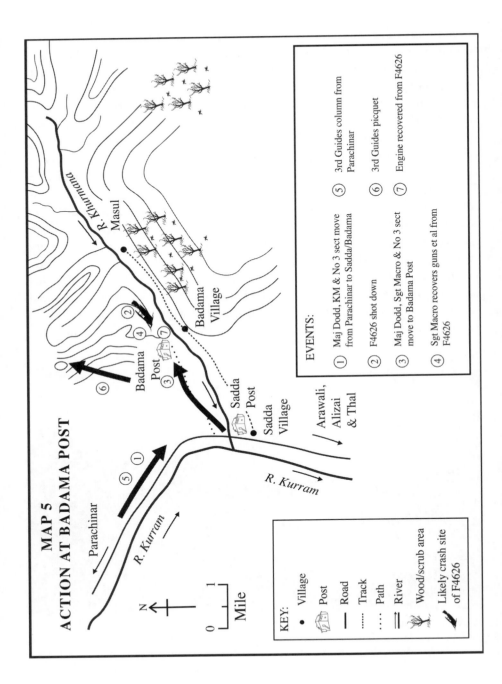

received from Alexander Molony. Although the information was probably fairly limited, this would have been something that Bill took seriously, especially as it was normally the task of a young officer. However, as has been noted, all of 22 MMG's sections were now commanded by non-commissioned officers. The section also probably had a quick talk through of the various drills which they would employ if they came into action. The prospect of action after a month in camp would have added to the sense of tension and doubtless most of the section would have been considering the possibility that this might be the last time they saw action before demobilisation and returning home.

Even though they were probably second nature after the nearly three years the section had been on the North West Frontier, the preparations took some time. Number 3 Section of 22 MMG departed Parachinar for Sadda at 2015 hours, well after nightfall, on 29 July. It is clear from Sergeant Macro's account and the various war diaries that the machine-gun section travelled separately from Major Dodd and the Kurram Militia mounted-infantry party. In the dark, and possibly travelling without using headlights, it is likely that that the trip of 20 or so miles to Sadda Post would have taken at least a couple of hours. Here, Number 3 Section spent the night, shaking out their blankets and getting what rest they could in the rather limited accommodation provided by the post.

On the morning of 30 July, with his mounted infantry, Percy Dodd scouted the environs of the Khurmana valley in the vicinity of Badama Post to relocate the gathering of tribesmen. The conduct of clearing patrols away from the fixed location of a post was a routine act performed every morning to ensure that tribesman were not exploiting the darkness to sneak up on the picquet and launch a surprise attack. Whilst under the cover of the rifles in the post, the patrol could proceed in relative safety. As soon as they moved out of range or sight of the post, the patrol would become a much more protracted affair. With only 50 mounted infantry, the patrol's ability to picquet the heights around the Khurmana valley would have been limited and the patrol's progress would have been slow. But, even if each picquet was only made up of five or six men, their deployment towards high ground was essential to protect the patrol in the tough terrain. And the terrain was very tough; it was rugged, dusty and rocky, with steep slopes and riven by dry ravines. Scrubby, stunted deciduous woods clung precariously to some of the slopes. The Khurmana river did not fill its bed but still rushed along foaming around the various rocks. It all provided perfect cover for an ambush and the tribesmen were adept at exploiting the terrain and the cover it provided. But there was to be no ambush of the patrol this morning. The only signs of the tribes the patrol found seemed to suggest they were withdrawing back up the Khurmana and into the mountains. This withdrawal may have been due to the arrival in Sadda and Badama of the reinforcements and their subsequent actions or it may have been due to the sudden presence of aircraft in the area over the previous two or three days. As the morning wore on, without having come into decisive contact with the enemy, Percy Dodd patrolled back to Badama Post. Subsequently, with a few of his militia, he headed back to Sadda in order to link up with Bill Macro and his machine guns.

Back in the headquarters in Parachinar, there were decisions to be made. With the immediate reinforcements deployed, there appeared to be no need to despatch the mobile column to the area. The aircraft of 20 Squadron, however, were available and were an extremely valuable resource that needed to be tasked effectively. Although few in numbers, only four aircraft available, their speed and range gave them a flexibility the British were starting to appreciate. The two obvious tasks were the escorting of the convoy and attacking the tribesmen in order to disperse them. Given that the continued safe running of the convoys was essential to sustaining both 20 Squadron and the ground forces in Parachinar, this should have been the priority task. And as the tribesmen had yet to commit an overtly hostile act, attacking them from the air was, supposedly, restricted under

A mountain pass near Jung in 1917. Ammunition boxes are carried on the rear of the combination. There is probably no link between the Battery and the camels beyond the combination, but the Battery would use whatever means it needed to in order to bring its guns into action. Mules were certainly used on occasions. (From E. W. Macro's album)

the terms of the Armistice. However, the majority of the accounts, and the official history in particular, indicate that the four Bristol Fighters operated together and that their primary task was to bomb the tribesmen. The beauty of the Bristol Fighter was that it carried bombs and machine guns, and it could conduct both escort and bombing tasks. There was also no reason that required all four aircraft to operate together, although operating as a pair was, subsequently, frequently found to offer a degree of mutual support and redundancy. Certainly, Sergeant Macro recalls seeing just a single aircraft,[11] and the 60 Infantry Brigade HQ war diary is clear that the aircraft were tasked with both escorting and bombing, although it is not specific as to how the aircraft were to operate or be divided between these tasks. The diary states, 'Aeroplane escort provided for convoy route Arawali [to] Sadda. Bomb Masul village.'[12] Whether they were tasked to do so or whether the senior officer of the squadron made the decision, it seems likely that the aircraft operated as singletons, probably keeping a permanent rotational presence over the convoy. As they were relieved of their patrol over the convoy or as their fuel supply reached low levels, each aircraft returned to Parachinar to refuel, with a detour into the Khurmana valley in order to search for the *lashkar* and bomb Masul village.

Captain George Eastwood, as a flight commander and one of the more senior officers of 20 Squadron, could have had his pick of the observers available in Parachinar that day. Why he and David Lapraik teamed up is not known, but it is likely this would not have been their first flight together. They would almost certainly have flown an aircraft up from Risalpur to Parachinar and had probably flown together in the air reconnaissance operations two days previously on 28 July. By this stage, they would have been starting to form a bond. Although younger and junior to his pilot, David Lapraik had more combat experience and at least one victory to his name; Eastwood would have quickly been starting to rely on him as an effective observer, capable of making and recording the detailed observations in conditions that were so different from France. Equally, Lapraik's confidence would have been growing that his pilot was safe and competent, despite the demanding high-altitude conditions. As they got airborne over Parachinar, probably sometime mid- to late-morning, there would have been nothing to indicate to them that their day was set to end so dramatically. Indeed, certainly for David Lapraik, without the menace of enemy aircraft or anti-aircraft artillery, the threat most have seemed very benign compared to the Western Front, even if the flying conditions were challenging. Their aircraft, Bristol Fighter F4626, would have been carrying a full load of fuel, which would have given it an endurance of a couple of hours. It would have been loaded with ammunition for both machine guns and, assuming

A Bristol Fighter over the Khyber probably in the second half of the 1920's. Possibly from 20 Squadron, although this is not confirmed. The aircraft appears to be painted in the silver colour used after 1923. F4626 would have been painted in the drab brown colour used on the Western Front.

they were available, Cooper bombs. As described in the opening of the book, Eastwood and Lapraik would have flown south from Parachinar until they picked up the convoy heading from Arawali up to Sadda. They would then have flown in escort above it for as long as they had sufficient fuel. At around midday, they broke away from the convoy and headed past Sadda towards Badama, with the intention of bombing the tribal gathering at Masul.

Number 3 Section, 22 MMG, according to the battery war diary, spent the morning of 30 July in Sadda Post, not leaving it until 1200 hours when they headed up to Badama. Although they had arrived late in the previous evening at Sadda, this seems unlikely, given Sergeant Macro had been ordered by Major Molony to patrol the road from Parachinar to Sadda. Having covered this road in the dark the previous night, it is much more likely that Number 3 Section deployed onto the ground during the morning of 30 July and patrolled a distance north towards Parachinar. They probably also headed south for a distance towards Alizai, in case they could locate and support the convoy moving north. Bill Macro also recalls that he made his rendezvous with Major Dodd outside the walls of the post, which suggests that both were outside the post when they met, otherwise it would have easier and safer to have a discussion within the post. It was during the course of this discussion that Sergeant Macro states 'Major Dodd reported that the tribesmen appeared to be dispersing owing to the arrival of the MMG section.'[13] The conference outside Sadda Post probably took place at around midday, which would fit with the statement in 22nd Battery's war diary. And while the conference was taking place, Eastwood and Lapraik overflew Sadda, heading towards Badama. Again, in his report Sergeant Macro states, 'This conference took place outside the walls of the post [Sadda], and while it was in progress, an aeroplane was seen to zoom down into a valley beyond Badama Post. As the plane did not reappear it was assumed it had been shot down and Major Dodd set off on horseback, accompanied by a few militiamen.[14]

Events started to happen quickly at this point. George Eastwood's aircraft would have covered the couple of miles from Sadda up to Badama in little more than a minute. It is known that the aircraft was shot down close to Badama Post, probably no more than half a mile to the east of it. The tribesmen, therefore, would have received little warning of F4626's approach, although it is possible there had been earlier bombing raids that would have warned them of aircraft being in the general area. However, locating tribesmen from the air proved difficult time and again as the official history records:

> The greatest credit is due to the officers of the Royal Air Force for the courage and skill which they displayed in performing their duties .... but in short-distance tactical reconnaissance they were of no great value. The terrain was difficult and the tribesmen soon learned how to break into small groups and to keep still when an aeroplane was overhead. The result of this was that bodies of the enemy were difficult to locate.[15]

While the official history states that the aircraft was engaged 'by a party concealed on the hill side,'[16] none of the war diaries are that specific. While an ambush by a group of tribesmen appears the most likely method of the tribesmen shooting down the Bristol Fighter, the possibility of a shot from a single tribesman cannot be ruled out. The 'No. 20 Squadron Operations Record Book' states the aircraft was 'shot down by snipers on the 29th July, 1919,'[17] although the date is certainly incorrect. Given the aircraft came down in close proximity to Badama Post, whoever shot it down must also have been fairly close to the post, in full daylight and on terrain which had been scouted in the preceding few hours. However, as has been identified already, the terrain around the post offers plenty of opportunities to conduct an ambush. The Bristol Fighter was a ruggedly constructed aircraft and, keeping in mind the punishment they had

taken on various occasions in air-to-air combat, it seems unlikely that even a
volley of rifle fire would do sufficient damage to the airframe to bring it down,
certainly in such a short timeframe. The aircraft was brought down because
one of the tribesmen got lucky and his bullet hit the most critical part of the
aircraft, the pilot. His casualty card records that George Eastwood received a
bullet in his left lung.[18] The injury was enough to render George unable to fly
the aircraft and so brought it down, although he was sufficiently in control to
get onto the ground in a manner which enabled both him and his observer to
survive. He certainly never got the chance to drop his bombs.

David Lapraik's injuries were almost certainly sustained as the Bristol Fighter
crash landed. His casualty card[19] records that he suffered the loss of three teeth
and his face and lip were cut; conceivably he could have sustained such injuries by
falling on rocks as he came back to Badama Post. The injuries of both Eastwood
and Lapraik are confirmed by most sources, including the 'No. 20 Squadron
Operations Record Book' which states 'The pilot, Capt. Eastwood was wounded
in the chest, and his observer 2/Lieut. Lapraik suffered a lacerated face.'[20] The
official history, however, suggests that the two aircrew 'had roughly dismantled
their machine'[21] before they were brought into Badama Post by the militia. This
seems highly unlikely. As George Eastwood had received a tribesmen's bullet in
his chest and David Lapraik had been bashed around the head and face, it is
probable that both would have also been suffering from shock, and David possibly
from concussion as well. Assuming both were still conscious, they would also
have been keenly aware that there were tribesmen close to where they were; they
would also certainly have been aware of how the tribesmen treated prisoners.
David Lapraik's efforts would doubtless have been focused on getting himself and
his more seriously wounded pilot out of the aircraft and into some sort of cover.
Help was also close at hand; as soon as the aircraft was seen to have crashed then
a *gasht* was mounted from Badama Post in order to rescue the aircrew should they
have survived. Subedar Gul Khan would have given the *gasht* the task of securing
the crash site and recovering as much of the aircraft as possible, particularly its
guns, ammunition and bombs. On the strength of his leadership in the earlier
attack on Badama, Gul Khan may well have led the *gasht* himself. Equally, the
tribesmen would have been looking to exploit their success and would have seen
a prime opportunity to acquire modern weapons and ammunition.

Just as the Kurram Militia at Badama Post acted promptly, so too did
Percy Dodd. Seeing the Bristol Fighter had not reappeared from the valley
beyond Badama Post, he immediately mounted his horse and headed in that
direction, accompanied by the mounted infantry that had been patrolling
with him. As he did so, he ordered Sergeant Macro to prepare his section

for action and follow him up to Badama Post. Even though they had been outside the post, this took Number 3 Section a few minutes. The track from Sadda to Badama village followed the southern or left-hand bank of the Khurmana river. Badama Post, however, was situated to the north of the river. There was no road from Sadda to the post, merely a goat track along the ridge. This made progress particularly difficult for Sergeant Macro's Ford lorries. Once his section was ready for action, they 'also set off for the post, but as there was no road, had to pick their way along the hilltop, and so did not arrive at the post until some minutes after Major Dodd.'[22] However, as Percy Dodd reached Badama Post, he had learnt that his militiamen had already deployed to the aid of the aircrew. He would have quickly become aware that the militia had already reached the airmen. It is not difficult to imagine Eastwood and Lapraik's relief as they found themselves surrounded by friendly militiamen, although having only been in India for a month or so, they probably had difficulty in communicating with them. Neither spoke Pashtu and few militiamen had more than a couple of words of English. Under fire and with tribesmen pressing in close upon them, no language would have been required to convey the urgency of the situation. The militia hustled and helped the two airmen towards Badama Post. There was insufficient time and not enough of the militia to secure the crash site or to make any attempt to recover parts of the Bristol Fighter. The focus was on recovering the casualties; David Lapraik was walking, although he required support. George Eastwood was sufficiently badly wounded to be beyond walking; the militia lashed together a rough *dhoolie* stretcher on which they dragged him back towards the post. Those militia men not helping the two British officers provided covering fire. They crouched for cover behind the rocks, firing at their pursuers whenever they presented a target and then sprinting to catch up with those helping the casualties. In the harsh surroundings, and uncertain of the size of the pursuing force, the men of the Kurram Militia would have been keen to keep the tribesmen at a distance. To be surrounded and brought to action at close quarters in such a situation would have been fatal.

Percy Dodd had reached the post ahead of Number 3 Section of 22 MMG. He and his accompanying mounted militia would have pushed straight on to link up with the *gasht* that was in the process of recovering the aircrew back to Badama Post. As he had already ridden two or more miles from Sadda to the post, and as the Bristol Fighter had come down so close to the Post, Percy did not go far beyond the post before he met his militia bringing the two airmen back towards him. He, therefore, came back to Badama Post and

Signalling Party. Walter Patrick is the taller soldier to the rear. The photo shows a heliograph on the left and a telescope behind the man on the right as well as the semaphore flags. In the days before radios this was still a common way of communicating. Training manuals required, 'All ranks should be efficient in Semaphore. In addition, 16 men per battery should be trained to send and read Morse with a flag only'. (Alex Bowell, from W. Patrick's album)

Combination fording a river in 1917. The picture gives a feel for how the Khurmana was forded near Sadda during the action at Badama Post. (From E. W. Macro's album)

it was here that Sergeant Macro and the MMG section caught up with him again. Bill Macro reported that his section:

> did not arrive at the post until some minutes after Major Dodd. He [Major Dodd] reported that some of his militia were bringing in the two wounded airmen, and Sgt Macro ordered one of his Ford vans to be cleared ready to take the airmen to hospital. The airmen, who were too badly injured even to help themselves, were given first aid, and dispatched to Kohut [sic].[23]

The arrival of the machine guns at the post significantly swung the balance of firepower in favour of the militia. Although the favoured technique was to dismount the gun from the sidecar and bring it into action on its tripod, when time was short it was quite possible for the combination to be parked up and the gun fired directly from its mount with the gunner still in his seat in the sidecar. The motorcycle rider would have dismounted and moved to assist his gunner. The crew members of the ammunition carrier combinations would have parked in whatever cover they could take nearby and would have brought over ammunition boxes of spare .303 cartridge belts. As the section commander, Sergeant Macro's role was to direct and supervise the men of the section. He also had to control the fire of both his guns and spot for the fall of shot. The drills had been thoroughly rehearsed over the previous four years and both guns would have been ready to open fire within no more than 30 seconds or so of pulling up. And whilst they lacked all the refinements of a fully prepared defensive position, such as defensive *sangars*, range cards and distance markers, the two machine guns would have been a formidable proposition for the tribesmen to attack. At this stage, the guns probably did not even open fire; if they did then they fired no more than a burst of a few rounds. There were insufficient tribesmen close to the post and the aircraft to press their attack, and those tribesmen pursuing the militia and the wounded airmen melted back into the broken terrain of the Khurmana valley.

Outside Badama Post, attention now turned to the two airmen and treating their injuries. There is no hard evidence which confirms that Number 3 Section was accompanied by one of 22 MMG's two attached Army Medical Corps personnel. However, given that the section were the only element of the battery deployed out of the camp at Parachinar, it seems a reasonable assumption that Major Molony would have instructed Sergeant Macro to take a medic when they deployed. Having been shot through the chest, George Eastwood's injuries were life-threatening; he required immediate hospital treatment. His injuries were beyond that which even the trained medic was capable of dealing with; he would not have had the modern equipment to conduct a needle decompression or plastics available to seal the sucking chest wound. Nor would a medic have

Gunner Walter Patrick on the gun. (Alex Bowell, from W. Patrick's album)

A machine gun team in action on the Frontier in 1919. From the album compiled by W K Fraser-Tytler. The prone figure, with binoculars, on the right of the photo, is believed to be A/Sgt E. W. Macro. (NAM 1953-02-31-174 Courtesy of the Council of the National Army Museum)

had means, such as breathing bags or bellows, to assist Eastwood's breathing or intravenous lines in order to get fluids into him. But if a medic had not been present, then it is likely George Eastwood would have died at Badama or certainly on route to hospital; the medical training of the British troops was minimal and that of the militia non-existent, apart from some tribal folklore. The medic had sufficient knowledge to attempt to seal the chest wound and to ensure Eastwood was lain with his injured side down so that gravity would assist in keeping his lung open. The initial first aid given stabilised his medical situation to give him the best possible chance of surviving being transported across rough terrain back to the road at Sadda and then some 100 miles (160km), via Thal, to Kohat in the back of a battered Ford van. David Lapraik's injuries were much less serious; his lacerations would have been bandaged and he would have been given water to drink. While first aid was being administered, Bill Macro had some of his troops clear the back of one of his two lorries. Once this was done, the two injured airmen were loaded as carefully as possible; the crew of the lorry were then briefed and provided with a couple of militia men to guide and escort them. Some 10 or 15 minutes after it had reached Badama Post, the Ford van was heading back to Sadda with its cargo of injured men.

It was now early afternoon, probably around 1400 hours; there was probably no more than three, possibly four, hours of daylight left. The tribesmen had secured a major victory by shooting down one of the scarce British aircraft. This was the first aircraft lost in the Kurram valley and the first Bristol Fighter ever shot down in India; the British do not appear to have made any further attempts to fly aircraft into the Khurmana during the remainder of the action at Badama Post. Certainly, there is no mention of them doing so in any of the ground unit war diaries or in the operational records of 20 Squadron. However, the British had managed to snatch the aircrew out of the clutches of the tribesmen, even though they were wounded. Although one of the wounded was seriously ill, both were now on the way to hospital, having been given some rudimentary first aid. The tribesmen would have been greatly heartened by their success, although it would not be sufficient to encourage Afghan regular forces to break the armistice and recross the Durand Line. On the ground, the tribesmen dominated the ground up the Khurmana valley, including, effectively, the wreck of the aircraft. They were now gathering their forces and preparing to push forward against Badama Post and Sadda again. They considerably outnumbered the British forces in the local area. If they could cut the link between Thal and Parachinar, they could cause major problems for the British. Although such an action in itself would be unlikely to trigger a fresh invasion by Afghan regular forces, it might be sufficient to inspire a more general uprising of the tribes. And a tribal uprising was the one event which might lead to another invasion by Afghan regular forces. The British, on the other hand, still held Badama and Sadda Posts securely, although they were not holding the ground where the wreck of Bristol Fighter F4626 lay. Although outnumbered, the arrival of the heavy machine guns was a significant factor in tipping the balance of firepower in favour of the British forces, both in terms of

Number 3 Section, gun pit, front view, near Morgah, Rawalpindi, January 1918. A/Sgt E. W. Macro, just to the left of the gun muzzle, is indicated by the X. (From E. W. Macro's album)

View of the rear of the same Number 3 Section gun pit near Morgah in 1918. A/Sgt E. W. Macro in the centre, indicated by the X. (From E. W. Macro's album)

Gun pit, probably also near Morgah in 1918. A/Sgt E. W. Macro on the left, so presumed to be Number 3 Section, probably with Gunner Charles Thomson in the centre, and possibly Gunner Edward Walton on the right. (From both E. W. Macro's and E. D. L. Walton's albums)

range and volume of fire. In the course of the war, the British had only rarely deployed in picquet positions or in isolated posts. Their arrival was, therefore, a factor which the tribesmen were unlikely to have anticipated. Attacking a position defended by the guns, particularly if they could use their superior range to sweep open ground, would have been a daunting and unwelcome prospect. Moreover, the motorcycle combinations gave the guns mobility which the tribesmen would struggle to match. Defensively, the guns could relatively easily be concentrated at Badama Post or Sadda Post depending on which was under threat. On the offensive, the motorcycles would enable the guns to be pushed forward aggressively, into positions from which they could dominate the ground at range. And the firepower could be used to suppress, fix or even disperse any concentration of tribesmen in order to enable the militia to close the range and launch an attack from close quarters. In short, at this stage of the action, the situation was finely balanced.

CHAPTER 9

Clearing the Aircraft

With the tactical situation so finely balanced, now was a time for bold action to gain the initiative. The tribesmen were not concentrated in sufficient numbers close to Badama Post to mount an immediate, overwhelming attack. However, if the initial estimate of 1500 tribesmen, given in the 60 Infantry Brigade HQ war diary, is correct then these men were probably within five miles of Badama Post. Later estimates of the tribesmen's strength placed it as high as 4000. If this is correct, and it does not seem unrealistic given the numbers that attacked Badama and Sadda in late May, these additional numbers must have been further up the Khurmana valley beyond Masul. Mullah Mahmud Akhinzada had three tactical options. First, he could concentrate his strength, which would take some time, probably the night; he could then launch an overwhelming attack on the posts once he had done so, at first light or in the early morning. His second option was to exploit the darkness with the numbers he had available, either to strip the crashed aircraft or to close the walls of the post and to then launch an escalade in the dark; the darkness would partially neutralise the firepower and range of the machine guns which had no night-fighting aides. Third, he could bank the success that had already been achieved and withdraw further up the Khurmana valley, in the knowledge that the British were unlikely to attempt to follow him deeper into the tribes' mountain strongholds. Where the mullah was located on the battlefield at this stage is not known. It seems unlikely that he would have been at the front of the action somewhere between Masul and Badama. It may well be that he was in Masul, in which case he would have been reasonably placed to learn of how the situation was developing and then make decisions on the tribes' next move. Alternatively, he might have been further still up the Khurmana valley, east of Masul, in which case, he would not have been well placed to influence the battle.

However, Masul was an obvious target and was already due to be bombed by the British aircraft, so he would have been safer further up the valley. As it would have taken some time, hours rather than minutes, for messages to be passed into the mountains, the fact the tribesmen did not immediately exploit their success suggests that Mullah Mahumud may well have been east of Masul.

As it was, the British reacted first and responded decisively and aggressively, on the ground at least. Bill Macro, having trained as a pilot the previous year, knew the value of the aircraft, and particularly its guns, ammunition and bombs, to the tribesmen. He states in his report:

> Sgt Macro, who had had RAF experience, realising that the wrecked plane would contain probably more than 1000 rounds of ammunition, possibly bombs and machine guns which would be of great value to the tribesmen, volunteered to go down to the wrecked plane, which was lying at the bottom of a dry river bed, to see what could be salvaged. Major Dodd said he would accompany him, and, although he hadn't sufficient men to picket the hillside, would bring a few men with him to carry back anything salvaged.[1]

Events on the ground were still moving fast, given that it was now early afternoon on 30 July, and there was, at the very best, no more than four hours of daylight left. With the injured aircrew now on their way to medical attention, the urgency was driven by both the need to salvage as much as possible from the aircraft, and the ordinance in particular, before night fell and by the requirement to counter the success of the tribes. The conversation between Percy Dodd and Bill Macro would have been brief; Dodd already knew the value of the mobility and firepower the machine guns put at his disposal and he would have been quick to recognise that in Sergeant Macro he now had technical expertise available to him that was completely beyond that normally available to the militia. Percy probably had time to issue very quick order to Badama Post's commander, Subedar Gul Khan. These would have been no more than instructions to secure the post and to keep overwatch of the troops deployed on the ground. He then ordered his small party of mounted militiamen to remount and prepared to move off towards the ravine where F4626 lay.

With the plan agreed, Sergeant Macro wasted no time. As Percy Dodd issued orders to his militiamen, so Bill gathered his motorcycle crews and gave quick battle orders. His remaining lorry was probably left within the shelter of the walls of Badama Post. The terrain was difficult enough for a motorcycle combination or troops mounted on horses; it was all but impossible for lorries. Having remounted, the motorcycle crews pushed out to the east of Badama Post, as fast as possible, in order to secure the ravine. The section split into two, each detachment taking a gun combination and

Bringing a gun into action on steep terrain, near Kohat. (From E. W. Macro's album)

its two supporting combinations carrying ammunition and spares. The detachments were positioned north and south of the crash site, on the lip of the ravine, so as to provide a measure of all-round security for the crash site. The guns would have been nestled in amongst the rocks, sited so that they could fire out across the ravine. Each detachment would also have been accompanied by a small group of the militia, perhaps six or eight. When the guns were sighted, the militia dismounted; every fourth man was a horse holder and he took his own beast and those of his three companions into shelter to the rear of the gun position. While the machine guns provided the long-range protection to the crash site, the purpose of the militia was to provide close protection to the machine-gun crews. Aside from the guns, the number one gunners and loaders in the machine-gun crews were armed only with pistols – the Webley Mk VI.455 for self defence. Although the ammunition carriers normally carried rifles, they were frequently too busy keeping the Vickers supplied with ammunition to be effective in protecting the gun crew. It may also have been that a few mounted militia were able to cross the ravine and patrol further east towards Masul, in order to provide early warning of the tribesmen's movements. However, isolated detachments such as this would have been vulnerable to being cut off; they would have taken care to ensure they remained within range of the cover which the machine guns could provide.

Once he had positioned his guns and ensured his instructions were clear, Sergeant Macro handed over command of Number 3 Section to his second in command, Corporal Ernest Warburton. This was to ensure that, should anything untoward happened to him, the section still had a clear chain of command and the ability to act as required if the situation changed suddenly. He must have been conscious that the ravine was deep and, once in it, he would be relatively isolated from the guns. The section was not equipped with radios; battlefield radio would not be in common use until World War II and the section generally used semaphore flags for communication beyond shouting range. Bill would also have been aware that, as Percy Dodd was accompanying him into the ravine, they were putting themselves in a position where the two senior commanders on the ground were both collocated and detached from their forces. It was not an ideal situation, but Bill was the only man with the technical expertise to strip the aircraft efficiently and Percy Dodd was not the sort of man to watch from a distance. He wanted to be at the key point. Bill Macro, in his report said he, 'positioned his two machine guns so that they could give covering fire if necessary, placed the section under the command of Cpl Warburton, and climbed down the hillside to the wrecked plane'.[2]

The descent must have been something of a trial for the two British men. Neither would have been particularly used to scrambling in rocks, Sergeant Macro making more regular use of the motorcycle and Major Dodd of his horse. Furthermore, both would have been shod in boots and, whilst Percy Dodd was probably wearing leather-soled riding boots, Bill Macro's boots were most likely equipped with hobnails. These would have provided minimal grip on the rocks and boulders that marked the side of the ravine and the gully by which they had to make their way down to the wreck of F4626. The mid-afternoon heat would not have made their task any easier, but at least, the

Effect of fire. The reach and firepower advantage given to British troops against the tribesmen is well illustrated. (From E. W. Macro's album)

rocks and boulders in the steep gully provided them with considerable cover during the descent. Dodd and Macro were accompanied by a small party of the Kurram Militia, perhaps five or six men; Percy Dodd had detailed them off to descend into the ravine with him so they could assist in recovering any equipment which Sergeant Macro might manage to strip from the aircraft. The militiamen may have had a slightly easier descent than the two British men; they were more used to both the rough terrain and the heat. There was no way by which a motorcycle could have been brought into the ravine; the gully was far too steep. Whether it crossed the minds of either Dodd or Macro that a rather groggy David Lapraik had, with the assistance of the militiamen, helped his badly wounded pilot up this same route not long previously, we will never know. Both men were probably now focusing on the task in hand; nevertheless, the steepness of the descent to the ravine would have brought home how fortunate the two aircrew were that the militia at Badama Post had come so quickly to their assistance.

When they eventually reached the bottom of the gully, the difficulties of the party started to increase. In the gully, they had been relatively sheltered from the eyes and fire of the tribesmen. The bottom of the ravine, however, although rough and covered in rocks and boulders, was a different prospect. Here the party were much more exposed. And it quickly became apparent that there were at least some tribesmen still in the vicinity, probably located in the rocks on the eastern lip of the ravine. As the party exposed themselves at the foot of the gully, they came under rifle fire. Given the proven marksmanship of the tribesmen, it is probable that they were relatively few in number and located at maximum effective range, perhaps half a mile or 800m distant, as none of the party were hit. It may have been that the machine guns were able to provide sufficient suppressive fire to impede the accuracy of the snipers, although the guns expended very little ammunition through the course of 30 July. The battery war diary records the section fired just 50 rounds in total.[3] All the same, the party promptly took cover where they could among the boulders on the floor of the ravine and at the base of the gully. Sergeant Macro's report states, 'The tribesmen, encouraged by their success, commenced to reassemble and the party was subjected to an increasing volume of sniping, but most of the party were able to lie under cover of the rocks and no one was hit.'[4]

In the middle of the ravine, slightly way from the base of the gully, the wreck of F4626 presented a sorry sight. 'The plane had crashed on its nose leaving the tail up in the air.'[5] The nose rested amongst the boulders, surrounded by the splintered remnants of the propeller and there was a steady drip of oil from the engine, which was spreading in a black pool. The ticking of cooling metal could still be heard from the engine. The smashed undercarriage lay just behind the aircraft and the rocks here were scarred and shattered, showing were George Eastwood had attempted to land the Bristol Fighter flat onto its belly, before it had tipped forward onto its nose. The wings were largely intact but had partially crumpled where the wooden bracing straights had snapped. The bombs still hung beneath the wings, which trailed several streamers of tattered covering fabric. A strong smell of petrol hung in the air, but there had been no fire. Although there was cover at the base of the gully, the aircraft itself was exposed, in full view of the edges of the ravine. There was, however, still no time for delay; nightfall was getting ever closer. Advancing the guns from Badama Post, positioning them in covering positions and descending into the ravine had probably taken about an hour. The time was now around 1500 hours.

Leaving the militiamen in the cover of the rocks at the base of the gully, Bill Macro and Percy Dodd dashed out across the ravine. As they did so, a bullet ricocheted off the rocks at their feet and wined off into the sides of the ravine. A fraction of a second later, the sound of the shot carried down the ravine as the pair threw themselves into the cover of the boulders around the Bristol Fighter. With a cursory glance at the bombs beneath the wings, Sergeant Macro scrambled into the cockpit. This was quite an effort; when normally on its wheels, the cockpit rim of the Bristol Fighter was nearly 2m off the ground. With the aircraft tipped forward, it was probably even more awkward, although he would have been able to use the lower wings to assist climbing up. It is also possible that Percy Dodd was able to boost him up into the cockpit. Doubtless, the thought of being in a sniper's sights speeded up Bill's progress as well. Once in the cockpit, he would have had some cover from view, which probably made him feel better, even if the fabric covering of the aircraft would do nothing to physically protect him from bullets. The cockpit, especially the control column, was sticky with George Eastwood's blood. Having trained on the B.E.2c, Bill was unfamiliar with the Bristol Fighter, but it would not have taken him long to locate the bomb release toggle and pull it. The toggle then pulled on a Bowden cable, which operated the release mechanism on the carrier in order to drop the bombs off the wings. As each bomb came off the carrier, it would have cleared the stop that prevented the vane, under the nose of the bomb, from rotating. The vane was now free to rotate around its spindle; 25 rotations would cause the striker to unmesh and arm the bomb, such that a sharp blow on the nose cap would push the striker into the detonator and explode the bomb. However, the short drop off the wing of F4626 was insufficient to cause more than a couple of rotations and the bombs remained safe. Sergeant Macro now climbed back out of the aircraft. He would not have had the safety wires available to stop the vanes from rotating while being handled on the ground, so he now had to decide whether to disarm the bombs or send them up to Badama Post with the vanes still free to spin. It is not recorded what decision he made but given that disarming the bombs would have involved removing each bomb's nose cap, unscrewing the fuse and removing the detonator, it is probable he decided to leave the fuse in place and trust the vane would not spin during transit.

Throughout this time, Bill, Percy Dodd and the Kurram Militia with them were under intermittent sniper fire, as indeed were the two gun detachments under the command of Corporal Warburton. Every now and again, there would be a burst of covering fire from the Vickers, as one or other of the gun detachments spotted tribesmen attempting to creep into a sniping position. Major Dodd called four or five of his militia men over to the Bristol Fighter and each was given a pair of bombs. They then slowly clambered back up the gulley and out of the ravine, doubtless with dire warnings ringing in their ears that the bombs were to be handled with care and above all not dropped or banged on the nose cap. Once the militia men were at the top of the gully, Corporal Warburton would have been able to direct a couple of the ammunition-carrier motorcycle combinations to carefully transfer the bombs across to Badama Post. The militia men then scrambled back down to the aircraft in order to help Percy and Bill continue to clear the aircraft. Bill's next task was to deal with the ammunition, and while the militia were carrying bombs out of the ravine, he climbed back into F4626. The forward-firing Vickers gun was loaded with a belt of .303 ammunition, so this was unloaded first and passed down to Percy Dodd. As any spare ammunition for this gun was also in the forward cockpit, this was passed out as well. Bill now climbed over the dividing partition and into David Lapraik's rear cockpit. Here the ammunition for the Lewis gun was stored in its round pan magazines, each of which held 47 rounds. Again, there was a magazine fitted to the gun, so it had to be unloaded and the magazine passed down. The spare magazines then had to be located from where they were scattered around the rear cockpit; they were also passed out to Major Dodd and gathered up.

Once the ammunition had been collected, the next task was to dismount the Lewis gun. This was mounted on a Scarff ring, which surrounded the rear of the cockpit, and enabled the observer to rotate and elevate the gun, whilst still supporting its weight. Dismounting the Lewis gun would have taken Sergeant Macro no more than a couple of minutes; he was doubtless thankful because the volume of sniper fire directed in his and Major Dodd's direction was starting to increase alarmingly. The time was moving on towards 1600 hours, the sun was dropping behind the mountains and the darkness was staring to encroach. The tribesmen were starting to use the gathering darkness to work their way stealthily closer to the scene of the action. The failing light meant that Corporal Warburton and the crews of the covering machine guns were finding it increasingly difficult to catch even a glimpse of the well-camouflaged tribesmen, and there were now very few bursts of automatic fire. By contrast, the volume of rifle fire was increasing. This from both the Kurram Militia scouts as they encountered tribesmen at increasingly shortened ranges and from the tribesmen in the general direction of the wreck of F4626 and towards the suspected locations of those covering the operation around the wreck. However, the gathering darkness was making accuracy increasingly difficult for both sides. The increasing darkness would also have started to provide a small measure of relief from the scorching heat of the day.

Bombs, ammunition and the observer's Lewis gun had now all been stripped from the wreck of F4626 and passed out to Major Percy Dodd and the waiting men of the Kurram Militia. Bill Macro now clambered back into the pilot's cockpit. The only gun now remaining on the aircraft was the forward-firing Vickers gun. This was mounted onto the centreline of the aircraft through the engine casing. The impact of the crash had caused the casing around the gun to buckle and Bill now discovered that he was unable to remove the gun complete. He, therefore, set about dismantling the gun from the rear, removing the body of the gun, its working parts and also the barrel. These too were passed down to Percy Dodd. Bill was still unable to remove the casing but had now recovered all of the weapons that would have been useful to the tribesmen. He scrambled out of the cockpit and hastily sought cover amongst the rocks. Stripping the wreck had probably taken about an hour but Bill's report sums it up in just a few lines:

> Sgt Macro climbed into the cockpit, released the bombs from the rack, and having examined them to see if they were safe to handle, sent them up to the post. He then handed out the boxes and drums of ammunition, dismounted the Lewis gun, dismantled the Vickers, and passed them out to the militia to carry away. The only part of the Vickers not salvaged was the barrel casing, which couldn't be got at because of the crashed engine.[6]

In the shelter of the rocks at the base of the gully, Major Dodd and Sergeant Macro now held another hasty discussion. Sniper bullets continued to ricochet off rocks around them, but fortunately, neither of them or the militia men were hit. It was now past 1600 hours and it would be dark in less than an hour. On the North West Frontier, twilight was almost non-existent. As the sun fell below the mountains, the transition from day to night was very swift. In the deep gully, the light had almost gone, even at this hour. Neither man was keen that their troops be caught out of the sheltering walls of the posts during the hours of darkness as this would significantly negate their firepower advantage. There was a possibility that the Mullah Mahmud might gather up the tribesmen and attempt to strip the remainder of the aircraft in the dark or even launch an assault on the posts. In either case, the prospect of being on the ground, outside the shelter of the posts, was distinctly unattractive. The two men would also have been conscious that their prompt action had, partially at least, wrested the initiative back from the tribesmen. They would also have been acutely aware of the value of the British aircraft. While the guns and ammunition

were of intrinsic value to the tribesmen, the fact remained that the British
had but a handful of aircraft in India. There were very few supplies and the
chain to obtain them was long and tortuous. The British had made plain
that they valued the recovery of their aircrew, but they had also issued
very clear instructions that, in the event of an aircraft crash, every effort
was to be made to recover every part possible of the aircraft. So, although
the guns, bombs and ammunition had been recovered, there remained the
engine and fabric of the Bristol Fighter, which were of considerable value
to the British. Nevertheless, as the tribesmen continued to press the rather
precarious position that Percy Dodd and Bill Macro now occupied, the pair
came to the considered conclusion that the game was not worth the candle.
They would not keep troops on the ground overnight but would withdraw
into the shelter provided by the posts at Badama and Sadda. In order to
discourage the tribesmen from either attempting to sneak up on the post, or
from looting the wreck of F4626, it was decided that flares should be fired
over the wreck throughout the course of the night. This was to be carried
out by the militia in Badama Post using a Very pistol. First, however, they
needed to get back into the shelter of the posts.

The ascent of the gully, back up to the lip of the ravine, was in every
way as perilous as the descent. It was almost dark and those climbing were
now burdened with all of F4626's ammunition, as well as the Lewis gun
and the parts from the Vickers, in addition to their rifles. Percy Dodd and
Bill Macro were carrying pistols, which they were able to holster, so at
least they were able to keep both hands free. But every small slip sent a fall
of loose stones down the gully, to the irritation of those of the party who
were below the culprit. More seriously, the rattle of descending stones drew
increased attention from the tribesmen snipers. The noise and muzzle flash of
the snipers' rifles then drew the attention of the machine-gun detachments
and the supporting militia, and within minutes, the ravine echoed anew
to the sound of gunfire. Everyone, however, was now firing by sound and
towards muzzle flash, so both the Kurram Militia men and the tribesmen
were adjusting their positions as soon as they had fired, in order to confuse
the other marksmen. The machine guns were almost certainly minimising
their fire by this stage; their muzzle flash would have presented a rather too
attractive target, especially when they did not have a clear aiming mark to
make it worth opening fire. And it was much harder to change the gun's
position than it was for a rifleman to move.

At the top of the gully, Major Dodd and Sergeant Macro issued orders for
a rapid withdrawal back to Badama Post. The Kurram Militia men called up

their horse holders, mounted up and trotted back towards the gates of the post. As the darkness fell, those advance scouts of the militia who had gone east of the ravine were already falling back under their own initiative. The Kurram Militia estimated that there were now around 300 tribesmen in the vicinity of Badama Post and the crash site.[7] This was too many for the scouts to risk tangling with in the dark. The machine-gun detachments of Number 3 Section also gathered together their soldiers, mounted up onto their combinations and, under the instructions of Sergeant Macro and Corporal Warburton, moved west to Badama Post. Once the troops had regrouped under the walls of Badama Post, it became apparent that there was insufficient room within Badama for all of Number 3 Section's vehicles and equipment. Percy Dodd and Bill Macro, therefore, decided that Number 3 Section should return to pass the night at Sadda, as they had the previous night, and that Percy should join them. Percy would have briefed Subedar Gul Khan to remain secure within the post and to maintain a watchful guard. Gul Khan was also to maintain overwatch of the crash site and to keep firing flares over it throughout the night. Percy, Bill and the Motor Machine Gun Section then headed back to Sadda Post.

It was probably at around this time, most likely on reaching Badama Post but possibly when he got to Sadda Post, that Percy Dodd discovered he was missing a man. The Kurram Militia war diary simply states, 'K. M. lose one Lance duffadar missing believed killed' and does not name him.[8] War diaries rarely name other ranks' casualties, and the Kurram Militia one is no exception, but this casualty is almost certainly Lance Daffadar Miru Mian. This was deduced by searching the Commonwealth War Graves Commission website; Miru Mian was the only Kurram Militia casualty, of any rank, listed for 30 July 1919 and a week either side of that date.[9] It seems likely, as he was reported missing, that none of his companions saw him fall. Had they done so, they would have made a vigorous attempt to recover the body, both to prevent it being mutilated by tribesmen and to recover Miru Mian's rifle. It is also possible, as he was reported 'believed killed', that Miru was seen to fall but none of his companions were able to reach his body. Taking this into account it seems most likely that the Lance Daffadar was either one of the scouts patrolling east towards Masul or he was providing protection to the machine-gun detachments. In either case, he was probably hit towards the end of the day, presumably in the final withdrawal back from the ravine to Badama Post; if he had been hit any earlier, Percy Dodd and the other members of the Kurram Militia would have been aware sooner and a determined effort to recover the body would have been made before darkness intervened. Nor does it seem likely that Miru Mian was in the party which climbed down to the wreck of F4626; or, if he was, then he must have been hit during the final withdrawal. Sergeant Macro's report specifically mentions that no one was hit whilst at the aircraft, and as Percy Dodd was also on site there, he would have known if one of his militia men had been hit while in the ravine or the gully.

At this point, however, there was nothing that could be done to assist the unfortunate Lance Daffadar. Percy Dodd, Bill Macro and Number 3 Section joined the Kurram Militia garrison in Sadda Post and settled down to spend the night there. At Badama Post, the garrison under Gul Khan maintained their guard and illuminated the crash site as best they could. Even if they had known exactly where Miru Mian lay, it probably would have been considered too dangerous to mount a patrol to recover him at night. However, Percy would have wanted to come up with a plan of action for the next day. From the telegraph at Sadda, he would now have been in communication with both his militia headquarters and the brigade headquarters in Parachinar and would have updated them on the situation. How much they knew of the situation on the ground up until this point is not clear, and indeed, there was a limit to the amount of information that could be conveniently passed via the telegraph. All of the war diaries of 60 Infantry Brigade HQ, the Kurram Militia and 22 MMG have just the briefest of accounts of the day's events. Nor is it clear how long after the events they were written up, although it cannot have been long, given it was 30 July and war diaries were submitted to the higher headquarters on a monthly basis. 60 Infantry Brigade HQ must have known that an aircraft was overdue soon after it had failed to return to Parachinar, even if they did not know that it had been shot down. Their diary suggests that the aircraft was shot down mid-morning, at 1000 hours, and that the relief column was on the road to Sadda just 40 minutes later. However, the diaries of the Kurram Militia and 22 MMG, while they are not specific, both suggest that the Bristol Fighter crashed around midday on 30 July. This is backed up by the report left by Sergeant Macro. And all the other accounts, including Sir George Fletcher MacMunn's *History of the Guides, 1846–1922* (Volume I), are specific that the relief column marched from Parachinar to Sadda overnight on 30/31 July. It is possible that the brigade headquarters gave instructions for the column to march and that it then took some hours for it to assemble, but as the column had been warned on 29 July, this seems unlikely. So, it can be concluded that the brigade headquarters in Parachinar learnt of the downing of Eastwood and Lapraik's Bristol Fighter, F4626, not long after the event occurred, probably in the early afternoon. Thereafter, they re-warned the ready column but did not order it to march at this stage. And, for whatever reason, they do not appear to have instructed the remaining aircraft of 20 Squadron to investigate the Badama Post area further. As the convoy, by now, would have passed north of Sadda on its way to Parachinar, maybe that is where Brigade attention had been focused. In the early evening, they then received an update from Major Dodd on the scene, so they were aware an aircraft was down, the crew had been recovered and the aircraft had been partially, but not fully, salvaged. At this point, the orders were given that the mobile column, led by two companies of 3rd Guides, was ordered to march and left almost immediately.

At Sadda Post, Major Percy Dodd now knew that a relief column was marching to help him. His priorities for the next day at this stage would have been first to defeat and drive Mullah Mahmud Akhinzada's *lashkar* back into the mountains beyond Masul. Second would have been to salvage the remains of F4626, so that nothing of value was left for the tribesmen and to give the best possible chance to the British of getting an airframe back in the sky. And third, but by no means least, for the sake of the morale of his men in the Kurram Militia, and in order to minimise the proliferation of modern firearms amongst the tribesmen, Percy would have wanted to recover the body of Lance Daffadar Miru Mian and, in particular, recover his rifle. The column that was heading towards Sadda was a powerful one. Having been in communication with Parachinar, Dodd would have known that the column consisted of two companies of 3rd Guides, a section of two guns from the Royal Field Artillery, another section of two pack guns from 28th Mountain Battery and an additional reinforcement of 60 infantry from the Kurram Militia. This was a considerable reinforcement in terms of both manpower and firepower to the force that Percy had available to him at the present. However, he would not have been certain of exactly when the column would reach him or, having marched around 20 miles, the state of the men. So, the plan that he came up with, probably in consultation with Sergeant Macro, was a simple one; there were minimal changes from that which they had carried out on 30 July, other than the reinforcing column would be exploited. The garrison of Badama Post would remain on overwatch from the walls of the post. The machine guns of Number 3 Section would be pushed forward to the lip of the ravine, so they could provide close covering fire across the wreck of F4626. The guns of the field section and the mountain battery would be held near the post, from which position they would be able to both fire across the ravine and onto the high ground to the north of the post. The two companies of additional infantry would give sufficient troops to secure the ground between the ravine and Masul, in order to allow a safe environment to salvage the remainder of F4626. It was also sufficient troops to be able to send a picquet onto the high ground a mile or so to the north of the ravine, which dominated both Badama Post and the crash site. To carry back the remains of the aircraft, a party of Kurram Militia would be used.

With the plan for the following day settled in outline, Percy Dodd and Bill Macro would now have briefed their troops again and overseen the preparations for renewing the battle. Horses would have been fed and watered. Motorbikes were checked and adjustments made; they were refueled and oiled where applicable. All weapons needed to be cleaned by pulling the barrels through and lightly oiling them. Ammunition was redistributed, so that everyone had an equal supply and replenished when stock was available. Although relatively few rounds had been fired from the machine guns, fresh belts of ammunition were made up. Filling the belts by hand was a long and laborious process, so it was always wise to have the maximum amount of ammunition already belted. Even using the automatic filling machine was not a quick process. Nevertheless, the men of 22 MMG had done this many times over the preceding three years, so it would not have taken long, even if they had been doing it by hand. Once the men had been briefed and equipment checked and replenished, there was time for feeding and, more importantly in the climate, rehydration; it had been a long, hot day and the

Filling cartridge belts using the Machine, Filling Belts, Maxim, .303-inch, Mk.II. One belt filling machine was carried by each section. Here it appears to be mounted on its carrying case. (Alex Bowell, from W. Patrick's album)

Filling cartridge belts by hand was a long, slow, laborious process. (Alex Bowell, from W. Patrick's album)

troops would have had little opportunity to take on water while they were in action. Finally, they would have had the chance to grab some sleep.

By the evening of 30 July, although still finely balanced, the tactical advantage was shifting back towards the British. Although the tribesmen had secured a major victory, by shooting down F4626, the British had managed to save both of the aircrew. Despite being heavily outnumbered, the British had also managed to salvage the most valuable items of weapons and munitions from the wreckage of the aircraft. Although they had suffered a further casualty through Lance Daffadar Miru Mian being missing, they now knew that reinforcements were on their way, and were located relatively securely for the night within the walls of Sadda and Badama Posts. After the initial success that appeared to have ended aerial operations against them, the tribesmen, by contrast, had had the initiative wrested from them by the prompt action of Percy Dodd and Bill Macro. The night would now cloak their movements; could they use this to exploit their initial success and regain momentum before the reinforcing column arrived from Parachinar?

CHAPTER 10

The Endgame: 31 July 1919

It was just a little after midnight on the night of 30/31 July 1919, along the road from Parachinar to Sadda. There were no lights, and the only sounds were the occasional whispered instruction to close up and the rhythmic thump of several-hundred marching feet. The dust, stirred up from the feet, rose from the road in a cloying pall; the breeze of the day had dropped so that the dust did not blow away but rather settled slowly onto the heads and faces of those towards the rear of the column. It coated heads, gummed up eyes, tickled nostrils and slid into mouths to dry out tongues and aggravate the excruciating thirst. At least the heat of the day had passed and the temperature had dropped from 45 C (110 F) to a more bearable 20 C (70 F). Even so, there were few stops for water. There was a sense of urgency in the air. The column had been warned to be ready to march towards Sadda and Badama, where the tribal gathering had been reported, on 29 July. It was known that a small party of Kurram Militia, along with a section of the motor machine gun battery had been despatched to assist. On 30 July, the news had come swiftly; a British aircraft had been shot down. The crew was safe, but there was a danger that the tribesmen would rise and capture the posts of Badama and Sadda. Help was required urgently. The column was to march. Consisting of two companies of 3rd Guides, numbering five British officers, three Indian officers and 279 other ranks, the column departed from Parachinar that evening. It was accompanied by two field guns, two mountain guns from 28th Mountain Battery and 40 *sowars* from the Kurram Militia.[1]

The 3rd Battalion, Queen Victoria's Own Corps of Guides (Frontier Force) (Lumsden's) Infantry, to give the battalion its full title, was, along with the 4th Battalion, the youngest of the battalions of the Corps of Guides. More commonly known as 3rd Guides, it was raised in Mardan, the home of the Corps of Guides, on 22 October 1917. Drafts of just

Officers of 3rd Guides at Mardan in early 1919, before deployment on the Third Afghan War. Seated on the right Captain J. H. Jameson DSO. Seated on the left Captain FE Ferguson MC. Standing row, 5th from left, Lieutenant A. J. H. Bourke.

under 40 Indian officers and soldiers were received from each of the 1st and 2nd Battalion depots. The battalion was a mixed-race unit with a half company each of Sikhs and Dogras, and one company each of Gurkhas, Pathans and Punjabi Mussulmans. The first Commanding Officer was Lieutenant-Colonel W. Villiers-Stuart of 1/5th Gurkha Rifles, who handed over to Major John Clementi in March 1918.[2] Clementi, who was the son of another Indian Army Officer, Captain Montagu Clementi, Bengal Staff Corps, had been born at Allahabad Garrison on 27 September 1877. He was first commissioned in September 1897 and married Augusta Mildred Warren Graham on 11 November 1907 in Rangoon. John Clementi was still in command of 3rd Guides at Mardan when the Third Afghan War broke out in May 1919.[3] Two days after they had mobilised, the battalion had moved by train to Kohat, where they remained for five days until 15 May. They had then moved, again by train, to Thal. Here, 3rd Guides spent another three days, employed in the enhancing of Thal's defences. When they moved again it was by foot; marching from Thal on 19 May, up the Kurram valley, eventually reaching Parachinar on 22 May. Here, the battalion was attached to 60 Brigade, under the command of Brigadier Fagan, and moved into a perimeter camp to the west of Parachinar Fort.[4] They were then involved in the defence of the Upper Kurram valley as has been described in Chapter 5 and particularly the operation to destroy the Afghan position at Amir Thana on 2 June.

The 3rd Guides element of the column, when it marched for Sadda on 30 July, consisted of B and D Companies, and the entire column was under the command of Captain J. H. Jameson DSO, B Company commander.[5] The commander of D Company was Captain F. Ferguson MC,[6] so it is highly likely that he was one of the four other British officers marching with the column that night. As the other two company officers of B and D Companies are listed in *History of the Guides 1846–1922* (Volume I) as Lieutenants Bourke and Harrison[7] respectively, they are likely to be two more of the five British officers. However, as new evidence is emerging that suggests that Harrison could not have been present at Badama Post; the identity of two of the five British officers remains a mystery at this time.

John Henry Jameson was born on 12 November 1889. His father was Creighton Edward Jameson, who presumably was in the army because both John and his brother William were born in India. The youngest brother, Cecil, was born in Ireland in about 1894. Their mother was Annie Jane, but she was widowed well before the war broke out because Creighton died in 1900. Commissioned into the Liverpool Regiment in 1915, John Jameson had won his DSO on the Somme in 1916, where as a lieutenant, acting captain, he had shown, 'conspicuous gallantry in action. He handled his company in the attack with the greatest courage and skill, himself remaining out with a few men in an exposed position. He has at all times set a splendid example of gallantry and leadership.'[8] In May 1917, he had been appointed on probation to the Indian Army, initially attached to 54th Sikhs (Frontier Force). John was confirmed in the Indian Army a year later, by which time he had almost certainly joined 3rd Guides.[9]

Fritz Eberhard Ferguson had been born around 1894 in Thirsk; the son of Dr Alfred Cornwall Ferguson and his wife Elizabeth. Elizabeth was German, so Fritz's name was likely a tribute to her heritage. Fritz was educated at St Peter's School in York, where he was captain of the school football and gymnastics teams. He was awarded sporting honours in rugby and rowing in his final years of school.[10] Fritz followed his father into medicine and is recorded as studying at Glasgow on 3 May 1912.[11] In his first year, he studied biology, natural philosophy and zoology, followed in his second year with classes in chemistry, anatomy and physiology.[12] While at Glasgow, he must have trained with the Officer Training Corps because when war broke out he was appointed a 2nd lieutenant (on probation) with 3rd Battalion, West Yorkshire Regiment, on 15 August 1914.[13] He arrived in France on 27 January 1915, presumably as part of 185th (2/1st West Riding) Brigade, and spent the majority of the next three years in France, probably with various of the West

Yorkshire battalions and probably seeing fighting on the Somme in 1916 and at Arras in April 1917. He was gazetted for the Military Cross on 1 February 1918,[14] the citation for which was, 'For conspicuous gallantry and devotion to duty. In the attack he commanded the leading company of the battalion, and by his energetic and gallant leading the objective was captured with little loss, his company's battle patrol clearing the woods in front of snipers. The operations in this sector resulted in the capture of five guns and seventy-three prisoners.'[15] Given the date at which the medal was gazetted, Fritz may have been serving with 2/6th West Yorkshires of 185th Brigade at the battle of Cambrai on 20 November 1917. The 2/6th West Yorkshires took the Germans' front trenches and entered Havrincourt. However, the Germans put up a stout resistance which took several hours to deal with. Fritz was transferred into the Indian Army on 1 June 1918.[16]

Likewise, Arthur Jonathon Henry Bourke had been born in Dublin to Arthur E. D. Bourke and his wife, Maude Margaret, *née* Mahon, on 9 May 1897. Arthur's father died on 31 January 1903 when Arthur junior was aged five. Arthur was educated at Christ Hospital School, West Horsham, and commissioned on 5 October 1914, aged 17½; he may well have lied about his age. He had military links on his mother's side of the family that may have helped his passage into the army; his mother, Maude, was the elder sister of General Sir Bryan Thomas Mahon. Bryon Mahon had commissioned into the 8th (King's Royal Irish) Hussars in 1883 and seen service in Sudan and the Boer War. Arthur junior had deployed to France on 14 May 1915 with 2nd Battalion, Royal Munster Fusiliers, according to his medal index card,[17] by which time his uncle had commanded the 2 (Sialkot) Cavalry Brigade and was preparing to go ashore in command of 10th (Irish) Division at Gallipoli. There is no evidence to suggest that uncle and nephew ever served together. If his medal index card is correct, then Arthur Bourke junior probably saw action with 2nd Battalion, Royal Munster Fusiliers, at Loos in September 1915 and on the Somme from mid-July 1916. He was appointed lieutenant on 5 July 1916. However, according to his own post-war service papers,[18] Arthur Bourke served with 2nd Battalion Connaught Rangers in France in 1915 and then in Mesopotamia in 1916, before transferring to the Indian Army in 1917. So, it is not completely clear whether he was involved in the initial attack at the Somme. His service papers indicated he was wounded twice, but again it is not clear whether this refers to his service in Mesopotamia, France or subsequent post-war service on the North West Frontier. What is clear is that Arthur was appointed to 3rd Guides on 24 October 1917, just after they had been formed.

THE ENDGAME: 31 JULY 1919 • 169

William Edgar Pringle Harrison also came from a military family and was born in Gonda, India, on 11 November 1891. His father was William Hugh Pringle Harrison who had been a lieutenant colonel with the Bengal Infantry. As a young officer, William senior had served during the China War of 1860 and was present at the capture of the Taku Forts. He had married Emma Maria Knowles in 1889 but there were 25 years between them. Although they had had two sons, Maitland the elder and then William junior, the marriage, sadly, did not last and William divorced Emma in 1899 on the grounds of adultery with Hugh Rose. William senior had custody of his boys but died in 1903; William junior was just 10 years old. His mother does not appear to have played a further part in his upbringing and William moved out to Canada. He enlisted as a soldier with the Canadian forces on 26 February 1916 and landed in England in February 1917. Whether he then proceeded out to France is not clear but, if he did, then he may well have fought in the Canadian Corps's first battle to seize Vimy Ridge in April 1917. William then underwent officer training and was commissioned on 31 October 1917. He joined 3rd Guides on 1 February 1918 and was appointed lieutenant on 31 October 1918. Although listed in *History of the Guides 1846–1922* (Volume I) as the second company officer for D Company,[19] at the start of the Third Afghan War in May, there is now evidence emerging that William Harrison may have been one of the very first officers permitted to proceed on leave from the battalion.[20] From the passenger manifest, it looks as if William was onboard the SS *Megantic,* of the White Star-Dominion Line, which sailed from Liverpool bound for Montreal, Canada, on 8 August 1919, with 978 passengers. The *Megantic* arrived at Quebec on 15 August at 2230 hours and disembarkation took place the following morning. If this is the case, then William Harrison would have left the North West Frontier in early July, before the action at Badama Post.

The marching column reached Sadda between 0700 and 0800 hours on the morning of 31 July 1919. They had marched through the night for a distance of about 22 miles (35km). At Sadda, the column was allowed to rest and recuperate for a few hours, while John Jameson conferred with Percy Dodd. Having discussed his plans with Sergeant Macro the previous evening, Percy Dodd would have been more than ready to brief his reinforcements and incorporate them into his plan. While the troops rested, he would have conferred with Jameson and Ferguson, as well as the officer in charge of the guns. Once the officers had been briefed, they would have passed on the orders to their junior officers and the sepoys.

The night had passed quietly at both Badama and Sadda Posts. There had been no attack on either location by the tribesmen. The customary dawn-clearance patrol would have been conducted at Badama, probably about the very time the 3rd Guides column reached Sadda. This patrol would probably have been the first indication the British received that the tribesmen had not been inactive through the night. Through the course of the night, despite the flares being fired from the post, the tribesmen had systematically stripped the wreck of F4626. They had removed almost all the fabric covering and dismantled and taken away the majority of the wooden framework of both the fuselage and the wings. All the wire control cables had been collected up and removed. The only thing left on the crash site was the Rolls-Royce Falcon III engine, sitting rather sadly in a slowly spreading pool of engine oil. The news would have been passed swiftly back to Percy Dodd and the troops in Sadda Post, which may have been why the troops were allowed to rest briefly before they pushed out of Sadda Post in order to recover what they could of the remains of F4626. In his report, Bill Macro states that Number 3 Section returned to Badama Post in the morning of 31 July. He implies it was the machine gun section who discovered that F4626 had been stripped during the night. However, all the war diaries, and Sir George MacMunn, are clear that no movement forward to Badama took place before midday. It seems unlikely that British Forces would have remained unaware through the morning that the aircraft had been stripped and probable that the Kurram Militia troops in Badama Post would have been the first to discover the fact.

It was, however, clear that there was no immediate concentration of tribesmen massing to attack either of the posts. It seems likely that the tribesmen were, by now, aware that the British in the area had been reinforced significantly and that the reinforcement had included artillery. With this knowledge, Mullah Mahmud Akhinzada was unlikely to attempt further direct attacks against the British. He may have hoped to complete the destruction of F4626 by recovering the engine the next night, although other than denying its use to the British, the engine itself, unlike the rest of the aircraft, was of little value to him. However, it seems more likely that he now intended to maintain his positions around Masul and wait for the next move from the British forces. He did not have long to wait.

Percy Dodd put his plans into action from about 1200 hours on 31 July. The troops from the column, accompanied by the machine guns of Number 3 Section, moved out from Sadda Post and up to Badama Post. Here, the guns of the field section and the mountain battery were held, in a position where the Kurram Militia on the wall of Badama Post could overwatch and protect them. The guns then opened fire in order to establish the range to their likely targets across the ravine and on the high ground to its north. The two companies of 3rd Guides pushed on from the post, working their way around and across the ravine in which the remains of F4626 lay. The fine detail of Percy Dodd's plan, and how it was implemented by John Jameson, is not known, but it is likely that a company will have gone south of the crash site, moving towards the north bank of the Khurmana river and then north-east towards Masul. This enabled them to secure the ground between the ravine and any tribesmen in Masul. By the convention of the day, this company on the right would have been the senior company; there is no evidence to confirm this, but if it is the case, it would have been Jameson's own B Company. It would also have made sense for Jameson, as the commander of the column, to place himself in the area which was closest to the last-known position of the tribesmen. Additionally, it offered him a position in which he would have been well placed to link in with Percy Dodd and those working on the aircraft. The other company, Fritz Ferguson's D Company, would have moved to the north of the crash site and crossed the ravine before pushing east. Both companies would have been careful to not over extend themselves beyond the covering fire of the guns.

To provide further security and early warning to the two companies, 3rd Guides pushed a picquet up onto the high ground a mile or so to the north of the ravine. This would probably have come from the company, believed to be D Company, on that northern flank of the operation. This was a typically sized picquet of 25 men, about two sections or half a platoon, and was under the command of one of 3rd Guides' Indian Officers, Jemadar Lalbahadur Gurung. A jemadar was the most junior of the Viceroy Commissioned Officers (VCO) and there were normally eight in a battalion. It was roughly the equivalent of a British lieutenant, although even the most senior VCO was junior to any British officer. The VCO was an Indian soldier who had worked his way up through the soldier ranks. Promotion was based on merit. Ten to 12 years was typical to achieve this rank. Lalbahadur Gurung had joined the army on 18 January 1906 and been appointed as a jemadar on 2 June 1918.[21] His name indicates he must have been a Gurkha. MacMunn confirms that, 'a piquet [sic] of twenty-five men of the Battalion under Jemadar Lal Bahadur [sic] Gurung was sent up the hill on the left of the nullah, a climb of two and a half hours in intense heat.'[22] Given they left Sadda at around midday, the picquet must have been on top of the hill between 1430 and 1500 hours. From here, they were in a position that dominated both Badama Post and the crash site. However, the rest of the force had not been idle while Gurung and his men had been making their climb.

The machine guns of Number 3 Section were pushed forward to the lip of the ravine, into positions close to those they had occupied the previous day. It would not have taken them long to get there, so it is safe to assume that they were in position well before Lalbahadur Gurung's picquet was in position on the heights. From these positions, having gone through the routine of coming into action, they were able to provide covering fire across the wreck of F4626. As soon as the crash site was protected by both close-in machine guns and a cordon formed from the infantry companies, and with the artillery ranged in and ready to fire, a party of militia were sent down the gulley into the ravine. Whether Percy Dodd accompanied them is not clear, but there seems little doubt he was close by. It seems likely that Sergeant Macro did not go back down to the wreck; his account simply states, 'The MMG Section gave covering fire, and a party of militiamen got to the plane, and managed to carry the engine to Badama Post.'[23] The Kurram Militia war diary is not specific as to who salvaged the engine, but the 60 Infantry Brigade HQ diary is specific that this was carried out by the militia. According to the same war diary, the militia were aided by 'skilled mechanics'.[24] This almost certainly refers to men of Number 3 Section because they would have been considered skilled mechanics. However, not only does Bill Macro not mention going down to the wreck himself on the last day of the operation, he also makes no mention of any of his men doing so. It is possible that the 60 Infantry Brigade HQ war diary has transposed Sergeant Macro's work of the previous day onto this day, and that the Kurram Militia recovered the engine without assistance. Equally, it may well have been the Kurram Militia were assisted by men of Number 3 Section and that Bill Macro simply failed to record it.

Whoever conducted the salvaging of the engine, it was, by any standards, a considerable feat. The Rolls-Royce Falcon III engine weighed over 300kg (700lb), so it was not a simple two-man lift. The troops had to get down into the ravine to the crash site and probably used the same gully that Bill Macro and Percy Dodd had used the day before. The war diaries, perhaps understandably, make no mention that the remains of the aircraft had been plundered overnight by the tribesmen. Bill Macro, however, is clear that, 'during the night, the tribesmen had managed to carry away all but the plane's engine'.[25] Given this, there was probably very little dismantling of the aircraft still required, although the Motor Machine Gun Section would have been able to provide a limited supply of tools to assist with any that was required. Perhaps more importantly, after three years' service in India, they would have been experienced at recovering their motorcycles and combinations with minimal equipment in every conceivable circumstance. These recovery skills would have been readily transferable to the current problem. And the soldiers of the Kurram Militia would have been well used to conjuring ingenious solutions for all the engineering problems they faced on the North West Frontier in the days before mechanisation. Shear legs would have been rigged to lift the engine off the ground and then doubtless, probably using wooden poles, a carrying frame would have been lashed around the engine. This would have enabled more men, at least four and probably six or eight, to help with the lifting. The engine still needed to be lifted up the gully out of the ravine. Fresh shear legs may have been rigged to enable the engine to be winched up to the top of the gully. Or it is possible there was a longer but flatter route to reach the crash site, perhaps by going to the bank of the Khumana and then entering the ravine from the south. If this was the case, then it is likely that the Machine Gun Section's lorry would have been pressed into action again. If that could have been driven to the crash site, then it would have made the recovery of the engine much easier than it might otherwise have been. Or the lorry may have been driven to the lip of the ravine and then used to recover the engine to Badama Post. If it was used, then the lorry introduced the fresh problem of lifting the engine from ground level onto the flat bed at the back, although this would probably have been easier than getting it out of the ravine via the gully.

What is not clear is the extent to which this part of the operation was opposed by the tribesmen. Had the recovery of the engine been conducted under fire, as the salvaging of the bombs, guns and ammunition had been the day before, then it would have been an extremely difficult and dangerous operation. Unopposed, the weight of the engine would have made difficulties but was an altogether simpler problem of engineering rather than a battle. The war diaries of both 60 Infantry Brigade HQ and the Kurram Militia record that the tribesmen offered, 'no resistance'[26] but MacMunn records that the ridges were shelled and the tribesmen were 'driven back'.[27] The 22 MMG war diary states that Number 3 Section expended 500 rounds of ammunition in covering fire.[28] As both artillery and machine-gun ammunition were too valuable a resource to be expended without any consideration, it seems likely there was something to fire at. From this, and the fact that Number 3 Section's machine guns, B and D Companies, and 3rd Guides were in position before Lalbahadur Gurung's picquet was, it is possible to deduce that a combination of artillery fire, machine-gun fire and the advancing infantry, drove back the tribesmen towards Masul. This then enabled the recovery of the engine from F4626 to proceed under a protective screen in a relatively secure location.

Recovering F4626's engine would have taken up the majority of the afternoon of 31 July, certainly three or four hours. It was probably around 1600 hours, or perhaps even a little later, by the time the engine was safely back at Badama Post. Once again, by this time, darkness would have been starting to come on. With a total force available to him of around 500 men and facing a *lashkar* reported to be of more than 3000 tribesmen, Percy Dodd would have again been keen that his forces were well-protected overnight. The option of continuing to push east in order to drive Mullah Mahmud Akhinzada further back into the hills beyond Masul does not appear to have been seriously considered. Instead, the cordon was collapsed and the troops, both regular and militia, withdrew back to Badama and Sadda Posts. 22nd Battery war diary records that Number 3 Section 'returned to Sadda Post' at 1700 hours[29]. The Kurram Militia and the 3rd Guides companies were a little later, between 1800 and 1900 hours. This was due firstly to it taking a little time to extract Lalbahadur Gurung's picquet off the high ground and secondly due to the requirement for the infantry and militia to scout and gain intelligence on the tribesmen's movements.

Extracting picquets off high ground was never an easy business. While on their post, frequently behind a hastily erected *sangar*, they were secure and protected. However, as the troops on lower ground whom they were protecting moved away, then the picquet was increasingly exposed. Tribesmen, ever the masters of camouflage and concealment, were capable of getting very close to the picquet position. The picquet troops then had to escape downhill, frequently over extremely difficult terrain, and without the benefit of supporting troops available to give covering fire. The difficulty of the terrain normally meant that it was impossible for the troops of the picquet to conduct any form of fire and movement; the tribesmen could get sufficiently close and in sufficient numbers, meaning any members of the picquet attempting to cover their companions with fire would simply be overwhelmed by a mass of tribesmen. Therefore, the recovery from a picquet position frequently ended up as a madcap dash down a steep, rocky hillside, with the troops desperately trying to avoid falling, frequently whilst they were being shot at. In this case, it seems unlikely that the tribesmen were in a position to intervene with the picquet but, even so, it would have been a nervous few minutes.

As for scouting out the tribesmen's movements this was likely done initially by the 3rd Guides companies. Once the guides started to withdraw back west across the ravine, the scouting would have been continued by the Kurram Militia. The mounted infantry would have pushed forward, probably as far as Masul, to try and maintain contact with the tribesmen. However, as dusk fell, they too would have returned towards Badama and Sadda, and the protection afforded by the posts. They would then have reported to Percy Dodd. Bill Macro's report states, 'The MMG Section returned to Sadda to await the return of scouts regarding the movements of the tribesmen. That evening the scouts reported that the tribesmen were dispersing and returning to their villages.'[30]

At some stage in the course of the afternoon of 31 July, as the British troops surged back and forth across the area in the vicinity of Badama Post, somebody came across the body of Lance Daffadar Miru Mian. The Kurram Militia war diary just records, 'Body of Kurram Militia Lance duffadar recovered.'[31] There is no information as to who found the body or where Miru was found. As discussed in the previous chapter, the body probably lay east of the ravine, so it is likely that it was discovered either by one of the companies from 3rd Guides or by some of the party of Kurram Militia Mounted Infantry who were accompanying them. Whoever found the body, it would have been immediately apparent whether or not the tribesmen had discovered it during the night. Given it was probably the far side of the ravine, the chances are high that the tribesmen had stumbled across it. If they had done so, then Miru Mian's rifle and ammunition would have been missing and, almost certainly, his body would have been mutilated. Once the body had been discovered, then the priority would have been to secure his rifle and ammunition, if they were still present. Thereafter, the body would have been taken back to Badama Post. Here, despite the ongoing action, the Muslim burial rites would have been performed. There was a need for haste as Miru had already been dead for about 24 hours when his body was recovered. The body would have been ritually washed, enshrouded, the prayer for the dead said and then buried. Whether Badama Post had a dedicated graveyard, either within or more likely without, the post is not known. The rites would have been hasty. First because of the risk of a fresh attack from the tribesmen, although the likelihood of this now seemed to be diminishing, and second, as darkness was falling, because Muslim rites require the burial to take place before sunset on the day after the death.

So, as darkness settled on to the area around Badama Post, the quiet gradually returned as well. B and D Companies of 3rd Guides returned to Sadda Post, where they now prepared to spend the night. The scouts of the Kurram Militia returned and reported to Percy Dodd that the tribesmen appeared to be dispersing beyond Masul. It appeared that Mullah Mahmud Akhinzada had given up on the opportunity to raise further trouble amongst the tribes in the vicinity of Badama and Sadda, and was retreating into the high mountains of the Safed Koh to the north and east of Badama. Although nothing is stated specifically, it is probable that Percy Dodd returned to Parachinar and his main headquarters at this stage. At Badama, he would have been feeling isolated from the rest of his command and conscious that 60 Infantry Brigade, his higher headquarters, was at Parachinar and closer to the bulk of his command than he was. He would also have been comfortable in the knowledge that Badama was reinforced with two companies of infantry, and artillery, each with an experienced company commander. Certainly, according to Bill Macro, Percy discussed Bill's performance with Alexander Molony, the commander of 22 MMG, and it seems likely that this sort of conversation would have taken place face-to-face rather than over the telegraph. The 22 MMG war diary is clear that Number 3 Section returned from Sadda Post to Parachinar at 1800 hours on 31 July,[32] although, in his report, Bill Macro states this took place 'the next day [1 August]'.[33] The column, meanwhile, remained in Sadda. The section of RFA guns returned to Parachinar on 1 August, and while Badama Post reported that all was quiet, Sadda Post recorded that the militia had exchanged some shots with villagers to the east of the Sadda to Arawali road.[34] On 2 August, the battalion's second in command, Major D. Bainbridge, arrived to take command. Douglas Bainbridge was aged about 31 and had been commissioned into 57th Wilde's Rifles (Frontier Force) in September 1908. He had been present at the 1911 Durbar and when war broke out had come back to Europe with his battalion. He had fought in France from November 1914 to December 1915. He had spent the following six months in Egypt before fighting in East Africa from July 1916 through to January 1917. Somewhere along the line, he had been mentioned in despatches and awarded the Military Cross.[35] He had then returned to India and been attached to 3rd Guides. However, there was no further contact with the tribesmen and the column was recalled on 4 August. They arrived back in Parachinar the same day, 'after a very hot and exhausting march'.[36]

So, the action at Badama Post concluded. A few days later, on 8 August 1919, the Armistice to end the Third Afghan War was formally ratified by the signing of the preliminary peace treaty at Rawalpindi. Badama Post was the last recorded action of the war in the Kurram theatre of operations, although in Waziristan, to the south of the central theatre, trouble with the tribes continued unabated, even after the signing of the treaty. This trouble eventually led to the campaign in Waziristan to put down the Mahsuds in the second half of 1919 and into 1920. The action at Badama Post changed nothing in the overall impact of the Third Afghan War but was typical of many of the minor actions fought throughout its course. It was also typical of many of the actions fought all along the North West Frontier, both before the war and subsequently. It was, broadly, a success for the British-Indian forces. The convoy route linking Thal and Parachinar had been protected from interference, despite the nearby presence of a large force of restless tribesmen. Most tellingly, that body of tribesmen had been forced to disperse into the mountains by a significantly smaller force of British and Indian troops. While the tribesmen of Mullah Mahmud Akhinzada had scored a major success in shooting down George Eastwood's Bristol Fighter, the adverse impact had been minimised. Both George Eastwood and David Lapriak had been swiftly recovered, alive, from the wreck of F4626. The prompt actions of Percy Dodd and Bill Macro, with the Kurram Militia and Number 3 Section of 22 MMG, had denied the tribesmen the chance to salvage the bombs, guns and ammunition from the aircraft. And the cost, the tragic loss of one Lance Daffadar, was relatively light. It could have been very different. While the loss of the aircraft was embarrassing for the British, the loss of the aircrew would have been much worse, both in terms of loss of British prestige and in terms of the damage to the morale of British aircrew in the earliest days of the fledgling RAF starting to police the Empire from the air. Additionally, the capture of machine guns and ammunition, in addition to bombs, would have been a welcome addition to the firepower and ordinance available to the Mullah's tribesmen. A more significant success for the tribesmen in the vicinity of Badama Post could have caused a much more serious general uprising of the tribes on the frontier; this uprising was the one thing that the amir of Afghanistan had been hoping to achieve and the British had been working hard to avoid. Had such an uprising come about, then it might well have threatened the peace negotiations in Rawalpindi. The desertion of the Waziristan Militia, in the face of Nadir Kahn's move down the Kaitu river in the days of late May had shown the potential fragility of militia morale. However, the Kurram Militia had fully justified the policy of recruiting from local tribes with proven loyalty. It had performed, almost perfectly, those tasks it had been formed to undertake, particularly when backed by regular troops and by the firepower of machine guns. Nowhere was this more so than at Badama Post. However, what happened to those involved in the action at Badama Post following the Third Afghan War is much harder to determine. This will be covered in the final chapter.

CHAPTER 11

And Afterwards

When Number 3 Section and Sergeant Macro returned to Parachinar on the evening of 31 July 1919, they were not to know that Badama Post was the last action of the Third Afghan War for 22 MMG. Bill Macro reported to Major Molony, his commanding officer:

> Sgt Macro reported to OC 22nd Battery MMG, Major Malony [sic], on the success of the mission. Major Malony complimented him on his handling of the situation, and said he had received an excellent report of his conduct from Major Dodd, and that he was being recommended for a DCM.[1]

The peace treaty was signed shortly afterwards and, with one notable exception, 22 MMG remained in camp at Parachinar throughout the month of August 1919. In the middle of August, the Viceroy and Governor-General of India, Lord Chelmsford, made a tour of inspection of the central theatre, visiting Thal and subsequently Parachinar on 14 and 15 August. His movements from Kohat were escorted throughout by 22 MMG. Number 1 Section travelled initially to Kohat on 13 August. The following day they escorted His Excellency from Kohat to Thal. Meanwhile Number 2 and 3 Sections moved from Parachinar down to Thal, collected the Viceroy and escorted him on to Parachinar, while Number 1 Section remained in Thal. The Viceroy then spent a day in Parachinar, during which he inspected the Kurram Militia and visited their camp on the border at Peiwar.[2] The escort process was then reversed on 16 August in order to return the Viceroy to Kohat. Number 2 and 3 Sections escorted him to Thal and then returned to Parachinar, while Number 1 Section continued the escort on to Kohat. Number 1 Section then finally returned to Kohat on 17 August.[3] The war diary gives no indication that there were any issues during the escort task, nor does it indicate if Alexander Molony commanded the escort in person or whether he left that to his section commanders. Given the importance of the visitor, it seems likely that he took command in person.

The war diary of 22 MMG ends on 31 August. Sometime shortly after this, the battery must have been released from the Kurram theatre of operations and returned to Rawalpindi. From here the process of disbandment and demobilisation kicked in almost immediately. As it had been for the rest of the army back in Europe, however, this was still a phased process. Those who had been first through the doors, the early volunteers to the Motor Machine Gun Service, were, generally, the first to leave. Doubtless, this was much to the relief of many who had spent more than three years away from their families without the chance to return home. The first out appear to have been passing through the demobilisation camps in late September and early October. Those who came back later were in the UK by early January 1920. Of course, there were some who wished to continue serving in the army, particularly in the new armoured car companies. There were opportunities for mechanically minded soldiers to follow this route, which would eventually lead them into the new Tank Corps. Others, generally those who had come out as replacements, were compulsorily transferred to other units as they had not served long enough to be entitled to discharge. Finally, Gunner John Travell Maton Gough, one of the editors of *Momagu*, although he had not deployed with 22 MMG to Parachinar during the Third Afghan War, chose to discharge but still remain in India. Why he did not deploy is not known; nor is his reason for remaining in India after the war. Sadly, he did not enjoy his release from the army for long. John Gough died on 28 August 1921 at the British Station Hospital, Murree. The cause of death is not known but he left over £4500 in his will to his father; a considerable sum at the time.[4] He was aged just 26.

Back in the Kurram valley, the situation was slowly returning to normal for the Kurram Militia as well. Leave was reopened on 23 August when 481 Infantry and 70 Mounted Infantry were allowed to take a month of leave from the headquarters.[5] At around the same time as 22 MMG returned to Rawalpindi, 3rd Guides was released from the Kurram. They moved south to Thal and then spent a couple of weeks in isolation in Kohat due to cholera cases. Once cleared, 3rd Guides then moved to Tank in Waziristan.[6]

Percy Dodd, meanwhile, remained the commandant of the Kurram Militia; he continued to hold this post for a further year and a half, until November 1920. His leadership of the militia during the war was recognised with a Distinguished Service Order and a Mention in Despatches.[7] The commander of the RAF in India, Air Commodore Norman MacEwen, also wrote to thank Percy for saving Eastwood and Lapraik at Badama Post. In a letter written from the RAF Headquarters in Simla in late October 1919, he states:

Dear Dodd

Colonel Minchin who commands the 52nd Wing, has just sent me a report in regard to your action on the occasion of Captain Eastwood's crash near Badama. I thought I would just write you a line to say how much we appreciate actions of this sort, and to ask you to realise that your initiative and rapid action is fully appreciated. Had it not been for the rapidity with which you came to Eastwood's assistance, we should have lost both officers and a perfectly good machine.

My thanks seem hardly to meet the case, but if it is any satisfaction to you to know that I am fully aware and very much appreciate what you did to save the officers and machine, I hope you will accept these few lines as being a very incomplete recompense for your determined action.

Please therefore accept my heartfelt thanks, with which is coupled my admiration for the way in which you held off some 4 to 500 men in difficult country, while salvaging the machine.[8]

There was, of course, no such similar letter for the family of Lance Daffadar Miru Mian, although doubtless the local nature of the militia and the tribal traditions of the frontier would have ensured his family was looked after. Miru Mian is remembered by the Commonwealth War Graves Commission on the Delhi Memorial (India Gate). He has no known grave but is not forgotten. Subedar Gul Khan, the commander of the post at Badama, was awarded the Indian Distinguished Service Medal; the first to be issued for the North West Frontier in 1920. No citation has been traced, but it is a reasonable deduction that his performance as the post commander was being recognised, both during the attacks of late May and during the late-July action at Badama Post. Gul Khan was also Mentioned in Despatches for the Third Afghan War. What happened to him after the war is not known.

In November 1920, Percy Dodd handed over as the commandant of the Kurram Militia to R. H. Wilson, who was appointed as a major. However, Dodd continued his military career in the Indian Army, rejoining his own regiment, 31st Duke of Connaught's Own Lancers, who had recently moved to perform garrison duties in Palestine. His appointment was as a temporary squadron commander, but Percy must have been the senior one as he was also the temporary second in command of the regiment. Percy only spent nine months in Palestine and that was punctuated by a fortnight in hospital in late May and early June for an unknown reason. He was then given a new appointment as a staff officer, the General Staff Officer (GSO) Grade II, with the Waziristan Field Force back in India in October 1921. As GSO II, Percy would have acted as the deputy to the GSO I, the lieutenant colonel who was the chief of staff. He was responsible for the preparation of orders and instructions as directed by the GSO I, the general organization and working of the 'G' office, and the detailing of duty officers at the headquarters. The

GSO II also coordinated, in consultation with the Administrative ('A' and 'Q') Staff, arrangements for moving the headquarters, details of movement by road and general policy regarding headquarters defence and the preparation and promulgation of the headquarters standing orders. Percy held this position for a year and a half until 31 March 1923.[9] It was not a small task and would have kept him extremely busy, particularly as during this period Waziristan was the focus of trouble on the frontier.

The Waziristan Revolt of 1919–20 had been sparked by the Third Afghan War and the defection of the Waziristan Militia in the face of Nadir Khan's invasion. After the Afghans had been defeated, the Waziri tribesmen continued to launch large-scale raids into the administered areas. By November 1919, they had killed over 200 people and wounded a further 200. The British launched operations against first the Tochi Wazirs and subsequently the Mahsuds. But the columns met heavy resistance as the largely inexperienced Indian units came up against determined, well-armed tribesmen. Many of the Waziri men were veterans of the Indian Army and used modern military tactics and firearms. In contrast, due to the denuding of the Indian army through overseas commitments during World War I, many of the battalions employed in this campaign were second-line units, with disproportionately large numbers of very young soldiers and inexperienced officers. The fighting continued for about 12 months and the British suffered a number of reverses, before Wana was reoccupied in December 1920. On a number of occasions, the British had to resort to using aircraft to suppress the tribesmen. The long-term plan for control of the district entailed building metalled roads along the lines of communication to a new central base at Razmak. In 1921, work began on the southern road up the Tank river from Jandola, under the protection of the Waziristan Force. The following year, work on the northern road from Tochi began at Idak, shielded by the Razmak force advancing to its objective. It was in these operations that Percy Dodd would have been particularly involved. And he must have done his work well because he was Mentioned in Despatches twice more, for operations in Waziristan in both 1921 and in 1922–23.[10] Eventually, in 1924, the two roads met and linked north and south Waziristan. This enabled the Indian Army to reorganise both areas into one military district. The Waziristan and Razmak field forces then disbanded to become brigades permanently based at Manzai, Razmak, Gardez and Bannu. By this time, however, Percy had taken a year of furlough out of India. He returned to his regiment, now amalgamated with the 32nd Lancers to become the 13th DCO Lancers, as a squadron commander, on 16 March 1924.[11]

Officers of 31st DCO Lancers. Thought to be Major Percy Dodd in the centre of the photo. Probably taken in the mid 1920s when he was a squadron leader. (With permission of Percy Dodd's daughters)

This time around Percy enjoyed a full two-year tour with his squadron. The 13th DCO Lancers remained in India throughout, although they do not appear to have been involved in any operations along the border during the period. However, there would have been a steady routine of field training exercises and the horses required daily exercise. This would still have left plenty of time for sport and recreation, and Percy Dodd would have enjoyed the usual range of activities such as polo and pig sticking. There would also have been a regular round of social engagements. Again, Percy must have been the senior squadron commander because he acted as the regimental second in command for the second half of 1925.[12]

Life changed greatly in March 1926; Percy left regimental duty and took up his next appointment as the Military Attache to the British Legation in Kabul. Here, in the capital of his former enemy, he would have worked closely with the ambassador, Sir Francis Humphrys. As Sir Francis was a former British and Indian Army officer who had spent much of his time as a political officer on the North West Frontier, the two men doubtless got on well together. The highlight of his tour was being placed on the deputation, with the ambassador, to accompany the king and queen of Afghanistan on their state visit to Great Britain and the continent of Europe from February through to May 1928. Percy was made a temporary lieutenant colonel for the duration of the trip, during which he was also appointed as a Member of the Fourth Class of the Royal Victorian Order. Along with Sir Francis, Percy had an audience with King George V and attended the state banquet held in honour of the king and queen of Afghanistan at Buckingham Palace on 13 March 1928. Percy's family still have a copy of the seating plan with his papers. Percy was seated opposite the admiral of the fleet, Sir Charles Madden, Bt, with Lady McMahon to his left. On his right was Brigadier General Ghulam Dastagir Khan, who commanded the 1st Division of the Kabul Corps. It must have been an impressive occasion. However, Percy left Kabul and returned to regimental duty in October 1928.[13] He, therefore, missed the 1928/29 Kabul airlift, organised by Sir Francis, when the Shinwari tribe attacked Jalalabad, cutting off its water supply and closing the Kabul–Peshawar road, and other disaffected tribesmen attacked Kabul.

Percy Dodd's last period at regimental duty was a short stint again as the regimental second in command of 13th DCO Lancers from late 1928 through to mid-1929. He was then appointed as the Military Attache to the British High Commission in Tehran. Whether his appointment was due to Sir Francis Humphrys moving from Afghanistan to Iran is not clear, but it would seem likely that having worked together previously, Sir Francis may well have asked for Percy Dodd as his military attache. At some stage in this period, Percy met his bride-to-be Norah Margueritte Wilson. Norah was the daughter of another army officer, Richard Chapman Wilson, and was born on 15 October 1906 in Alexandria, Virginia, to Marguerite Nungovic, *née* McWatt. She was 21 years Percy's junior. The pair were married on 20 October 1929 in Bombay. Before getting married, Percy had already taken up his appointment in Tehran. He was accommodated in a house in the summer legation grounds at Gulhek. His service papers,[14] held by Army Personnel Centre Glasgow, contain a series of letters between Percy, the Treasury, HM Office of Works, the India Office and the War Office attempting to work out how much rent Percy should pay. Eventually, the sum of £200 per annum was agreed upon.

Tehran was Percy's last tour as an army officer and he retired in 1933,[15] possibly as Marguerite was pregnant with their first child, and returned to settle in south-east England. Over the years, the area of Sussex and Kent become the Dodd family home. His first daughter, Angie, was born in December 1933 and Percy took up teaching at Parkfields School at Haywoods Heath. The couple's second child, Libby, was born in 1935 and soon after this Percy left Parkfields and set up as a farmer near Eastbourne. When World War II broke out, Percy offered his services as an officer on the Indian Army Reserve Officers (IARO) list and the War Office initially looked to employ him in

Percy Dodd and Norah Margueritte Wilson at their wedding 20 October 1929, in Bombay. (With permission of Percy Dodd's daughters)

the Intelligence Corps. However, by the time they came around to offering him a job, Percy had already been accepted by the Air Ministry into the RAF Volunteer Reserve. He was employed as an intelligence flying officer in Fighter Command at Stanmore.[16] He was, therefore, removed from the IARO list.[17] Percy Dodd died in Tonbridge, Kent, in late 1967.

Like Percy Dodd, Alexander Molony had been a professional soldier before the war. He would, therefore, have had a reasonable expectation of continuing in his career after the war had finished. However, that all changed when, at the end of the war in November 1918, Sinn Féin secured a majority of 73 Irish seats in the general election. In January the next year, 27 Sinn Féin MPs assembled in Dublin and proclaimed themselves unilaterally as an independent parliament of an Irish Republic. This was ignored by Britain. The Irish War of Independence (1919–21) ensued. Britain went ahead with its commitment to implement Home Rule by passing a new Fourth Home Rule Bill, the Government of Ireland Act 1920. This formalised dividing Ireland into Northern Ireland and Southern Ireland. The latter never functioned but was replaced under the Anglo-Irish Treaty by the Irish Free State which later

Percy Dodd's 1929 passport photo. (With permission of Percy Dodd's daughters)

became the Republic of Ireland. It was agreed that the six former Southern Ireland regiments would be disbanded on 31 July 1922, including Alexander's regiment, the Royal Dublin Fusiliers. With the outbreak of the Irish Civil War, some thousands of their ex-servicemen and officers chose to enlist in the Free State government's newly formed national army. Others, particularly the officers, were offered the chance to transfer to other regiments in the British Army. Alexander did not follow either of these routes; instead, he returned to Britain in October 1919[18] to discharge, having handed over command of 22 MMG to Captain Max Roescher.

On becoming a civilian on 21 February 1920, Alexander attempted to contact Bill Macro, possibly intending to offer the latter a job. Bill, however, was training or working as a teacher, and never made contact. Alexander then returned to India. His subsequent paperwork, initially signed in 1928, to be listed on the Officers Emergency Reserve includes the information that he, 'Resided in India in [a] civil capacity from 1921 to 1928.' It also includes the information that, on leaving the army, he became a 'trainer of racehorses and managed [a] large racing stable'[19]. Sadly, the details of the stables are not recorded. As the document also includes the information that Alexander was in South Africa in 1937, it was updated after Alex had signed it. Presumably, this took place when he was called up for emergency service in World War II. In June 1934, he passed his 50th birthday and received his letter from the War Office informing him that his name was being released from the Regular Army Reserve Officer list. This letter still gives his address as Fitzwilliam Street, Dublin. During World War II, he served in India from 7 August 1940 to 18 January 1943, although in what capacity is not recorded.[20] After the war, probably around the time India gained independence, Alex returned to the UK. He died in Winchester in 1957. So far as can be established, he never married or had children.

George Eastwood, despite his injuries, made it alive to Kohat. Here, he was transferred to alternative transport, which may well have been a train, for onward movement to hospital at Simla. His casualty card records him as being in Simla on 6 August and confirms his injuries as a gun-shot wound to the left lung. The card also records George as 'doing well'.[21] Meanwhile, the 22 MMG lorry which had carried him to Kohat, via Thal, returned eventually to rejoin the battery in Parachinar. At least, it is assumed it did, as neither Bill Macro's report or the battery war diary makes further mention of it. George was removed from the dangerously ill list on 12 August, but it was still a little over a month before he was well enough to be transferred back to England. He was evacuated from Bombay in September 1919 on the SS *Bremen*.[22] So far as is known, he never flew again. His place as a flight commander in 20 Squadron was taken by Captain Arthur Glenny DFC and MC*, formerly of the Army Service Corps.[23]

Born 2 March 1897 in Newry, Co Down, Arthur Glenny had won his first MC as an observer attached to 5 Squadron in December 1915. He had then trained as a pilot in July 1916, qualifying for his 'Wings' on 4 August 1916. With 50 Squadron out of Dover, he had taken on 12 Zeppelins attacking London on the night 23–24 September 1916 by flying his B.E.2c pilot-only to save weight. He had then served in France with 52 Squadron, 9 Squadron, the R.E.8 equipped 7 Squadron and finally 'M' Squadron. After serving in 20 Squadron as a flight commander, he had about a year as a staff officer in Headquarters RAF India before commanding 28 Squadron from July 1922 to December 1923. He retired as an air commodore at the start of World War II, having been Air Officer Commanding, No 1 (Indian) Group and died in Switzerland in January 1947.[24]

George Eastwood was transferred to the unemployed list on 2 December 1919.[25] Thereafter, he is difficult to track. It is believed that he married a Constance Coker, born 27 (or possibly 17) July 1897, in Peterborough in 1926.

George and Constance had a son, Michael John Eastwood, who was born 21 March 1929 in Northamptonshire. At this time, George appears to have been working as a commercial traveller and been away from home a great deal. Certainly, the 1939 census has a Constance Eastwood living at 145 Cromwell Road, Peterborough; she was married and her date of birth was given as 27 July 1897. Also in the household were her son Michael J. Eastwood and what appears to be her parents, George T. Coker, born 31 January 1867, married, a retired railway bookstall manager, and Betsy Anise Coker, born 21 January 1865, married.[26] George was not listed as present at this address; he is in residence in Newcastle upon Tyne, married and with his occupation listed as a commercial traveller.[27] No details have been established as to how the family were involved in World War II and how it impacted them. Nor is it clear when or why they moved down to the south-west of England, but this may have been due to the war. It is believed that George Eastwood died in Truro in 1977. Constance also appears to have died in Truro, just before him, in 1976. Details are even more sketchy for their son, Michael John. He appears to have passed away in quarter 2 of 2004, also in Truro. He probably married in 1954, again in Truro, to a Loveday J Hocking, whose birth appears to have been registered in Truro for quarter 3 of 1933. It appears the couple may have divorced and Loveday remarried but currently there is no firm evidence.

David Lapriak was rather more fortunate than his pilot. His casualty card records from Simla that by 6 August he too was 'doing well'.[28] Neither the card nor his officer papers make clear when David was sufficiently recovered to return to 20 Squadron, but he was certainly back with the squadron by mid-September.[29] The 'No. 20 Squadron Operations Record Book' records the he was involved in successfully bombing a village south-east of Spalga. His pilot on this occasion was Captain Paul Elbridge Bishop flying BF4446; the first Bristol Fighter to take to the skies in India.[30]

Horace Lale, Edmund Britton and Lieutenant S. P. de M. Bucknall were all involved in bombing missions at this stage, during which the squadron was supporting army ground operations in Waziristan. Spalga lies in Waziristan to the south-east of Spinwam, so it is probable that these flights were flying out of Bannu rather than Parachinar. The complete squadron moved to Bannu in late September, concentrating from Parachinar and Risalpur, although the condition of the lines in Bannu was reported to be very poor and unsanitary compared to Parachinar. B Flight was then pushed further south-east in order to operate from Tank. Support of the army in Waziristan consisted of flying bombing missions, engaging concentrations of tribesmen or cattle with small arms fire and reconnaissance missions, both general and photographic. During the course of October 1919, 20 Squadron dropped eight 112lb bombs, 144×25lb Cooper bombs, fired 3000 rounds of small arms ammunition and exposed 419 photographic plates, while conducting around 50 bombing and reconnaissance missions. David Lapraik is officially recorded as flying on at least two of these missions, on 7 and 8 October, each time with Paul Bishop as his pilot.[31] It is likely that he flew on rather more. In December, the squadron then moved to link up at Tank, where the 'No. 20 Squadron Operations Record Book' describes their accommodation as 'what appeared to be disused mule sheds'. It must have at some point around this time that David Lapraik left 20 Squadron and shipped home. He was discharged from the RAF on 18 May 1920.[32] 20 Squadron, however, remained in India operating along the North West Frontier for the whole of the inter-war period. Its Bristol Fighters were replaced by Wapitis in 1932 and these, in turn, by Audaxes in 1935 and Lysanders in 1941. The squadron re-equipped with Hurricanes in March 1943 and thereafter saw action against the Japanese.

David Lapraik is listed on the 1939 census as living at 10 The Heights, Northolt Park, Harrow, Middlesex.[33] He is shown as married, but his wife is not listed, although she appears on the 1939 Harrow electoral roll, with David, at the same address. David's occupation in the census is given as Chief Estimator Civil Engineering Contractor and he is noted as being RAF Emergency Reserve. He was, as World War II broke out, just short of his 40th birthday, but what part he played in that war is not known. He was still shown at the same address in 1940, still without his wife.[34] When David married is not known; his wife was Elizabeth Simpson who is thought to have been born 20 February 1901, although her maiden name and parents have not been identified. David died on 4 August 1966 at the Radcliffe Infirmary in Oxford at the age of 66. His occupation at the time is given as a retired newsagent. Elizabeth outlived David by nearly 30 years; she passed away at St Andrews Nursing Home, Headington, Oxford, on 22 February 1995. So far as can be established, it is believed that the couple were childless.

At some stage after the Third Afghan War, John Henry Jameson, who had commanded the 3rd Guides column and B Company at Badama Post, returned to the UK. He was probably taking leave and putting his affairs in order because he had been able to maintain his commission in the Indian Army. He shipped back to India in early 1921, onboard the P&O steamer the SS *Dongola*. She departed London for Bombay on 28 January 1921, under the command of C. R. A. Newby. John Jameson then appears to return to London in August 1922 on the SS *Narkunda*. John is shown on the passenger list, still as an Indian Army captain, residing on the North West Frontier. His movements and life thereafter are difficult to track, but he does not appear to have married or had children. He had died before MacMunn's *History of the Guides* was published in 1938, as he is listed as 'since died.[35] It is believed that this was in the last quarter of 1933 and that John was residing in Hastings at the time. John Jameson's brothers are just as difficult to track. William Arthur Jameson appears to have gone to sea. He is believed to have married Elizabeth Ada. The date of the marriage is unknown but was probably 1928 or slightly earlier. The couple had a son, John W. Jameson, born 6 February 1929. William died at sea during World War II, when the MV *Western Chief*, on which William was the 2nd Officer, was torpedoed and sunk in the Atlantic on 14 March 1941 by the Italian submarine *Emo*. The youngest Jameson brother, Cecil, has proven even more elusive; the last firm trace of him is from the 1901 census, in a Preston boarding house with his two elder brothers. His involvement in World War I, whether he married, had children or even the date of his death, have not been established.

In contrast, John Jameson's fellow company commander, Captain Fritz Eberhard Ferguson MC was never able to resume his medical studies. He was killed in action in Waziristan on 6 October that year.[36] 3rd Guides arrived in Tank in late September. They had sent a mixed company out on 1 October in a vain attempt to prevent some raiding tribesmen from escaping into the hills after the latter had burnt the village of Parapure. A few days later, 6 October 1919, Fritz Ferguson took out a mixed company of 155 other ranks, with two Indian officers, in support of a column under the command of Major John Bostock, Bhopal Lancers. The column, which consisted of Fritz's company from 3rd Guides, a squadron from the Bhopal Lancers and one company from 1/109th Infantry, was ordered to Kaur Bridge to collect the wounded and bury the dead from a previous engagement. As the column completed the task and was getting ready to move off, it was ambushed. The tribesmen inflicted heavy casualties on the flank and rear guards, the Bhopal Lancers and the 1/109th Infantry, and the flank guard closed on the rear guard. This deprived the main body of the column, the 3rd Guides company, of its protection and in a short time 20 men were killed and around a dozen wounded. According to MacMunn, Fritz Ferguson:

> grasped the situation, occupied some low sand-hills and formed a defensive flank; then, seeing that the platoon in rear of the mules and camels was hard pressed, he went across to it, being wounded *en route*, and ordered a charge with the bayonet, urging on the men with

a hunting horn. He was then again hit and fell. Seeing now that a withdrawal had become inevitable, Captain Ferguson continued with the utmost gallantry to give all necessary orders, but he was hit a third time and killed before the retirement began. The command of the company then devolved on Subadar Sukhbir Gurung (Gukha) and Jemadar Sultan Muhammad (Yusafzai), and these Indian officers conducted the withdrawal to Kot Azam.[37]

Fritz Ferguson's body was recovered and buried when Lieutenant Colonel Clementi, the Guides commanding officer, took a column out to Kot Azam on 24 October. Fritz is remembered on a tablet in the Church of St Mary, Thirsk, which was unveiled on 28 May 1921.

Arthur Bourke, who was almost certainly John Jameson's company subaltern during the action at Badama Post, is not mentioned subsequently in MacMunn's *History of the Guides 1846–1922* (Volume I). However, he continued to serve with the Indian Army. Arthur Bourke's Indian Army service papers have not been located. However, those post-World War II service papers held by Army Personnel Centre, Glasgow,[38] confirm that he transferred to the Prince of Wales's Own 8th Punjab Regiment in 1921.[39] Bourke saw further action on the North West Frontier between 1936 and 1938, although it is not clear in what capacity he was serving. He commanded 4/8th Punjabs from 1938 to 1941. He then took command of the newly formed 2nd Burma Brigade. He held this command, until relieved by Brigadier Roger Ekin of 2nd Burma Brigade, defending Moulmein (now Mawlamyine) from the Japanese in January 1942.[40] Despite this, Arthur retained administrative responsibility for his brigade, and eventually get out of Burma and back to India. Here, he was involved in the formation at Shillong, Assam, in June 1942 of 39th Light Indian Division. This was done by redesignating the remnants of 1st Burma Division. The division formed as a 'light' division, consisting of only two brigades, with six mule and four jeep companies rather than the conventional transport establishment. It trained at Shillong and Ranchi for a deep-penetration role until the Infantry Committee, India, sitting from 1–14 June 1943, decided it would be given a training role to properly prepare units for active service in Burma. It was at this time, between March and August 1943, that Arthur Bourke acted as the divisional commander. The division was redesignated as a Training Division on 14 June 1943 at Ranchi. Divisional HQ then moved to Saharanpur, internal training started from 1 October and the first drafts from regimental centres arrived from 1 November.[41] Arthur retired, after World War II and the subsequent gaining of independence by India and its partition, in April 1949. He was retained, on a voluntary basis, on the Regular Army Reserve of Officers, as a substantive colonel, holding the honorary rank of brigadier. Arthur was retired from this reserve list on his 58th birthday on 9

May 1955. So far as can be determined, Arthur was the longest-lived veteran of the action at Badama Post; he died in Finchampstead, Berkshire, on 12 June 1986, aged 88 years. There is no trace of him getting married or having children. His elder sister, Eleanor Louise, however, is believed to have married in April 1922 to the Dublin born, Indian civil servant, Maurice Stewart Collis. Just before World War I, Collis was posted to Burma; following the war he was an administrator there until he returned to England in 1934. He then authored a number of works on Southeast Asia, China and other historical subjects and took up painting. Eleanor and Maurice had two children; a girl, Louise Edith, born in 1922, and a boy, David Arthur Collis, born in Burma on 4 June 1929.

Mullah Mahmud Akhinzada, who had orchestrated the tribesmen during the action at Badama Post, continued to be a thorn in the British side on the North West Frontier. In particular, he mobilised Orakzai *lashkars* against the Shia tribes in 1923 and 1927. In 1923, he was also heavily implicated in the kidnapping of Molly Ellis, the daughter of a British Officer, although Mullah Akhinzada was subsequently partially instrumental in securing the young lady's release. His origins, however, and what happened to him after 1927, have not been traced.

Corporal Ernest Warburton was the second in command of Number 3 Section, certainly at Badama Post. Apart from Majors Dodd and Molony, Ernest Warburton is the only person mentioned by name in Bill Macro's account – when Bill handed command of the section to Corporal Warburton while he recovered the guns and ammunition from the crashed BF4626. Ernest Warburton was discharged from the army on 1 January 1920.[42] On his Medal Index Card, his address, presumably around 1924 as this when his India General Service Medal and North West Frontier 1919 bar was issued, is recorded as being Woodbank, 53 Mersey Road, Rock Ferry, Birkenhead.[43] No trace has been found of his service papers and, without a date of birth, to date it has proven impossible to establish any further information about Ernest.

Bill Macro on the other hand was discharged on 8 December 1919. Once 22 MMG had returned to Rawalpindi, he would have travelled south by train towards Delhi and onwards to Bombay via the demobilisation camps. His photo album contains pictures of the camps and the docks at Bombay. Having thought he was going home after his pilot training had finished as the war ended on the Western Front, he doubtless was excited at the prospect of going home nearly a year later. He was certainly keen to see his girlfriend Avis Prosser, with whom he had maintained a roughly weekly correspondence throughout the previous four years. Bill's album also includes pictures of HMT *Huntsgreen*, so it is assumed that this is the ship he returned to England on. HMT *Huntsgreen* was originally the German SS *Derflinger*; a 9060- ton ship, with a top speed of 14 knots and accommodation for just over 2100 passengers. The maiden voyage had been from Bremen to New York in May 1908, after which SS *Derflinger* had operated on the Bremen, via Suez, to Far East service. The ship was captured by the British at Port Said in 1914, renamed and then used as a troopship. HMT *Huntsgreen* supported the Gallipoli landings in 1915 and the Salonika campaign in 1917. In 1919, and probably through to early 1922, HMT *Huntsgreen* was used to transport troops to and from India.

When Bill was discharged, he was immediately granted an honorary commission as a 2nd Lieutenant in the RAF, in recognition of his having completed his pilot training. He was also Mentioned in Despatches, dated 3 August 1920. Presumably, he was written up for the Distinguished Conduct Medal by Alexander Molony and Percy Dodd; the citation cannot have been strong enough to secure the award of a medal but must been downgraded to a Mention. Bill, however, had more pressing issues on his mind. He briefly

Ernest William Macro and Avis Mary Prosser at their wedding 23 July 1921. (Macro family)

resumed his engineering studies at University College, London, but then transferred to teacher training at the London Institute of Education. He subsequently managed to find employment at a London County Council school in Islington. Initially, he was living with his parents, George and Adelaide, at 35 Fortis Green, Finchley. He married Avis Prosser on 23 July 1921 at the East Finchley Congregational Church. The following year, the couple were living with Avis's parents, Thomas and Ada, at 22 Beresford Road, Finchley. A couple of years later and they were in their own home at 55 Leicester Rd, still in East Finchley. Bill and Avis only had one child, a son, John Anthony Macro, who was born in Barnet in July 1931. While he taught in Islington, Bill Macro continued to maintain his interest in sports. At various times, he was director of the London Schools' annual life-saving competition, and a judge at the London Schools' Amateur Boxing Association, the London Schools' Amateur Swimming Association and the Royal Life Saving Society. He was appointed chairman of Islington School Athletic and Football Association in 1937.

In 1939, as World War II broke out, Bill was evacuated out to Peterborough with a number of the senior boys from Islington. Peterborough is now in Cambridgeshire, but in the 1930s, it was part of Northamptonshire. Initially,

Bill Macro, with his son John, about 1939. (Macro family)

certainly for the 1939 census, Bill, Avis and John lived at the Manor House, High Street, Eye, just outside Peterborough. By 1940, they had moved to a house which they called the Billet, located on the Peterborough Road, still in Eye. Bill taught at Eastholm Senior School and also coached football, boxing and swimming. His son attended the Kings School Peterborough. It appears Bill had no idea that he was living so close to the wife and son of the pilot he had assisted in rescuing at Badama Post; certainly, if he did know, he made no mention of it to his family. As the phoney war ended and the British army was evacuated from Dunkirk, Bill joined the Local Defence Volunteers, more commonly known as the Home Guard. He enlisted into D Company of 2nd Northampton Battalion Home Guard on 16 June 1940. With his previous military experience, he was accepted as an officer and was soon commanding D Company.[44] Fortunately, the Home Guard was not called to action but, to overcome the deficiencies of their equipment, Bill, with one of his sergeants, a Jim Jarret, built an 'armoured car'. This was probably a standard car with some boiler plate welded on, similar to the first armoured cars of World War I and possibly inspired by the armoured cars which Bill would have seen operating on the North West Frontier.

Major Bill Macro, seated centre, with the officers and NCOs of D Company, of 2nd Northampton Battalion Home Guard, probably in 1944 or 1945. (Macro family)

Once World War II was over, Bill and Avis decided to settle in the Peterborough area. Bill continued his teaching, but they moved a little further out of Peterborough to the village of Thorney. Here, they lived in a house which had originally been a coaching inn called the White Hart in the 1700s; now it was simply the White House. His son, John, completed his National Service in the 14th/20th King's Own Hussars, before completing Sandhurst and commissioning into the Royal Army Service Corps. He subsequently was transferred into the Royal Corps of Transport and served a full career in the army. Bill, meanwhile, retired from teaching in 1959. He continued to tend the large garden at the White House through the 1960s into the 1970s. He survived to see all three of his grandchildren but died, peacefully, at the White House on 5 May 1974.

APPENDIX I

Short History of the Various Anglo-Afghan Conflicts

The First Anglo-Afghan War, also known by the British as the Disaster in Afghanistan, was one of the first major conflicts during the Great Game; the 19th-century competition for power and influence in central Asia between Britain and Russia. The war was fought between the British East India Company and the Emirate of Afghanistan from 1839 to 1842. Initially, the British successfully intervened in a succession dispute between amir Dost Mohammad (Barakzai) and former amir Shah Shuja (Durrani), whom they installed upon conquering Kabul in August 1839. The Army of the Indus, which included 21,000 British and Indian troops under the command of John Keane, 1st Baron Keane (subsequently replaced by Sir Willoughby Cotton and then by William Elphinstone) set out from Punjab in December 1838. They were accompanied by William Hay Macnaghten, the former chief secretary of the Calcutta government, who had been selected as Britain's chief representative to Kabul. The force also included an immense train of 38,000 camp followers and 30,000 camels, plus a large herd of cattle. By late March 1839, the British forces had crossed the Bolan Pass, reached the southern Afghan city of Quetta and begun their march to Kabul, setting up camp at Kandahar on 25 April 1839. After reaching Kandahar, Keane decided to wait for the crops to ripen before resuming his march, so it was not until 27 June that the Army of the Indus marched again. On 22 July 1839, in a surprise attack, the British-led forces captured the fortress of Ghazni; they suffered 200 men killed and wounded, while the Afghans lost nearly 500 men and a further 1600 Afghans were taken prisoner. Ghazni was well supplied, which considerably eased the continuing advance of the British to Kabul. Following this, in August 1839, Shuja was again enthroned in Kabul.

The majority of the British troops now returned to India, leaving 8000 in Afghanistan; however, it soon became clear that Shuja's rule could only be maintained with the presence of a stronger British force. The Afghans resented the British presence and the rule of Shah Shuja. As the occupation continued, William Macnaghten, as the East India Company's chief representative and first political officer, allowed the soldiers to bring their families to Afghanistan to improve morale; this further infuriated the Afghans, as it appeared the British were setting up a permanent occupation. Meanwhile, Dost Mohammad waged a guerrilla war, being defeated in every skirmish he fought, but allegedly taunted Macnaghten in a letter with the boast: 'I am like a wooden spoon. You may throw me hither and yon, but I shall not be hurt.'[1] He eventually surrendered and was exiled to India in late 1840. At the same time, there was a general lowering of Anglo-Russian tension, which made holding Afghanistan an expensive luxury for the British because it no longer seemed essential to have a friendly government in Kabul. The occupying British force vacated the fortress of Bala Hissar and relocated to a cantonment built to the northeast of Kabul. The chosen location was indefensible, being low and swampy with hills on every side. To make matters worse, the cantonment was too large for the number of troops camped in it and had a defensive perimeter almost two miles long. In addition, the stores and supplies were in a separate fort, 275m from the main cantonment. The British commander, Major-General William Elphinstone, who arrived in April 1841 was bed-ridden most of the time with gout and rheumatism. Between April and October 1841, disaffected Afghan tribes were flocking to support Dost Mohammad's son, Akbar Khan, in Bamiyan and other areas north of the Hindu Kush mountains, and were organised into an effective resistance. Then in September 1841, Macnaghten reduced the subsidies paid out to Ghazi tribal chiefs in exchange for accepting Shuja as amir and to keep the passes open; this immediately led to the Ghazis rebelling and a *jihad* being proclaimed. On the night of 1 November 1841, a group of Afghan chiefs met at the Kabul house of one of their number to plan the uprising, which began in the morning of the next day. A mob assembled outside of the house of the East India Company's second political officer, Sir Alexander 'Sekundar' Burnes, and he was shot down. The British were then besieged within their cantonment and their situation deteriorated further when Afghans stormed the poorly defended supply fort inside Kabul on 9 November.

In the following weeks, the British attempted to negotiate with Akbar Khan; Macnaghten secretly offering to make him Afghanistan's vizier in exchange for allowing the British to stay. Simultaneously Macnaghten was disbursing gold to have Akbar assassinated. A meeting for direct negotiations between Macnaghten and Akbar was held near the cantonment on 23 December, but

Macnaghten and the three officers accompanying him were seized and killed by Akbar Khan. Macnaghten's body was dragged through the streets of Kabul and displayed in the bazaar. On 1 January 1842, General Elphinstone reached an agreement with Akbar that provided for the safe exodus of the British garrison and its dependents from Afghanistan. Five days later, the withdrawal began. The departing British contingent numbered around 16,500, of which about 4500 were military personnel and over 12,000 were camp followers. They were attacked by Ghilzai warriors as they struggled through the snowbound passes. On the first day, the retreating force made only five miles. On 9 January, Lady Sale and the British woman and children were escorted back to Kabul by Akbar as hostages, but the vast majority of the column was almost completely annihilated while retreating, before reaching Jalalabad. At Gandamak, some 20 officers and 45 other ranks of the 44th Regiment of Foot, together with some artillerymen and sepoys, armed with only 20 muskets and two rounds of ammunition per man, made a final stand at dawn on 13 January. The ground was frozen, the men had had no shelter and little food for weeks. The British formed a square, defeated the first couple of the Afghan attacks, before running out of ammunition, fighting on with their bayonets and swords, before being overwhelmed. The Afghans took prisoner Captain James Souter, Sergeant Fair and seven soldiers; the remainder were killed. The only British soldier to reach Jalalabad was Assistant Surgeon Dr William Brydon, with, over the following nights, a few sepoys.

As the garrison at Kabul was attacked, Afghan forces besieged the other British contingents in Afghanistan, at Kandahar, Jalalabad and Ghazni. This last was stormed, but those at Kandahar, the largest British force in Afghanistan, and Jalalabad, to which a force had been sent from Kabul in October 1841 as the first stage of a planned withdrawal, held out until relief forces arrived from India in spring 1842. Akbar Khan was defeated near Jalalabad and plans were laid for the recapture of Kabul and the restoration of British dominance. Meanwhile, there had been a change of government back in Britain and Lord Auckland, who had suffered a stroke, had been replaced as governor-general by Lord Ellenborough. Ellenborough was under instructions to bring the war to an end and ordered the forces at Kandahar and Jalalabad to leave Afghanistan after inflicting reprisals and securing the release of prisoners taken during the retreat from Kabul. In August 1842, General William Nott advanced from Kandahar, pillaging the countryside and seizing Ghazni, whose fortifications he demolished. Meanwhile, General George Pollock, who had taken command of a demoralised force in Peshawar used it to clear the Khyber Pass to arrive at Jalalabad, where General Sale had already lifted the siege. From Jalalabad,

Pollock inflicted a further crushing defeat on Akbar Khan and took Kabul in September 1842. A month later, having rescued the prisoners and demolished the city's main bazaar as an act of retaliation for the destruction of Elphinstone's column, they withdrew from Afghanistan through the Khyber Pass. Dost Muhammad was released from exile in India and resumed his rule in Kabul.

The second occasion the British invaded Afghanistan was the Second Anglo-Afghan War; this was fought between the British Raj and the Emirate of Afghanistan from 1878 to 1880, when the latter was ruled by Sher Ali Khan of the Barakzai dynasty, the son of former amir Dost Muhammad Khan. After tension between Russia and Britain in Europe ended with the June 1878 Congress of Berlin, Russia turned its attention to central Asia and sent an uninvited diplomatic mission to Kabul. The amir of Afghanistan, Sher Ali Khan, tried unsuccessfully to keep them out but the Russian envoys arrived in Kabul on 22 July 1878. On 14 August, the British demanded that Sher Ali accept a British mission too. However, the amir refused to receive a British mission and threatened to stop any that were despatched. Lord Lytton, the Viceroy of India, ordered a diplomatic mission to set out for Kabul in September 1878; the mission was turned back as it approached the eastern entrance of the Khyber Pass. This then triggered the Second Anglo–Afghan War.

In the first phase of the war, a British force of about 50,000 fighting men, mostly Indians, was divided into military columns, which penetrated Afghanistan at three different points. The first was in the Khyber Pass where the British forces, under Lieutenant-General Sir Samuel James Browne, attacked and captured the fortress of Ali Masjid on 21 November 1878; despite the fortress being defended by 24 cannons, the Afghan forces, under Ghulam Haider Khan, withdrew overnight. This meant that the northern approach to Kabul was left virtually undefended by Afghan troops. General Browne was able to reach Loe Dakka with relative ease and spent the winter camped safely in Jalalabad. Perhaps more significantly, the Kurram valley Field Force advanced north out of the Kurram valley and fought the Battle of Peiwar Kotal from 28 November through to 2 December1878. The British forces under Major-General Sir Frederick Roberts outmanoeuvred the Afghans and seized the strategic Peiwar Kotal leading into Afghanistan from the top of the Kurram valley. Roberts's force then spent four days collecting the stores and weapons left by the Afghans in the Peiwar Kotal position and sending the wounded back to Kurram. On 6 December 1878, the force moved on to Ali Khel, from where Roberts reconnoitered the Shutagardan Pass. However, this was considered too exposed, so the Kurram Valley Field Force then fell back and wintered in the Peiwar and Kurram positions. Once winter passed, Roberts gathered supplies and transport for the final advance on Kabul. Meanwhile, in southern Afghanistan, the third British Force advanced over the border via the Khojak and Bolan passes, occupied Quetta and then Kandahar. They were harassed by the mountain tribes, but there was no serious resistance from the Afghan regular forces.

Alarmed, Sher Ali attempted to appeal in person to the Russian Tsar for assistance, but unable to do so, he returned to Mazar-i-Sharif, where he died on 21 February 1879. With British forces occupying much of the country, Sher Ali's son and successor, Muhammad Yaqub Khan, signed the Treaty of Gandamak in May 1879 to prevent a British invasion of the rest of the country. According to this agreement and in return for an annual subsidy and vague assurances of assistance in case of foreign aggression, Yaqub relinquished control of Afghan foreign affairs to Britain. British representatives were installed in Kabul, British control was extended to the Khyber Pass, and Afghanistan ceded various North West Frontier province areas and Quetta to Britain. The British army then withdrew. However, on 3 September 1879, an uprising in Kabul led to the slaughter of Sir Louis Cavagnari, the British representative, along with his guards and staff. This provoked the next phase of the Second Afghan War.

The second phase of the Second Afghan War was initiated when General Roberts led the Kabul Field Force over the Shutargardan Pass into central Afghanistan. Roberts then defeated the Afghan army at Charasiab on 6 October 1879. Two days later, he occupied Kabul. This provoked a further uprising by Ghazi Mohammad Jan Khan Wardak who, with a force of 10,000, attacked British forces to the north of Kabul and besieged them in the Sherpur Cantonment in December 1879. However, rather than maintain the siege, Jan Khan Wardak shifted his focus to Roberts' force, and this resulted in the collapse of the rebellion. Yaqub Khan, suspected of complicity in the massacre of Cavagnari and his staff, was obliged to abdicate. The British considered a number of possible political settlements, including partitioning Afghanistan between multiple rulers or placing Yaqub's brother, Ayub Khan, on the throne but ultimately decided to install his cousin Abdur Rahman Khan as amir instead. The following year Ayub Khan, who had been serving as governor of Herat, rose in revolt, defeated a British detachment at the Battle of Maiwand in July 1880 and besieged Kandahar. Roberts then led the main British force from Kabul and decisively defeated Ayub Khan on 1 September at the battle of Kandahar, bringing his rebellion to an end. Abdur Rahman then confirmed the Treaty of Gandamak, leaving the British in control of the territories ceded by Yaqub Khan and ensuring British control of Afghanistan's foreign policy in exchange for protection and a subsidy. Abandoning the provocative policy of maintaining a British resident in Kabul, but having achieved all their other objectives, the British then withdrew.

The end of the Second Afghan War marked the beginning of almost 40 years of good relations between Britain and Afghanistan under the leadership of Abdur Rahman Khan and Habibullah Khan, during which time the British attempted to manage Afghan foreign policy through the payment of a large subsidy. The background to the Third Afghan War and the course of its events are described in this book. The Third Afghan War resulted in the Afghans winning back control of foreign affairs from Britain and the British recognising Afghanistan as an independent nation. However, the British effectively achieved a minor strategic victory because the Durand Line was confirmed as the political boundary between Afghanistan and British India. Further, the Afghans agreed not to ferment trouble on the British side of the line.

The conflicts in Afghanistan which followed the Third Afghan War cannot be described as Anglo-Afghan conflicts. British forces have been involved in them, most notably the current campaign of the 'Fourth War' but always as part of a coalition with the United States and other NATO nations. The 50 years which followed 1919 were relatively peaceful ones for Afghanistan. The country was not drawn into World War II. However, discontent with the monarchy grew in the urban areas of Afghanistan from the early 1970s; a communist military coup took place 27 April 1978. This became known as the Saur Revolution, and the People's Democratic Party of Afghanistan (PDPA) took power. Following the Saur Revolution, much of Afghanistan experienced uprisings against the PDPA government. In December 1979, the forces of Soviet Russia crossed the border from the north, in order to prop up the ailing left-wing government. British and American governments backed the *Mujahideen* resistance fighters but assistance was rendered very covertly, frequently through Pakistan. The Russians eventually withdrew in February 1989. The Soviet-backed Afghan communist government survived for three more years. In 1992, the Afghan political parties agreed on the Peshawar Accords; these established the Islamic State of Afghanistan and appointed an interim government. However, a number of militias opposed the Accords and instigated bombing campaigns in Kabul. Although by early 1995 the Islamic State had managed to defeat most of the militias around Kabul, the Taliban then emerged as a new faction to threaten the capital.

In September 1996, the Taliban, with military and financial support from Pakistan, took power in Kabul and established the Islamic Emirate of Afghanistan. Backed by Al-Qaeda fighters from Arab countries and central Asia, the Taliban imposed religious extremist rule. Following the 9/11 attacks, based on the understanding that the Taliban were sheltering Osama Bin Laden, the United States backed an alliance of war lords who rose to overthrow the Taliban government. The United States and Britain both sent troops in support. In 2006, concerned that the Taliban was re-establishing itself in the south of Afghanistan, the British sent more forces to Helmand Province. It was the start of a long and bloody campaign. 2014 saw the end of British combat operations in Helmand, but British involvement continues in supporting roles, focussed on Kabul and the running of the Afghan National Army Officer Academy (Sandhurst in the Sand). Most notably, at the time of writing, British forces were providing the backing for the Kabul Security Force.

Nominal Roll 22nd Battery Motor Machine Gun Service

Largely based on information supplied by Mr David Murdoch

Service number	Rank	Name	Served NWF 1919	At Badama Post	Remarks
42817	Major	Alexander Weldon Molony	Y	N	1st Royal Dublin Fusiliers
	Lieut	Max Henry Roescher	Y	N	9th King's Royal Rifles
	2nd Lieut	Edward Percy Windsor	Y	N	18th Royal Fusiliers
	2nd Lieut	James Hargreaves	N	N	RNAS (RNVR)
	2nd Lieut	Charles Robert Herbert Farmer	N	N	18th Hussars
MMGS					
619	Sergeant	Herbert George Pearsall	N	N	Commissioned, deployed to France
903	Act. Sgt	Percy Butt	Y		
1068	Gunner	John Travell Maton Gough	N	N	
1239	Gunner	Alexander Carmichael	Y		
1276	Gunner	George Learmouth Harkness	Y		
1368	Gunner	Alexander Cunningham Young	Y		
1390	Gunner	Thomas Boulton	Y		
1397	Gunner	James May Clark	Y		
1408	Gunner	James Baldie Draper	N	N	
1422	Gunner	William Ferguson Bennet	Y		
1439	Gunner	Harry Hargreaves	Y		
1441	Gunner	Alexander Kilgour	Y		

Service number	Rank	Name	Served NWF 1919	At Badama Post	Remarks
1442	Gunner	Charles C. Keddie	Y		
1443	Gunner	Robert Louden	N	N	
1445	Gunner	David Griffith Lawrie	Y		
1529	Gunner	Robert Philip Malcolm	N		
1565	Act. Cpl	James Petrie Jamieson	N	N	No 1 Section
1567	Gunner	William Lafferty	Y		Later Tank Corps
1570	Gunner	Reginald Moss	N	N	
1587	Act. Sgt.	Sydney John Powell	N	N	
1591	Sergeant	Joseph Reginald Slater	Y		
1592	Corporal	Arthur Sutcliffe	Y		
1594	Gunner	David Summers	N	N	
1599	Cpl Act. Sgt	Thomas Stewart	N	N	
1600	Gunner	William Frederick Telfer	Y		
1604	Cpl Act. WO2	Albert Ward	Y	N	Presumed to be Battery Sergeant Major
1609	Corporal	Ernest Warburton	Y	Y	
1615	Gunner	Norman Smeal	N	N	
1618	Gunner	Alexander Morrison Dowie	N	N	Commissioned
1621	Act. Cpl	Walter Patrick	N	N	No 1 Section
1622	Gunner	Edward Collins	Y		
1623	Gunner	Harold John Haycock	N	N	
1624	Gunner	Thomas Collins	Y		
1636	Gunner	John Alexander Galt	N	N	
1641	Gunner	Alex Chisholm	Y		
1644	Gunner	James Gibson Hepburn	N	N	
1645	Gunner	Hector McDonald	Y		
1647	Gunner	Archibald Joseph Purves	N	N	
1650	Gunner	Charles Thomson	N	N	
1652	Sgt	William Welsh	N	N	Commissioned
1658	Cpl Act Sgt	Ernest William Macro	Y	Y	No 3 Section, Pilot Training
1660	Gunner	James Muir Roger	N	N	
1751	Gunner	Edward Dennys Losco Walton	N	N	Discharged 18 April 1919
1753	Gunner	Ralph Henry Weston	Y		

Service number	Rank	Name	Served NWF 1919	At Badama Post	Remarks
1875	Gunner	Harry Young	N	N	
1878	Gunner	James George Warren Tyler	N	N	
2220	Sergeant	Alfred A. T. Barton	N	N	Probably commissioned Tank Corps
2298	Gunner	Harry Edward Laws	Y		
2370	Gunner	Charles Joseph McDonald	Y		
2398	Act. Sgt	Philip Bolger	Y		
2400	Gunner	James Alexander Lyon	Y		
2410	Act. Cpl	James Lindsay	Y		Lindsey on Indian General Service roll
2419	Gunner	George Botterill	N	N	
2420	Gunner	Allan Gilmour	N	N	Silver Wound Badge 418433 Discharged 18 June 1918
MGC (M)					
113344	Private	William Burke	Y		Liverpool Reg, MGC
163649	Private	Arthur Fovargue	Y		Kings Own Royal Lancashire Reg
118816	Private	George Norman Burns	Y		MGC
163654	Gunner	William Lobley	Y		Loyal North Lancs. Reg.
79566	Gunner	James Arthur Bartholemew	Y		
68955	Gunner	William James Hitchcock	Y		MGC
TC	Transferred Tank Corps, but believed with 22nd MMG Battery for NWF 1919				
191847	Private	William John Jones	Y		Army Service Corps, Tank Corps
163651	Gunner	John William Rigg	Y		East Lancs. Reg., Tank Corps
163655	Gunner	Thomas Wilson	Y		Loyal North Lancs Reg, Tank Corps
62185	Private	Thomas Garrity	Y		Tank Corps
61542	Gunner	Joseph Walker	Y		North Staffs., Tank Corps
191854	Gunner	Thomas Lloyd Williams	Y		Tank Corps
61694	Gunner	John Allan	Y		2nd Black Watch, Tank Corps

Service number	Rank	Name	Served NWF 1919	At Badama Post	Remarks
10861	Private	John B. Adams	Y		Royal Fusiliers, Tank Corps
ASC	Attached 22nd MMG Battery				
M2/100503	Sgt	Alfred James Fielder		N	
M2/102138	Private	Harry Albert Cutler	Y		
M2/097864	Private	John Girdwood	Y		
M2/115535	Private	Edgar William Davis	Y		
M2/101516	Private	William Arthur Cordwell	N	N	Died 5 April 1918
Others	Not yet identified				
	Gunner	Parker			Probably 1900
		Ross			Possibly 1330, 2044, 2059
	Sgt	Kellet			
	Sgt	Whitfield			
		Duncan			Army Service Corps
		Frank Taylor			Royal Army Medical Corps
		J. Thomson			Royal Army Medical Corps

APPENDIX 3

Report by Sergeant Macro

On July 30th 1919 a report was received in Parachinar by Major Malony, OC 22nd Battery, MMG, that large numbers of tribesmen were collecting in the Khurmana valley for the purpose of attacking a convoy expected to pass along the Thal-Parachinar Rd.

On receipt of this message Major Malony detailed Sgt Macro to take No 3 Section, 22 Battery MMG and patrol the road from Parachinar to Sadda, and there to rendezvous with Major Dodd to exchange information.

The rendezvous was effected in the late afternoon, and Major Dodd reported that the tribesmen appeared to be dispersing owing to the arrival of the MMG section.

This conference took place outside the walls of the post, and while it was in progress, an aeroplane was seen to zoom down into a valley beyond Badama Post. As the plane did not reappear it was assumed it had been shot down and Major Dodd set off on horseback, accompanied by a few militiamen. No 3 Section MMG prepared for action and also set off for the post, but as there was no road, had to pick their way along the hilltop, and so did not arrive at the post until some minutes after Major Dodd. He reported that some of his militia were bringing in the two wounded airmen, and Sgt Macro ordered one of his Ford vans to be cleared ready to take the airmen to hospital. The airmen, who were too badly injured even to help themselves, were given first aid, and despatched to Kohut.

Sgt Macro, who had had RAF experience, realising that the wrecked plane would contain probably more than 1000 rounds of ammunition, possibly bombs and machine guns which would be of great value to the tribesmen, volunteered to go down to the wrecked plane, which was lying at the bottom of a dry river bed, to see what could be salvaged. Major Dodd said he would accompany him, and, although he hadn't sufficient men to picket the hillside, would bring a few men with him to carry back anything salvaged. Sgt Macro positioned his two machine guns so that they could give covering fire if

210 • ACTION AT BADAMA POST

necessary, placed the section under the command of Cpl Warburton, and climbed down the hillside to the wrecked plane.

The tribesmen, encouraged by their success, commenced to reassemble and the party was subjected to an increasing volume of sniping, but most of the party were able to lie under cover of the rocks and no one was hit. The plane had crashed on its nose leaving the tail up in the air. Sgt Macro climbed into the cockpit, released the bombs from the rack, and having examined them to see if they were safe to handle, sent them up to the post. He then handed out the boxes and drums of ammunition, dismounted the Lewis gun, dismantled the Vickers, and passed them out to the militia to carry away. The only part of the Vickers not salvaged was the barrel casing, which couldn't be got at because of the crashed engine.

It was now beginning to get dark, and the tribesmen, getting bolder, were closing in along the hillsides, so the party withdrew to Badama Post. This was too small to hold the MMG Section, so this withdrew to Sadda, where Major Dodd also spent the night.

The following morning the section returned to Badama and found that, despite flares having been fired over the wreck at intervals during the night, the tribesmen had managed to carry away all but the plane's engine. The MMG Section gave covering fire, and a party of militiamen got to the plane, and managed to carry the engine to Badama Post. The MMG Section returned to Sadda to await the return of scouts regarding the movements of the tribesmen. That evening the scouts reported that the tribesmen were dispersing and returning to their villages, so the next day No 3 section MMG returned to Parachinar.

Sgt Macro reported to OC 22nd Battery MMG, Major Malony, on the success of the mission. Major Malony complimented him on his handling of the situation, and said he had received an excellent report of his conduct from Major Dodd, and that he was being recommended for a DCM. However, nothing was ever heard of this.

APPENDIX 4

The Vickers Machine Gun: History and Specifications

The Vickers machine gun, or Vickers gun, was the water-cooled .303 inch (7.7mm) machine gun produced by Vickers Limited, originally for the British army. The machine gun typically required a six- to eight-man team to operate; one fired the gun, one fed the ammunition, the rest helped to carry the weapon, its ammunition and spare parts. The Vickers gun was based on the successful Maxim gun of the late-19th century. Vickers purchased the Maxim company in 1896. Having done so, Vickers then took the design of the Maxim gun and improved it. The British army formally adopted the Vickers gun as its standard machine gun under the name Gun, Machine, Mark I, Vickers, .303-inch on 26 November 1912. However, there were still great shortages when World War I began, and the British Expeditionary Force was still equipped with Maxims when it deployed to France in 1914.

As the British army's numbers increased during the war, the Vickers gun became the army's primary machine gun. It was used on all fronts during the conflict. It was also employed as an aircraft-mounted weapon system, including on the Bristol Fighter. When the Lewis Gun was adopted as a light machine gun and issued to infantry units, the Vickers guns were redefined as heavy machine guns. They were withdrawn from infantry units and grouped into companies within the new Machine Gun Corps (MGC). When heavier 0.5 inch (12.7mm) calibre machine guns appeared, the tripod-mounted, rifle-calibre machine guns, like the Vickers, became medium machine guns. The MGC was disbanded following World War I and the Vickers returned to infantry units. Before World War I, there were plans to replace the Vickers gun. The Bren gun became the army's light machine gun and the Mauser Besa machine gun eventually became the standard tank-mounted machine gun. However, the Vickers remained the standard medium machine gun and stayed in service with the British army until 30 March 1968. Its last operational use was in Radfan during the Aden Emergency. Its successor in UK service was the L7 General Purpose Machine Gun.

The weight of the gun varied dependent on what attachments were employed; it was generally 25–30lb (11–14kg) with a 40–50lb (18–23kg) tripod. The ammunition boxes for the 250-round ammunition belts weighed 22lb (10kg) each. In addition, the gun required about 7.5 imperial pints (4.3l) of water in its evaporative cooling system to prevent overheating. The heat of the barrel boiled the water in the jacket surrounding it. The resulting steam was taken off by a flexible tube to a condenser container; this had the benefit of avoiding giving away the gun's position. It also enabled re-use of the water, which was very important in hot, dry conditions such as India.

In British service, the Vickers gun fired the standard .303 inch cartridges used in the Lee–Enfield rifle. These were generally hand loaded into the cloth ammunition belts, although there was a loading machine produced. The Mark VIIIz cartridge, which had a boat-tailed spitzer 'steamlined' bullet, could be used against targets at a range of approximately 4500 yards (4115m). The bullet jackets were generally made of an alloy of cupro-nickel and gilding metal.

The Vickers gun was 3 feet 8 inches (112cm) long and its cyclic rate of fire was between 450 and 600 rounds per minute. In practice, it was expected that 10,000 rounds would be fired per hour, and that the barrel would be changed every hour—a two-minute job for a trained team. The muzzle velocity was around 2500ft/s (770m/s), depending on the type of ammunition being fired.

Motorcycles and Sidecars of 22nd Battery Motor Machine Gun Service

The early batteries of the Motor Machine Gun Service had made considerable use of Enfield machines, both as single bikes and as carrier combinations. However, by the time 22 MMG shipped to India in February 1916, the army had settled on two principal manufacturers for the majority of its bikes. These were the Triumph Model H for single seater use (largely despatch riding) and the Clyno combination for carrier machines. These were the equipment that deployed to India with 22nd Battery.

The first Triumph motorcycle of 1902 used a Belgian Minerva engine, but within a few years, the Coventry firm, originally a bicycle manufacturer founded by German immigrants Siegfried Bettman and Maurice Schulte, was building its own power units. The company was soon involved in racing; Jack Marshall won the 1908 Isle of Man TT single-cylinder class for Triumph, having finished second the previous year. The publicity generated by competition's success greatly stimulated sales. Triumph's 3½hp model had first appeared in 1907. With an original capacity of 453cc, its sidevalve engine was enlarged to 476cc in 1908 and finally to 499cc in 1910. This was then superseded by the 550cc 4hp Model H, with an air-cooled four-stroke single-cylinder engine in 1914.

At the start of World War I, the British government was looking for a motorcycle for use by despatch riders. Various makes and models were trialled for suitability and the Triumph Model H was selected. With the rear wheel driven by a belt, this was the first Triumph that was a true motorcycle, not being fitted with pedals. Engine differences from the previous Model A included a single cam wheel with two cams replacing separate cam wheels for the inlet and exhaust valve, and new design of cylinder casting. The valve head diameter was enlarged and the valves were spaced further apart. The Model H was fitted with a Sturmey-Archer three-speed countershaft gearbox operated by a hand gear-change lever. More than 30,000 Triumph Model H motorcycles had been produced by the end of the war in 1918. It became known as the 'Triumph Trusty' or 'Trusty H' by the troops.

Specifications of the Triumph H were:

- Engine/transmission
  Configuration: Single-cylinder side valve
  Capacity: 550cc (33.6cu in)
  Bore/stroke: 85mm/97mm (3.35in/3.82in)
  Gears: Three
  Clutch: Multi-plate

- Chassis
  Front wheel: 26 inch multi-spoke
  Rear wheel: 26 inch multi-spoke
  Front tyre: 26 inch × 2.3 inch
  Rear tyre: 26 inch × 2.3 inch

- Dimensions
  Fuel tank: 6.8 litres (1.5 galUK/1.79 galUS)

- Performance
  Maximum power: 4.1PS (4bhp–3kW)

Clyno was founded in 1909 by two cousins, Frank and Ailwyn Smith, at Thrapston, Northamptonshire, to produce a variable-speed drive for motorcycles, using a pulley with inclined faces. The Clyno name is derived from the word 'inclined'. The firm soon progressed to producing complete motorcycles and in 1915 were asked by the War Office to investigate the manufacture of a motorcycle combination with machine gun. This was done in conjunction with Vickers Ltd and the result was the Clyno combination. Initially, they were made in large numbers, but by summer 1916, the relationship between Clyno and Vickers had broken down and the partnership was annulled in October that year.

As World War I transitioned from a war of movement to the stalemate of the trenches, the rationale for employing motorcycle machine guns became increasingly difficult to sustain. Although the combination had been designed so that the gun could be fired while mounted, it was found that the terrain meant the sidecar did not offer a sufficiently stable platform for firing the gun. Frequently, the gun was dismounted from the sidecar and set up on the ground on its tripod. The three crews of a sub-section normally operated so that one carried the gun, one carried reserves of fuel, ammunition and water and the other machine was a spare should one of the other combinations be put out of action.

In 1917 and 1918, Clyno continued to supply military equipment; they also signed an agreement with the Russian Imperial Army for the supply of solo and sidecar machines without guns. During 1918 and 1919, they also produced a small number of ABC Dragonfly aero engines. However, after the war, the market for motorcycles collapsed with a shortage of material and large numbers of ex-army machines flooding the market. The Russians then failed to pay their bills and Clyno went bankrupt by 1920.

A History and Description of the Major British Aircraft Types Involved

B.E.2

The Royal Aircraft Factory B. E. (Bleriot Experimental) 2 was a single-engine, tractor, two-seat biplane designed and developed at the Royal Aircraft Factory. Most production aircraft were constructed under contract by various private companies, both established aircraft manufacturers and firms that had not previously built aircraft. Around 3500 were manufactured in all. Early versions of the B.E.2 entered squadron service with the Royal Flying Corps in 1912 and the aircraft served throughout World War I. It was initially used as a front-line reconnaissance aircraft and light bomber. In most variants, the pilot flew the aircraft from the rear cockpit. Some were modified to become single-seat night fighters, in which configuration it was responsible for the destruction of several German airships.

By late 1915, the B.E.2 was overmatched by German fighters such as the Fokker Eindecker. Although obsolete, it remained in front-line service while replacements were developed and brought into service. Once withdrawn from operations, the aircraft served in various second-line roles, seeing use as a trainer and communications aircraft, as well as performing anti-submarine coast patrol duties. It was at this time, late 1915, that 31 Squadron was formed and shipped to India with B.E.2s. They were airborne from January 1916.

The B.E.2c variant was designed to be 'inherently stable'. This was useful when the aircraft conducted artillery observation and aerial photography missions. The pilot was able to fly without constant attention to the flight controls and conduct the mission. However, rapid manoeuvring was difficult, which made the aircraft vulnerable in a dog fight. The situation was compounded as the observer, whose primary role was to defend the aircraft, occupied the front seat, where he had a limited field of fire for his gun. Indeed, he was often not carried because of the aircraft's poor payload.

General characteristics
- Crew: Two – pilot and observer
- Length: 27ft 3in (8.31m)
- Wingspan: 37ft 0in (11.28m)
- Height: 11ft 1½in (3.39m)
- Wing area: 371ft^2 (34.8m^2)
- Empty weight: 1370lb (623kg)
- Loaded weight: 2,350lb (1068kg)
- Powerplant: 1×RAF 1a air cooled V-8 engine, 90hp (67kW)

Performance
- Maximum speed: 72mph (63 knots, 116km/h) at 6500 ft (1980m)
- Endurance: 3hr 15min
- Service ceiling: 10,000ft (3050m)
- Rate of climb to 3500ft (1070m): 6½ minutes
- Rate of climb to 10,000ft (3050m): 45¼ minutes
- Power/mass: 0.038hp/lb (63W/kg)

Armament
- Guns: Normally 1×.303in (7.7mm) Lewis gun for observer
- Bombs: 224lb (100kg) of bombs (with full-bomb load usually flown as a single-seater, without machine gun)

F.E.2

The first F.E.2 (Farman Experimental 2), designated the F.E.2a, was developed as a fighter by the Royal Aircraft Factory and made its maiden flight in February 1914. It was a single-engine, pusher, two-seat biplane A production order for 12 machines was placed in August 1914 and the aircraft entered service as the F.E.2b in May 1915. The designation was then changed to 'Fighting Experimental 2'. The crew of two consisted of the observer, armed with a forward-firing .303 Lewis machine gun, who was accommodated in the nose of the aircraft. The pilot sat above and behind the observer, in front of the engine. A second Lewis machine gun was mounted to fire rearwards over the top wing; its operation required the observer to stand on his seat. The F.E.2b also carried a small bomb load and, as a night bomber variant, was given the designation F.E.2c.

The first F.E.2bs were powered by a Beardmore in-line engine of 120hp, soon upgraded to 160hp, with the final model in the series, the F.E.2d, being fitted with a Rolls-Royce Eagle of 250hp. This more powerful engine facilitated the carriage of an additional one or two forward-firing Lewis guns operated by the pilot.

The F.E.2b equipped 16 squadrons in France and six in England. It was well-liked by pilots for its handling characteristics and remained a difficult opponent for its adversaries. By autumn 1916, however, the machine was being outperformed by the new generation of German fighters. Early in 1917, it was withdrawn from offensive patrols, although the F.E.2d continued to carry out this role. The F.E.2b continued to serve as a night fighter on anti-Zeppelin patrols over England and was heavily used as a dedicated night bomber through to the end of the war. A total of 2325 F.E.2b/c/ds were built with the majority constructed by private aircraft companies.

General characteristics
- Crew: Two – pilot and observer
- Length: 32ft 3in (9.83m)
- Wingspan: 47ft 9in (14.55m)
- Height: 12ft 8in (3.85m)
- Wing area: 494ft^2 (45.9m^2)
- Empty weight: 2,061lb (937kg)
- Loaded weight: 3037lb (1380kg)
- Powerplant: 1×Beardmore six-cylinder in-line piston engine, 160hp (119kW)

Performance
- Maximum speed: 80 knots (91.5mph, 147km/h)
- Endurance: 3hr
- Service ceiling: 11,000ft (3353m)
- Rate of climb to 10,000ft (3048m): 39¾ minutes
- Power/mass: 0.053hp/lb (86W/kg)

Armament
- Guns: 1 or 2×.303in (7.7mm) Lewis gun for observer (one mounted in front and one firing back over the top wing) and 1 or 2×.303in (7.7mm) Lewis gun sometimes mounted for the pilot's use in the F. E.2d
- Bombs: up to 517lb (235kg) of bombs

Bristol Fighter 2B

The Bristol F.2 Fighter was a two-seat biplane fighter and reconnaissance aircraft developed by Frank Barnwell at the Bristol Aeroplane Company. The prototype Bristol Type 12 F.2A was first flown on 9 September 1916 at Filton, fitted with a newly available 190hp Rolls-Royce Falcon I in-line engine. Bristol had already received an order for 50 aircraft by the time the second prototype flew on 25 October 1916, this time fitted with a Hispano-Suiza power unit. Although the type was intended initially as a replacement for the B. E.2c reconnaissance aircraft, the newly available Rolls-Royce Falcon V12 engine gave it the performance of a fighter.

The aircraft was a twin-cockpit biplane, with the fuselage suspended mid-way between the wings. The pilot was seated forward. The observer/gunner was in the rear equipped with a Scarff-mounted machine gun. A forward-firing Vickers gun was mounted on the fuselage centreline. The F.2B featured a fully covered lower-wing centre section and downward sloped longerons in front of the cockpit to improve the pilot's view when landing. Despite being a two seater it was an agile dog-fighter which had superiority over many of its single-seater opposition.

General characteristics
- Crew: Two – pilot and observer/gunner
- Length: 25ft 10in (7.87m)
- Wingspan: 39ft 3in (11.96m)
- Height: 9ft 9in (2.97m)
- Wing area: 405ft^2 (37.62m^2)
- Empty weight: 2145lb (975kg)
- Loaded weight: 3243lb (1474kg)
- Powerplant: 1×Rolls-Royce Falcon III liquid-cooled V12 engine, 275hp (205kW)

Performance
- Maximum speed: 123mph (107 knots, 198km/h) at 5000ft (1500m)
- Endurance: 3hr
- Service ceiling: 18,000ft (5500m)
- Rate of climb: 889ft/min (4.5m/s)
- Power/mass: 0.085hp/lb (139W/kg)

Armament
- Guns: 1×.303 in (7.7mm) forward-firing Vickers machine gun in the upper fuselage and 1 or 2×.303 in Lewis Guns in the observer's cockpit
- Bombs: 240lb (110kg)

Glossary

Bhishti – water carrier

Bhoosa – straw

Dhoolie – carrying chair or stretcher

Durbar – literally an Indian court; more normally a public reception held by an Indian prince or a British governor or viceroy in India

Fakir – a holy man

Feringhee – a European foreigner; literally, 'Frank', a term applied by Muslims to Europeans

Firman – a royal proclamation or edict

Gasht – a patrol or reconnaissance; can be used as a verb, 'to gasht'

Hartal – strike, mass protest, civil disobedience

Jezail – old fashioned long-barrelled matchlock

Jihad – Islamic, holy war

Jirga – tribal assembly or parliament

Khassadar – un-uniformed tribal levy, armed with his own rifle

Kotal – pass

Lambardar – landowner

Lashkar – a tribal armed force

Mujahideen – guerrilla fighters in Islamic countries, especially those who are fighting against non-Muslim forces; denoting persons who fight a *jihad*

Mullah – man learned in the Koran, a preacher. Not a 'priest'; Islam has no priesthood

Nullah – gully, ravine or watercourse

Tangi – defile, gorge or ravine

Samadhi – Hindi, mausoleum, tomb, cremation site or monument for a deceased guru

Sangar – protective stone wall or breastwork

Sowar – junior rank in an Indian cavalry regiment, a Trooper, literally 'a rider'

Surra – parasitic disease of camels and other mammals, transmitted by biting flies and occurring chiefly in North Africa and Asia

Endnotes

Prologue

1   General Staff Branch, Army Headquarters India, *Third Afghan War 1919 Official Account* (Naval & Military Press, 2004 reprint of original 1926 edition), p. 70.
2   Casualty Card, Lieutenant G. Eastwood, 30 July 1919, RAF Museum Story Vault, http://www.rafmuseumstoryvault.org.uk/archive/7000242779-eastwood-g.-george, accessed 23 July 2017.

Chapter 1 Strategic Background

1   General Staff Branch, Army Headquarters India, *Third Afghan War 1919 Official Account*, p. 18.
2   Brian Robson, *Crisis on the Frontier, The Third Afghan War and the Campaign in Waziristan 1919–20* (Spellmount, 2007), pp. 5–8.
3   Robson, *Crisis on the Frontier,* p. 9.
4   *Ibid,* pp. 9–12.
5   Charles Chenevix Trench, *The Frontier Scouts* (Jonathon Cape, 1985), pp. 28–30.
6   Private letter Chelmsford to Montagu, quoted in T.A. Heathcote, *The Afghan Wars, 1839-1919* (Spellmount, 2007), p. 178.
7   Robson, *Crisis on the Frontier,* pp. 9–18.
8   General Staff Branch, Army Headquarters India, *Third Afghan War 1919 Official Account*, p. 2.
9   Robson, *Crisis on the Frontier,* p. 21.
10   General Staff Branch, Army Headquarters India, *Third Afghan War 1919 Official Account*, p. 2.
11   Robson, *Crisis on the Frontier,* p. 22. For useful tables of the communication routes between Afghanistan and India and internal Afghan communications see General Staff Branch, Army Headquarters India, *Third Afghan War 1919 Official Account*, p. 3 and p. 5.
12   General Staff Branch, Army Headquarters India, *Third Afghan War 1919 Official Account*, p. 4.
13   Robson, *Crisis on the Frontier,* pp. 31–32.
14   *Ibid,* p. 21.
15   Encyclopaedia Britannica, Khyber Pass, https://www.britannica.com/place/Khyber-Pass, accessed 18 July 2018.
16   General Staff Branch, Army Headquarters India, *Third Afghan War 1919 Official Account*, p. 95.
17   Robson, *Crisis on the Frontier,* p. 107.
18   *Ibid,* p. 107.
19   *Ibid,* pp. 115–16.
20   *Ibid,* pp. 147–50.

21   *Ibid*, p. 93.
22   General Staff Branch, Army Headquarters India, *Third Afghan War 1919 Official Account*, p. 6.
23   *Ibid*, pp. 22–24.
24   Chitral Scouts, Mohmand Militia, two battalions of the Khyber Rifles, Kurram Militia, North Waziristan Militia and South Waziristan Militia.
25   Also with low velocity .303 rifles.
26   General Staff Branch, Army Headquarters India, *Third Afghan War 1919 Official Account*, pp. 16–20.
27   *Ibid*, p. 17.
28   Robson, *Crisis on the Frontier*, pp. 25–28.
29   General Staff Branch, Army Headquarters India, *Third Afghan War 1919 Official Account*, pp. 20–21.
30   Robson, *Crisis on the Frontier*, p. 27.
31   AIR 27/258/1, 'No 20 Squadron: Operations Record Book' with appendices, National Archives, Kew, May 1919
32   General Staff Branch, Army Headquarters India, *Third Afghan War 1919 Official Account*, p. 22.
33   Robson, *Crisis on the Frontier*, pp. 43–48.
34   *Ibid*, pp. 48–50.
35   *Ibid*, pp. 50–52.
36   General Staff Branch, Army Headquarters India, *Third Afghan War 1919 Official Account*, pp. 34–35
37   More normally the commander of the 10 Cavalry Brigade at Risalpur. For a detailed explanation of 'The Baldwin Affair', see Robson, *Crisis on the Frontier*, Annex A to Chapter V.
38   Robson, *Crisis on the Frontier*, p. 55. For a detailed description, see T. R. Moreman, *The Army in India and the Development of Frontier Warfare, 1849–1947* (Palgrave Macmillan, 1998).
39   *Ibid*, pp. 55–62.
40   General Staff Branch, Army Headquarters India, *Third Afghan War 1919 Official Account*, pp. 40, 42 and 48.
41   *Ibid*, pp. 46–47.
42   Robson, *Crisis on the Frontier*, pp. 73–76.
43   4th Division, 12 Mounted Brigade, and various other internal security and lines of communication forces. Additionally, Wapshare's forces were reinforced substantially in mid to late May by four battalions of infantry, two cavalry regiments, guns and machine guns. General Staff Branch, Army Headquarters India, *Third Afghan War 1919 Official Account*, pp. 96–97.
44   Robson, *Crisis on the Frontier*, p. 108.
45   *Ibid*. The figures in the *Third Afghan War 1919 Official Account* are contradictory and Monro's despatch gives different figures again.
46   *Ibid*, p. 109.
47   *Ibid*, pp. 109–10.

Chapter 2 The War in the Kurram

1   The fifth Mughal emperor who reigned from 1628 to 1658.
2   Robson, *Crisis on the Frontier*, p. 93.
3   *Ibid*, p. 94.
4   *Ibid*.
5   General Staff Branch, Army Headquarters India, *Third Afghan War 1919 Official Account*, pp. 52–53.
6   *Ibid*, pp. 54–55.
7   Robson, *Crisis on the Frontier*, p. 96.
8   General Staff Branch, Army Headquarters India, *Third Afghan War 1919 Official Account*, pp. 56–57.

9   Robson, *Crisis on the Frontier*, p. 97.

10 *Ibid*, p. 98

11 General Staff Branch, Army Headquarters India, *Third Afghan War 1919 Official Account*, pp. 60–61.

12 *Ibid*, p. 63.

13 Robson, *Crisis on the Frontier*, pp. 100–101.

14 *Ibid*, pp. 52–53.

15 General Staff Branch, Army Headquarters India, *Third Afghan War 1919 Official Account*, p. 50.

16 Robson, *Crisis on the Frontier*, p. 76.

17 General Staff Branch, Army Headquarters India, *Third Afghan War 1919 Official Account*, pp. 50–51.

18 *Ibid*, p. 25.

19 Robson states that the force included three sections (six armoured cars) from 22 MMG. This is not correct. 22 MMG had three sections of motorcycle combinations, each with two machine-guns, and no armoured cars. However, there is photographic evidence that armoured cars were present in Parachinar at this time (mid May); they were probably from 1st Armoured Motor Battery.

20 Robson, *Crisis on the Frontier*, p. 101.

21 General Staff Branch, Army Headquarters India, *Third Afghan War 1919 Official Account*, pp. 64–67.

22 *Ibid*, pp. 67–68.

23 *Ibid*, pp. 69–70.

24 *Ibid*, p. 70.

Chapter 3 Military Motorcycling and Raising 22nd Battery Motor Machine Gun Service

1   *Mechanical Transport Committee Annual report 1908/9*, Royal Logistic Corps Museum, Ref RLCS 5813, p. 55.

2   G. Winton, *Theirs Not to Reason Why: Horsing the British Army 1875 to 1925* (Helion and Company, 2013), p. 198.

3   *Mechanical Transport Committee Annual report 1910/11*, Royal Logistic Corps Museum, Ref RLCA 5815, p. 11–12.

4   *Report of the Advisory Committee on Motorcyclists (Technical Reserve)*, National Archives, 1911, Ref WO 33/3026.

5   Martin Gregg, *War Bike: British Military Motorcycling 1899–1919* (Lightning Source UK Ltd, 2015), pp. 10–13.

6   Perhaps even better known for being the first man to successfully fly an aircraft off a moving ship.

7   Bruce I. *Gudmundsson, On Armor (Greenwood Publishing, 2004)*, pp. 3–4.

8   Michael Carragher, *San Fairy Ann? Motorcycles and British Victory 1914–1918* (FireStep Press, 2013), p. 256; citing *The Motor Cycle*, 29 April 1915.

9   Army Order 480, Other Arms (Code 14 (J)): *Formation of Machine Gun Corps*, National Archives, Kew, Ref WO 32/11239, 1915.

10 David Fletcher, *War Cars* (HMSO), p. 92 and The Long Long Trail Website, www.longlong-trail.co.uk/army/regiments-and-corps-in-the-first-world-war/motor-machine-guns, accessed 15 March 2018.

11 F. H. Rood, quoted in C. E. Crutchley, *Machine Gunner 1914–1918, Personal Experiences of the Machine Gun Corps* (Pen & Sword, reprinted 2013), pp. 216–17.

12 *Eastbourne Gazette*, 29 September 1915, p. 4. Accessed at http://media.thekeep.info/gb179/EASTBOURNE%20GAZETTE_19150929.pdf, accessed 8 June 2017.

13 Stated by the Rosher family to M Cassell. See: https://www.greatwarforum.org/topic/249544-22-battery-machine-gun-corps-motors/?tab=comments#comment-2527672.

14 Bernard Burke, *1912 Edition Genealogical and Heraldic History of Landed Gentry of Ireland*, (Harrison & Sons, 1912) via the Digital Archive, www.archive.org, accessed 15 March 2018.

15 *The London Gazette.*

16 *The London Gazette.*

17 Service papers of Alexander Weldon Molony, obtained from Army Personnel Centre, Glasgow.

18 Philip Lecane, *Beneath a Turkish Sky* (History Press Ireland, 2017), pp. 164–165, quoting Alexander Weldon Molony from Wylly, Colonel H.C. *Neill's Blue Caps*, Vol III 1914–22, reprinted Cork 1996, p. 29.

19 *The London Gazette.*

20 Army Form B199A, P/42817 Maj A. W. Molony, and related papers, obtained from Army Personnel Centre, Glasgow.

21 *England, Select Births and Christenings, 1538–1978*, www.ancestry.com, accessed 16 April 2018.

22 British Army WWI Service Records, 1914–1920, M2/100503 Alfred James Fielder, www.ancestry.com, accessed 12 Apr 2018.

23 *The Motor Cycle*, 1 July 1915, p. 11, Boston Public Library, www.archive.org, accessed 25 April 2018.

24 Marriage Certificate, Fielder–Matthews, London, England, Church of England Marriages and Banns, 1754–1932, Reference p83/js1/012, London Metropolitan Archives, www.ancestry.co.uk, accessed 12 April 2018.

25 As related to the author by his father, Major (Retired) J. A. Macro, Bill's son.

26 *The Motor Cycle*, 1 July 1915, p. 10, Boston Public Library, www.archive.org, accessed 26 April 2018.

27 Stephen Pope, *The First Tank Crews* (Helion & Company, 2016), pp. 170–72.

28 Major A. H. Molony, Lieut M Roesher [sic], 2nd Lieutenants P. Windsor, J. Hargreaves and R. H. Farmer.

29 WO 25/3544, Embarkation Returns, At Home for Abroad – Jan. to Mar 1916, National Archives, Kew, accessed 17 July 2017.

30 Rood, quoted in C. E. Crutchley, *Machine Gunner 1914–1918*, p. 217.

31 *Ibid.*

32 http://www.poheritage.com/Upload/Mimsy/Media/factsheet/92802BELTANA-1912pdf.pdf, accessed 5 April 2019.

Chapter 4 22nd Battery in India 1916 to 1919

1 Peter Hopkirk, *On Secret Service East of Constantinople* (John Murray, 1994), pp. 66–71 and pp. 81–84.

2 *Ibid,* p. 63 and pp. 98–99.

3 *Ibid,* pp. 149–154.

4 General Staff Branch, Army Headquarters India, *Third Afghan War 1919 Official Account*, p. 12.

5 So named by taking the first two letters of each of Motor Machine Gun.

6 First edition of *Momagu,* reproduced in *The Motor Cycle* (Vol. 20), 28 March 1918, p. 310, https://archive.org/stream/motorcycle20lond_/motorcycle20lond#page/n393/mode/1up, accessed 7 November 2018.

7 The Great War Forum, 22nd Battery Machine Gun Corps (Motors), https://www.greatwarforum.org/topic/249397–22nd-battery-machine-gun-corps-motors/? page=17&tab=comments#comment-2543432, accessed 20 August 2017.

8   Francis Ingall, *The Last of the Bengal Lancers* (Pen and Sword, 1989), p. 26.
9   *Ibid*, pp. 26–30.
10   *The Motor Cycle* (Vol. 17), 13 July 1916, p. 35, https://archive.org/stream/motorcycle17lond_/motorcycle17lond#page/n84/mode/1up , accessed 7 November 2018.
11   *Ibid.*
12   First edition of *Momagu*, reproduced in *The Motor Cycle* (Vol. 20), p. 310.
13   WO339/38479, Long Service papers, Lieutenant Max Henry Roescher, Machine Gun Corps, National Archives, Kew, accessed 17 July 2017.
14   Richard J. Popplewell, *Intelligence and Imperial Defence: British Intelligence and the Defence of the Indian Empire 1904–1924* (Routledge, 1995), p. 201.
15   John W. Cell, *Hailey: A Study in British Imperialism, 1872–1969* (Cambridge University Press, 2002), p. 67.
16   Nigel Collett, *The Butcher of Amritsar: General Reginald Dyer* (A&C Black, 2006), pp. 234.
17   Charles Townshend, *Britain's Civil Wars: Counterinsurgency in the Twentieth Century* (Faber and Faber, 1986), p. 137.
18   Collett, *The Butcher of Amritsar*, pp. 252–53.
19   *Ibid*, pp. 254–55.
20   *Ibid.* pp. 262–63.
21   Report of Captain J. A. S. Ewing, 19th Lancers, on operations with mobile column in Sialkot area during the Punjab disturbances. *Evidence taken before the Disorders Inquiry Committee: Volume V: Gujranwala, Gujrat, Lyallpur and Punjab Provincial*, 1920, p. 200, HathiTrust Digital Library, https://babel.hathitrust.org/cgi/pt? id=umn.31951d00850875e; view=1up; seq=214, accessed 12 November 2018.
22   *Ibid.*
23   *Ibid.*
24   *Ibid.*

Chapter 5 The Kurram Militia and Major Dodd

1   Charles Chenevix Trench, *The Frontier Scouts* (Jonathan Cape, 1986), p. 12.
2   Roos-Keppel subsequently went on the be chief commissioner of the North-West Frontier province during the Third Afghan War.
3   Charles Jasper Blunt, "Tirah Campaign" in Hugh Chisholm, *Encyclopaedia Britannica*, Vol. 26, 11th edition (Cambridge University Press, 1911), pp. 1005–6.
4   Trevelyan, Christopher, King-Emperor.com The Indian Army on Campaign 1900–1939, http://www.king-emperor.com/Photographs%20-%20Mohmand%20Blockade%201916–17.html, accessed 21 November 2018.
5   I. A. F. Z-2041, Record of Service Lieut. Col. P. C. R. Dodd, I. A., 24 August 1935, held by the Dodd family.
6   1901 England Census, Class: RG13, Piece: 2784, Folio: 64, p. 59, www.ancestry.com, accessed 21 November 2018.
7   I. A. F. Z-2041, Record of Service Lieut. Col. P. C. R. Dodd, I. A.
8   John Gaylor, "13th Duke of Connaught's Own Lancers", *The Defence Journal*, November 1999, http://www.defencejournal.com/nov99/13th-duke.htm, accessed 21 November 2018.
9   I. A. F. Z-2041, Record of Service Lieut. Col. P. C. R. Dodd, I. A.
10   WO 100; Piece: 400, UK, Military Campaign Medal and Award Rolls, 1793–1949, National Archives, Kew, www.ancestry.com, accessed 21 November 2018.

11 I. A. F. Z-2041, Record of Service Lieut. Col. P. C. R. Dodd, I. A.

12 *Ibid.*

13 Army Headquarters India, *Indian Army List January 1919*, Volume 1 (Naval and Military Press, reprinted 2001), p. 95.

14 https://www.revolvy.com/page/Frederick-Walter-Champion, accessed 16 November 2018.

15 Major Robert John Wingfield Heale, born 24 September 1876, died 4 March 1962. From Who was Who http://oxfordindex.oup.com/ and Gravestone Photographic Resource https://www.gravestonephotos.com/, accessed 25 November 2018.

16 WO 95/5392, War Diary Kohat-Kurram Force: Force Troops: Commandant KURRAM Militia (April–July 1919), National Archives, Kew, 9 May.

17 WO 95/5392, War Diary Kohat-Kurram Force: Commandant KURRAM Militia, 16 May.

18 *Ibid*, 24–25 May.

19 *Ibid*, 26 May.

20 WO 95/5392, War Diary Kohat-Kurram Force: Force Troops: 22 Motor Machine Gun Battery (May–August 1919), National Archives Kew, 27 May.

21 *Ibid*, 28 May.

22 WO 95/5392, War Diary Kohat-Kurram Force: Commandant KURRAM Militia, 28 May.

23 WO 95/5392, War Diary Kohat-Kurram Force, 22 Motor Machine Gun Battery (May–August 1919), 28 May.

24 WO 95/5392, War Diary Kohat-Kurram Force: Commandant KURRAM Militia, 28 May.

25 *Ibid*, 29–30 May.

26 *Ibid*, 30 May–1 Jun.

27 WO 95/5392, War Diary Kohat-Kurram Force: 22 Motor Machine Gun Battery (May–Aug 1919), 1–2 Jun.

28 *Ibid*, 2 Jun.

29 WO 95/5392, War Diary Kohat-Kurram Force: Commandant KURRAM Militia, 2 Jun.

30 WO 95/5392, War Diary Kohat-Kurram Force: 22 Motor Machine Gun Battery (May–August1919), 3 Jun.

31 WO 95/5392, War Diary Kohat-Kurram Force: Commandant KURRAM Militia, 5–8 Jun.

32 *Ibid*, 23–26 Jun.

Chapter 6 20 Squadron Royal Flying Corps: Formation to September 1917

1 Richards, Clive, "Substitution or Subordination? The Employment of Air Power Over Afghanistan and the North-West Frontier, 1910–1939" in *Royal Air Force Historical Society Journal*, Vol. 48 (2010), pp. 71 and 75.

2 AIR 27/258/1, 'No 20 Squadron: Operations Record Book' with appendices, National Archives, Kew, 29 July 1919.

3 Sellwood, Robert, *Winged Sabres*, (Pen & Sword Books, 2018), pp. 1–4.

4 The Martinsyde Scout was a protype Serial No 4735, which had been provided to 20 Squadron for evaluation. It was not a success and the aircraft was returned to depot before the end of March. The type was subsequently relegated to training duties.

5 Sellwood, *Winged Sabres,* pp. 5–8.

6 *Ibid*, pp. 10–11.

7 AIR 27/258/1, No 20 Squadron, 15 February 1916.

8   Sellwood, *Winged Sabres*, p. 11.
9   AIR 27/258/1, No 20 Squadron, 23 April 1916.
10 *Ibid,* 21 March 1916.
11 Sellwood, *Winged Sabres*, p. 19.
12 *Ibid,* p. 27.
13 *Ibid,* pp. 29–30.
14 AIR 27/258/1, No 20 Squadron, 2 Jun 1916.
15 Sellwood, *Winged Sabres*, p. 33.
16 AIR 27/258/1, No 20 Squadron, 1 July 1916.
17 Sellwood, *Winged Sabres*, p. 37.
18 *Ibid,* p. 38 and p. 45.
19 *Ibid,* pp. 38–39.
20 AIR 27/258/1, No 20 Squadron, 1 July 1916.
21 Sellwood, *Winged Sabres*, p.43 and p. 49.
22 *Ibid,* p. 53.
23 *Ibid,* pp. 45–46.
24 *Ibid,* p. 61.
25 http://www.mottersheadstatueappeal.co.uk/themen.html, accessed 11 December 2018.
26 Sellwood, *Winged Sabres*, p. 59.
27 *Personal Memoires of Sydney Attwater*, Imperial War Museum Document Archive.
28 *The London Gazette*, 9 February 1917, Gazette Online Archive, accessed 24 October 2018.
29 http://www.mottersheadstatueappeal.co.uk/themen.html, accessed 11 December 2018.
30 From Boisdinghem, which the squadron had moved to in January. AIR 27/258/1, No 20 Squadron, 19 January and 15 April 1917.
31 Sellwood, *Winged Sabres*, pp. 77–78.
32 *Ibid,* pp. 79–89.
33 *Ibid,* pp. 91–118.
34 *Ibid,* p. 94.
35 *Ibid,* pp. 121–123.
36 Jon Guttman and Harry Dempsey, *Pusher Aces of World War I* (Osprey Publishing, 2009), p. 86.
37 Sellwood, *Winged Sabres*, p. 122.
38 *Ibid,* pp. 125–126.
39 *The London Gazette*, 17 September 1917, Gazette Online Archive, accessed 24 October 2018.
40 *The London Gazette*, 17 July 1917, Gazette Online Archive, accessed 24 October 2018.
41 *The London Gazette*, 14 September 1917, Gazette Online Archive, accessed 24 October 2018.
42 Guttman and Dempsey, *Pusher Aces of World War I*, p. 80.
43 Sellwood, *Winged Sabres*, p. 149.
44 AIR 27/258/1, 27 July 1917.
45 *The London Gazette*, 9 January 1918, Gazette Online Archive, accessed 16 December 18.
46 *The Edinburgh Gazette*, 10 January 1918, Gazette Online Archive, accessed 16 December 18.
47 Sellwood, *Winged Sabres*, 128–129.
48 AIR 27/258/1, No 20 Squadron, 27 July 1917.
49 *Ibid.*
50 Sellwood, *Winged Sabres*, p. 131.
51 *Ibid,* pp. 134–35.
52 *Ibid,* pp. 145–46.
53 *Ibid,* pp. 153–55.

Chapter 7 20 Squadron Royal Flying Corps and Royal Air Force: Third Ypres to India

1   BAE Systems Heritage Website, www.baesystems.com/en/heritage/bristol-f2b-fighter, accessed 16 December 2018.
2   Sellwood, *Winged Sabres*, p. 146.
3   *Ibid*, p. 156.
4   *Ibid*, p. 163.
5   *Ibid*, p. 147.
6   *Ibid*, pp. 163–68.
7   AIR 27/258/1, No 20 Squadron, October 1917.
8   Sellwood, *Winged Sabres*, p. 168.
9   *Ibid*, p. 174.
10   British Army WWI Pension Records 1914–1920, WO 364; Piece: 2046, www.ancestry.com, accessed 17 December 2018.
11   AIR 1/526/16/12/36, *The Employment of the Royal Flying Corps in Defence*, 16 January 1918. National Archives, Kew.
12   Sellwood, *Winged Sabres*, p. 190.
13   AIR 27/258/1, No 20 Squadron, March/April 1918.
14   Sellwood, *Winged Sabres*, p. 198.
15   See: https://news.google.com/newspapers? nid=1368&dat=19300327&id=pGVQAAAAIBAJ& sjid=8Q4EAAAAIBAJ&pg=4274,4836593, accessed 18 December 2018.
16   AIR 27/258/1, No 20 Squadron, 13 April 1918.
17   Sellwood, *Winged Sabres*, pp. 202–3.
18   *Ibid*, p. 203.
19   The Aerodrome, http://www.theaerodrome.com/aces/usa/beaver.php, accessed 22 December 2018.
20   The Aerodrome, http://www.theaerodrome.com/aces/scotland/mather.php, accessed 22 December 2018.
21   AIR 27/258/1, No 20 Squadron, May 1918.
22   Sellwood, *Winged Sabres*, p. 221.
23   *Ibid*, pp. 239–40.
24   *Ibid*, pp. 55–56.
25   AIR 76/288/71, Air Officers Service Record, Lapraik, David McGeachie. National Archives, Kew, accessed 17 July 2017.
26   AIR 27/258/1, No 20 Squadron, 11 August 1918.
27   Sellwood, *Winged Sabres*, p. 242.
28   *Ibid*, pp. 243–44.
29   *Ibid*, p. 246.
30   *Ibid*, p. 250.
31   AIR 27/258/1, No 20 Squadron, 16 Sep 1918.
32   *Ibid*, 24 Sep 1918.
33   Sellwood, *Winged Sabres*, p. 258.
34   *Ibid*, pp. 261–262.
35   AIR 27/258/1, No 20 Squadron, 7 October 1918.
36   Sellwood, *Winged Sabres*, p. 263.
37   *Ibid*, pp. 263–65
38   AIR 27/258/1, No 20 Squadron, 25 October 1918.

39 Sellwood, *Winged Sabres*, p. 265.
40 The Aerodrome, http://www.theaerodrome.com/aces/england/boothroyd.php, accessed 3 January 2019.
41 Sellwood, *Winged Sabres*, p. 266.
42 *Ibid*, pp. 267–68.
43 *Ibid*, p. 269.
44 AIR 27/258/1, No 20 Squadron, 16 November and 23 December 1918.
45 Air of Authority, http://www.rafweb.org/Biographies/Russell_JC.htm, accessed 4 January 2019.
46 AIR 27/258/1, No 20 Squadron, 14 May 1919.
47 *Ibid*, 14–15 May 1919.
48 *Ibid*, June 1919.
49 *AIR 76/145/88*, Air Officers Service Record, Eastwood, George. National Archives, Kew, accessed 17 July 2017.
50 1901 England Census, Class: RG13, Piece: 3135, Folio: 118, page: 30, www.ancestry.co.uk, accessed 4 January 2019.
51 1911 England Census, Class: RG14, Piece: 27935, www.ancestry.co.uk, accessed 4 January 2019.
52 WO339/65591, Officers Service Record, Eastwood, George. National Archives, Kew, accessed 17 July 2017.
53 AIR 76/145/88, Air Officers Service Record, Eastwood, George. accessed 17 July 2017.
54 AIR 27/258/1, No 20 Squadron, 19 June 1919.
55 *Ibid*.
56 *Ibid*, 14 Jul 1919.
57 *Ibid*, July–Aug 1919.

Chapter 8 Action at Badama Post – 29 and 30 July 1919

1   General Staff Branch, Army Headquarters India, *Third Afghan War 1919 Official Account*, The *Third Afghan War 1919 Official Account*, p. 70.
2   NAM-2009-12-06, *Report by Sgt Macro*, copies held by the National Army Museum and the Macro family.
3   WO 95/5392, War Diary Kohat-Kurram Force: 22 Motor Machine Gun Battery (May–Aug1919), 29 July.
4   WO 95/5392, War Diary Kohat-Kurram Force: Commandant KURRAM Militia, 29 July.
5   WO 95/5392, War Diary Kohat-Kurram Force: Force Troops: HQ 60 INF BDE (June–July 1919), National Archives, Kew, 28 July.
6   WO 95/5392, War Diary Kohat-Kurram Force: Commandant KURRAM Militia, 29 July.
7   WO 95/5392, War Diary Kohat-Kurram Force: HQ 60 INF BDE (June–July 1919), 29 July.
8   General Staff Branch, Army Headquarters India, *Third Afghan War 1919 Official Account*, The *Third Afghan War 1919 Official Account*, p. 70.
9   *Report by Sgt Macro*.
10 *Ibid*.
11 *Ibid*.
12 WO 95/5392, War Diary Kohat-Kurram Force: HQ 60 INF BDE (June–July 1919), 30 July.
13 *Report by Sgt Macro*.
14 *Ibid*.
15 General Staff Branch, Army Headquarters India, *Third Afghan War 1919 Official Account*, The *Third Afghan War 1919 Official Account*, p. 183.

16 *Ibid,* p. 70.
17 AIR 27/258/1, No 20 Squadron, 29 July 1919. Note this date is incorrect.
18 Casualty Card, Lieutenant G. Eastwood, 30 July 1919.
19 Casualty Card, 2/Lt D. McG Lapraik, 30 July 1919, RAF Museum Story Vault, http://www.rafmuseumstoryvault.org.uk/archive/lapraik-d.mcg.-david-mcgachie, accessed 23 July 2017.
20 AIR 27/258/1, No 20 Squadron, 29 July 1919.
21 General Staff Branch, Army Headquarters India, *Third Afghan War 1919 Official Account, The Third Afghan War 1919 Official Account,* p. 70.
22 *Report by Sgt Macro.*
23 *Ibid.*

Chapter 9 Clearing the Aircraft

1 *Report by Sgt Macro.*
2 *Ibid.*
3 WO 95/5392, War Diary Kohat-Kurram Force: 22 Motor Machine Gun Battery (May–August 1919), 30 July.
4 *Report by Sgt Macro.*
5 *Ibid.*
6 *Ibid.*
7 WO 95/5392, War Diary Kohat-Kurram Force: Commandant KURRAM Militia, 30 July.
8 *Ibid.*
9 Commonwealth War Grave Commission, https://www.cwgc.org/find/find-war-dead/results? regiment=Military%2bPolice%2band%2bLevies&dateFrom=20–07–1919&dateTo=08–08–1919, accessed 1 August 2017.

Chapter 10 The Endgame: 31 July 1919

1 Lt Gen Sir George MacMunn, *The History of the Guides 1846–1922,* Volume I (Gale and Polden, 1938), p. 258.
2 Later changed his name to Merris, see *The London Gazette,* issue 34214, 29 October 1935.
3 MacMunn, *The History of the Guides 1846–1922,* p. 254.
4 *Ibid,* p. 255.
5 *Ibid,* p. 258.
6 *Ibid,* p. 255.
7 *Ibid,* p. 255.
8 *The London Gazette,* supplement 29940, 13 February 1917, p. 1537, www.thegazette.co.uk, accessed 24 January 2019.
9 *The London Gazette,* issue 31230, 14 March 1919, p. 3491, www.thegazette.co.uk, accessed 24 January 2019.
10 The University of Glasgow Story, First World War Roll of Honour, https://www.universitystory.gla.ac.uk/ww1-biography/? id=301, accessed 24 January 2019.
11 The Wellcome Trust, London, *Medical and Dental Students Register;* Reference Number: b24389535_i13753496, www.ancestry.com, accessed 24 January 2019.
12 The University of Glasgow Story, First World War Roll of Honour, accessed 24 January 2019.

13 *The London Gazette*, issue 28892, 4 September 1914, p. 7005, www.thegazette.co.uk, accessed 24 January 2019.

14 *The London Gazette*, supplement 30507, 1 February 1918, p. 1603, www.thegazette.co.uk, accessed 24 January 2019.

15 *The London Gazette, Supplement 30780,* dated 2 July 1918, p. 7905, www.thegazette.co.uk, accessed 24 January 2019.

16 *The London Gazette, Issue 31162,* dated 4 February 1919, p. 1816, www.thegazette.co.uk, accessed 24 January 2019.

17 British Army Medal Roll Index Cards 1914–20, A. J. H. Bourke, https://www.ancestry.com/interactive/1262/30850_A000180–01448, accessed 24 January 2019.

18 Army Form B199A, P/342086 A. J. H. Bourke, late Indian Army, Army Personel Centre, Glasgow, accessed 16 April 2018.

19 MacMunn, *The History of the Guides 1846–1922*, p. 255.

20 Shipping records SS *Megantic* departing Liverpool for Quebec, 15 August 1915.

21 Army Headquarters, India, *Indian Army List January 1919*, Volume 2, Andrews UK Limited, 2012, pp. 970–1

22 *The History of the Guides 1846–1922. Vol I. Op Cit,* p. 258.

23 *Report by Sgt Macro.*

24 WO 95/5392, War Diary Kohat-Kurram Force: Force Troops: HQ 60 INF BDE (June–1919 July), 31 July.

25 *Report by Sgt Macro.*

26 WO 95/5392, War Diary Kohat-Kurram Force: Force Troops: Commandant KURRAM Militia, 31 July.

27 MacMunn, *The History of the Guides 1846–1922*, p. 258.

28 WO 95/5392, War Diary Kohat-Kurram Force: 22 Motor Machine Gun Battery (May–August 1919), 31 July.

29 *Ibid,* 31 July.

30 *Report by Sgt Macro.*

31 WO 95/5392, War Diary Kohat-Kurram Force: Commandant KURRAM Militia, 31 July.

32 WO 95/5392, War Diary Kohat-Kurram Force: 22 Motor Machine Gun Battery (May–August 1919), 31 July.

33 *Report by Sgt Macro.*

34 WO 95/5392, War Diary Kohat-Kurram Force: Commandant KURRAM Militia, 1 August.

35 WO 329, Piece 2391, WWI Service Medal and Award Rolls, National Archives, Kew, www.ancestry.co.uk, accessed 24 January 2019.

36 MacMunn, *The History of the Guides 1846–1922*, p. 258.

Chapter 11 And Afterwards

1 *Report by Sgt Macro.*

2 WO 95/5392, War Diary Kohat-Kurram Force: Commandant KURRAM Militia, 15 August.

3 WO 95/5392, War Diary Kohat-Kurram Force: 22 Motor Machine Gun Battery (May–August 1919), 13–17 August.

4 England and Wales, National Probate Calendar (Index of Wills and Administrations), 1858–1966, 1973–95, www.ancestry.com, accessed 6 February 2019.

5 WO 95/5392, War Diary Kohat-Kurram Force: Commandant KURRAM Militia, 23 August.

6   MacMunn, *The History of the Guides 1846–1922*, p. 258.
7   I. A. F. Z-2041, Record of Service Lieut. Col. P. C. R. Dodd, I. A.
8   *Ibid*, Letter MacEwen to Dodd, dated 28 October 1919, Simla.
9   I. A. F. Z-2041, Record of Service Lieut. Col. P. C. R. Dodd, I. A.
10 *Ibid.*
11 *Ibid.*
12 *Ibid.*
13 *Ibid.*
14 Service Papers of Percy Charles Russell Dodd, Army Personnel Centre, Support Division, Glasgow.
15 *Ibid.*
16 *Ibid.*
17 *The London Gazette*, issue 335019, 20 December 1940, p. 7134, www.thegazette.co.uk, accessed 24 January 2019.
18 Army Form B199A, P/42817 Maj A. W. Molony, and related papers, obtained from Army Personnel Centre, Glasgow.
19 *Ibid.*
20 *Ibid.*
21 Casualty Card, Lieutenant G. Eastwood, 30 July 1919.
22 AIR 76/145/88, Air Officers Service Record, Eastwood, George, accessed 17 July 2017.
23 AIR 27/258/1, No 20 Squadron, 16 September 1919.
24 Air of Authority – A History of RAF Organisation, Air Commodore A. W. F. Glenny, http://www.rafweb.org/Biographies/Glenny.htm, accessed 4 February 2019.
25 AIR 76/145/88, Eastwood, George.
26 RG 101/6293E, 1939 Register, National Archives, Kew, www.ancestry.co.uk, accessed 12 February 2019.
27 RG 101/2930G, 1939 Register, National Archives, Kew, www.ancestry.com, accessed 12 February 2019.
28 Casualty Card, 2/Lt D. McG Lapraik, 30 July 1919.
29 AIR 76/288/71, Officers Service Record, Lapraik, David, National Archives, Kew, accessed 17 July 2017.
30 AIR 27/258/1, No 20 Squadron, September 1919.
31 *Ibid,* October 1919.
32 AIR 76/288/71, Officers Service Record, Lapraik, David.
33 RG 101/785J, 1939 Register, National Archives, Kew, www.ancestry.co.uk, accessed 12 February 2019.
34 London City Directories, London Metropolitan Archives, www.ancestry.co.uk, accessed 12 February 2019.
35 MacMunn, *The History of the Guides 1846–1922*, p. 312.
36 *Ibid,* p. 312.
37 *Ibid,* p. 259.
38 Army Form B199A, P/342086 A. J. H. Bourke.
39 In 1921, the regiment was still the 92nd Prince of Wales's Own Punjabs. In 1922, they amalgamated with other Punjabi regiments to become the 4/8th Punjabs.
40 Alan Warren, *Burma 1942, The Road from Rangoon to Mandalay* (Bloomsbury Continuum, 1 December 2011), p. 66.
41 Chris Kempton, *Loyalty & Honour: The Indian Army, September 1939–August 1947, Part I: Divisions.* (Military Press, 2004).

42 WO 329, Piece 1771, WWI Service Medal and Award Rolls, National Archives, Kew, www.ancestry.co.uk, accessed 12 February 2019.

43 WO 372/20/214293, Medal Index Card of Warburton, Ernest, National Archives, Kew, www.ancestry.co.uk, accessed 12 February 2019.

44 Local Defence Volunteers Service Papers of Ernest William Macro, Army Personnel Centre, Glasgow.

Appendix 1 Short History of the Various Anglo-Afghan Conflicts

1   James Perry, *Arrogant Armies; Great Military Disasters and the Generals Behind Them*, (Castle Books, 2005) p. 120.

Bibliography

Unpublished sources

Held by the daughters of Percy Dodd:

- I. A. F. Z-2041, Record of Service Lieut. Col. P. C. R. Dodd, I. A., dated 24 August 1935 and other personal papers

Army Personnel Centre, Support Division, Glasgow:

- Army Form B199A, P/342086 A. J. H. Bourke, late Indian Army
- Service Papers of Percy Charles Russell Dodd, R Dub Fus and MGC (M), and related correspondence
- Army Form B199A, P/42817 Maj A. W. Molony, and related papers
- Local Defence Volunteers Service Papers of Ernest William Macro

Imperial War Museum Document Archive:

- Personal Memoires of Sydney Attwater

National Archives, Kew:

- AIR 1/526/16/12/36, The Employment of the Royal Flying Corps in Defence, 16 January 1918
- AIR 27/258/1, No 20 Squadron Operations Record Book with appendices
- AIR 76/145/88, Officers Service Record, Eastwood, George
- AIR 76/288/71, Air Officers Service Record, Lapraik, David McGeachie
- WO 32/11239, Army Order 480, Other Arms (Code 14 (J)): Formation of Machine Gun Corps, 1915
- WO 33/3026 Report of the Advisory Committee on Motorcyclists (Technical Reserve), 1911

- WO 100; Piece: 400, UK, Military Campaign Medal and Award Rolls, 1793–1949
- WO 95/5392, War Diary Kohat-Kurram Force: Force Troops: 22 Motor Machine Gun Battery (1919 May–August)
- WO 95/5392, War Diary Kohat-Kurram Force: Force Troops: Commandant KURRAM Militia (1919 April–July)
- WO 329 WWI Service Medal and Award Rolls
- WO339/38479, Officers Service Record, Roescher, Max
- WO 339/65591 Officers Service Record, Eastwood, George
- WO 364, British Army WWI Pension Records 1914–1920, Piece: 2046

National Army Museum:

- NAM-2009-12-6, Report by Sgt Macro

The RAF Museum, Hendon, Story Vault:

- Casualty Card, Lieutenant G Eastwood
- Casualty Card, 2nd Lieutenant D. McG Lapraik.

The Royal Logistic Corps Museum:

- RLCS 5813 Mechanical Transport Committee Annual report 1908/9
- RLCA 5815 Mechanical Transport Committee Annual report 1910/11

Useful websites

The Aerodrome: www.theaerodrome.com

Air of Authority – A History of RAF Organisation: https://www.rafweb.org/index.html

Ancestry: www.ancestry.co.uk

The Digital Archive: www.archive.org

Gravestones Photographic Resource: https://www.gravestonephotos.com/

The Great War Forum: www.greatwarforum.org

The HathiTrust Digital Library: https://www.hathitrust.org/digital_library

King-Emperor: www.king-emperor.com

The Long Long Trail: www.longlongtrail.co.uk

P&O Heritage: http://www.poheritage.com/

The RAF Museum Story Vault: http://www.rafmuseumstoryvault.org.uk

Who Was Who: http://oxfordindex.oup.com

Published sources

Journals/articles:

Gaylor, John, "13th Duke of Connaught's Own Lancers", *The Defence Journal*, November 1999

The Eastbourne Gazette, accessed via http://www.eastsussexww1.org.uk/eastbourne-gazette/

The London Gazette

The Motor Cycle, London

Richards, Clive. "Substitution or Subordination? The Employment of Air Power Over Afghanistan and the North-West Frontier, 1910–1939" in *Royal Air Force Historical Society Journal*, Vol. 48, (2010), pp. 63–87

Books:

Army Headquarters India, *Indian Army List January 1919*, Volume 1 (Naval and Military Press, reprinted 2001)

Army Headquarters, India, *Indian Army List January 1919*, Volume 2 (Andrews UK Limited, reprinted 2012)

Army Headquarters India, General Staff Branch. *Third Afghan War 1919 Official Account* (Naval & Military Press, 2004 reprint of original 1926 edition)

Carragher, Michael. San Fairy Ann? Motorcycles and British Victory 1914–1918 (FireStep Press, 2013)

Cell, John W. *Hailey: A Study in British Imperialism, 1872–1969* (Cambridge University Press, 2002)

Chenevix Trench, Charles. *The Frontier Scouts* (Jonathan Cape, 1986)

Collett, Nigel. *The Butcher of Amritsar: General Reginald Dyer* (A&C Black, 2006)

Crutchley, C. E. *Machine Gunner 1914–1918, Personal Experiences of the Machine Gun Corps* (Pen & Sword Books, reprinted 2013)

Fletcher, David. *War Cars* (HMSO, 1987)

Gregg, Martin. *War Bike: British Military Motorcycling 1899–1919* (Lightning Source UK, 2015)

Gudmundsson, Bruce I. *On Armor* (Greenwood Publishing Group, 2004)

Guttman, Jon and Dempsey, Harry. *Pusher Aces of World War I* (Osprey Publishing, 2009)

Heathcote, T.A. *The Afghan Wars, 1839-1919* (Spellmount, 2007)

Hopkirk, Peter. *On Secret Service East of Constantinople* (John Murray, 1994)

Ingall, Francis. *The Last of the Bengal Lancers* (Pen & Sword Books, 1989)

Lecane, Philip. *Beneath a Turkish Sky* (The History Press Ireland, 2017)

MacMunn, Lieutenant General Sir George. *History of the Guides 1846–1922*, Volume I (Gale and Polden, 1938)

Moreman, Tim. *The Army in India and the Development of Frontier Warfare, 1849–1947* (Palgrave Macmillan, 1998)

Perry, James. *Arrogant Armies; Great Military Disasters and the Generals Behind Them* (Castle Books, 2005)

Pope, Stephen. *The First Tank Crews* (Helion & Company Limited, 2016)

Popplewell, Richard J. *Intelligence and Imperial Defence: British Intelligence and the Defence of the Indian Empire 1904–1924* (Routledge, 1995)

Robson, Brian. Crisis on the Frontier, *The Third Afghan War and the Campaign in Waziristan 1919–20* (Spellmount, 2007)

Sellwood, Robert. *Winged Sabres* (Pen & Sword Books Ltd, 2018)

Townshend, Charles. *Britain's Civil Wars: Counterinsurgency in the Twentieth Century* (Faber and Faber, 1986)

Warren, Alan. *Burma 1942, The Road from Rangoon to Mandalay* (Bloomsbury Continuum, 1 December 2011)

Winton, G. *Theirs Not to Reason Why: Horsing the British Army 1875 to 1925* (Helion & Company, 2013)

Wylly, Colonel Harold C. *Neill's Blue Caps*, Vol III 1914–22 (Naval & Military Press, 2006)

Index

General